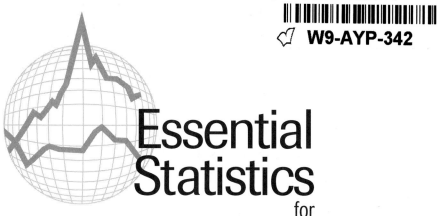

Essential
Statistics
for
Public Managers and
Policy Analysts

Evan M. Berman
University of Central Florida

CQ PRESS

A Division of Congressional Quarterly Inc.
Washington, D.C.

CQ Press
A Division of Congressional Quarterly Inc.
1255 22nd Street, N.W., Suite 400
Washington, D.C. 20037

(202) 822-1475; (800) 638-1710

www.cqpress.com

♾ The paper used in this publication meets the minimum
requirements of the American National Standard for Information
Sciences—Permanence of Paper for Printed Library Materials, ANSI
Z39.48-1992.

Printed and bound in the United States of America

05 04 03 02 01   5 4 3 2 1

Library of Congress Cataloging-in-Publication Data

Berman, Evan M.
  Essential statistics for public managers and policy analysts / Evan M. Berman.
    p.cm.
  Includes bibliographical references and index.
  ISBN 1-56802-647-1 (alk. paper)
  1. Social sciences—Statistical methods. I. Title.

HA29 .B425 2001
519.5—dc21

                                                                2001004917

Essential
Statistics

*This book is dedicated to Rosa ("Lala") Delgado
and in memory of Mario ("Geraldo") E. Rodriguez,
whose words and wisdom impacted my work.*

TABLE OF CONTENTS

TABLES

FIGURES

IN GREATER DEPTH

PREFACE

Although many practitioners and students feel that statistics are neither practical nor easy, those who routinely use statistics often believe otherwise. This book, and its accompanying workbook and instructor's manual, emphasizes conceptual understanding and practical application. Key statistical ideas are presented in a short, concise manner, and examples are presented in an accessible and economical style that will strengthen students' understanding and improve their application skills without the intimidation that a course in statistics is known to bring. In the text it is assumed that students will use computers to make most of the calculations.

The approach followed in this set of materials is consistent with two ongoing developments in the field of quantitative methods. First, the availability of statistical software that is more affordable and user friendly than in the past limits the rationale for doing hand calculations. On all but rare occasions, the text restricts hand calculations to situations in which they strengthen and enhance students' understanding of basic statistical concepts. Second, in many programs, students have limited time, and they demand a high degree of practical application. This book gets quickly to the point and shows them multiple applications they will need on the job. The brevity and clarity of presentation also promotes flexibility so that material can be added or adjusted to meet specific instructional needs.

The material covered in this set is designed for courses that are part of an analytical methods requirement that lasts either one or two semesters. When the entire program requirement is only one semester, such courses will need to emphasize research methods as well as quantitative methods. Such courses normally will spend two to five weeks on Chapter 1 ("Why Research? An Introduction") at the expense of Chapter 4 ("Measures of Association") and Chapter 8 ("Advanced Statistics"). By contrast, when the analytical requirement is for two courses, as is increasingly the case, research methods are usually not much discussed in the course that focuses on statistics. In such cases the course will require only cursory treatment of Chapter 1 (on research methods), allowing ample time for other chapters. In fact, professors may also want to include some nonstatistical techniques in such courses. To this end, the text provides spreadsheet exercises. Syllabi for a variety of situations are included in the instructor's manual. Although this well-integrated set is intended to support professors in their need for consistent teaching material, practitioners will find it a ready reference source for their on-the-job needs.

A UNIQUE LEARNING PACKAGE

This textbook is part of a unique resource set consisting of several valuable teaching tools. Developed in tandem with one another, each piece has been crafted as part of a larger learning package to enhance and reinforce lessons learned in the classroom. The whole set includes the following:
- *Essential Statistics for Public Managers and Policy Analysts,* the textbook, provides concise and clear discussions of statistical concepts and examples.
- *Exercising Essential Statistics,* the workbook, encompasses, for each textbook chapter, a summary of main points, application questions, hands-on exercises, examples of write-ups of research in practice, and further readings. The workbook includes a CD-ROM (with data sets in various formats) as well as a chapter on spreadsheet applications.
- *Instructor's Manual with Solutions* (for professors only) includes sample syllabi, lesson plans, answers to questions, and test questions.

Essential Statistics for Public Managers and Policy Analysts. The textbook includes statistics that are customarily taught in analytical methods courses. Each chapter comprises ten to twelve sections and subsections, which constitute teaching points. In each chapter the rationale for statistics is provided along with explanations, applications illustrated by "real world" examples, and numerous tables, charts, and graphs. "Learning Objectives" at the beginning of each chapter list exactly what will be covered in that chapter. Key terms are highlighted in bold italics in the text and are listed at the end of each chapter for quick and easy reference.

Exercising Essential Statistics. The accompanying workbook complements the textbook. Its aim is to strengthen students' learning and extend their ability to apply the material. Chapters 1–8 of the workbook correspond to the textbook and cover the same "Learning Objectives" listed in each textbook chapter. Each workbook chapter consists of five parts, which facilitate learning, testing, and application. The first part, called "Q & A," identifies key learning points and helps students test their comprehension of these points by providing them in a question-and-answer format. This section also helps in test reviews. The second part, called "Critical Thinking," contains open-ended questions designed to stimulate students' thinking and deepen their insight. The questions carry the material further and are excellent for in-class teaching and as homework assignments. The third part, "Data-Based Exercises," includes computer-based applications that use the data sets provided on CD-ROM to help students get used to working with data. The fourth section, "Research in Practice," provides practitioner applications, as well as examples drawn from the scholarly literature. Often, these models increase students' ability to apply and benefit from the material. The fifth section, "Suggested Readings," lists other textbooks, resources, and examples for anyone interested in further research.

The data sets reflect students' and professors' preferences for real-life data that shed light on the kinds of problems and issues that arise when working with data. The data sets cover experiences of federal, state, and local governments. They are based on employee and citizen surveys as well as environmental, welfare, and public safety data for policy making. In a few instances, plausible hypothetical data are also used. The sets include both cross-sectional and time-series data. The data sets contain complete documentation, including survey instruments, which many readers will find useful. Data are provided in SPSS, STATA, SAS, and SYSTAT formats. Of course, other statistics software packages are also widely used, and nothing in the textbook or workbook is specific to any software program. But recognizing the widespread use of SPSS, the workbook includes a chapter on using SPSS (Chapter 9). Some master's programs also require the extensive use of spreadsheets. To this end, an additional chapter (10), a guide to using spreadsheets for data analysis, is provided. Chapter 11 of the workbook provides documentation for the data sets on the CD-ROM.

The workbook and data sets span a wide range of areas and are designed to support integration with other areas of studies in master's degree programs in public policy and in public administration. The workbook covers many examples from human resource management, organizational behavior, budgeting, and public policy. The problems are written with those students in mind who have not yet taken these courses. And, of course, the data sets are quite extensive, enabling professors to develop additional applications in the areas they choose to emphasize.

Instructor's Manual with Solutions. The manual supports professors in teaching this course and provides all the answers to the workbook exercises. Instructors will also find test questions, sample syllabi, handouts, and lesson plans to assist them in class preparation. Many professors like to add their own material, and we are happy to provide them with additional approaches and suggestions.

ACKNOWLEDGMENTS

As always, numerous people contributed to this project. I would like to thank Charisse Kiino (acquisitions editor, CQ Press) for her unwavering support for this project; Amy Briggs (assistant editor, CQ Press) for suggestions and support of the review process; Joanne S. Ainsworth (Ainsworth Editorial Services) for her tireless editing; Amy Eastin (City of Maitland) for developing the bonus PowerPoint presentation (on the CD-ROM); and David Laney (doctoral candidate) for support in collecting data, assisting in the SPSS chapter of the workbook, and gathering copyright permissions. I also want to thank the following academic reviewers of this project: Professors Januar Hakim (Indiana University), who also did the final technical review of the manuscript; Richard Feiock (Florida State University), who also generously converted the data sets from SPSS into other formats that are now on the CD-ROM; Janet Kelly (University of Tennessee, Knoxville); Kurt Thurmaier (University of Kansas); and Sandra Emerson (California Polytechnic State University, Pomona). Despite all the help that I received from this most superb team, all errors are mine.

In addition, I give special thanks to the faculty and administrators of the University of Central Florida for their continued support of my work. Important lessons were gained in creating effective teaching materials through teaching in the master of public administration program, as well as in the interdisciplinary doctoral program in public affairs of the College of Health and Public Affairs, which provides a stimulating and collegial atmosphere. I acknowledge Professor Ray Surrette for his support. What I learned from these past efforts has served me well throughout the development of this project. I also acknowledge Dean Sprague, Michelle DelValle, and Ben

Hardcastle for their professionalism in public administration and for their support. I continue to be indebted to Professors Jonathan West and Bill Werther (both of the University of Miami) for enriching my career in more ways than can be enumerated here. Finally, I want to thank hundreds and hundreds of former students who indirectly contributed to this book through their feedback. They have never been shy in expressing themselves.

Evan M. Berman
Florida, USA
berman@mail.ucf.edu

Statistics Roadmap

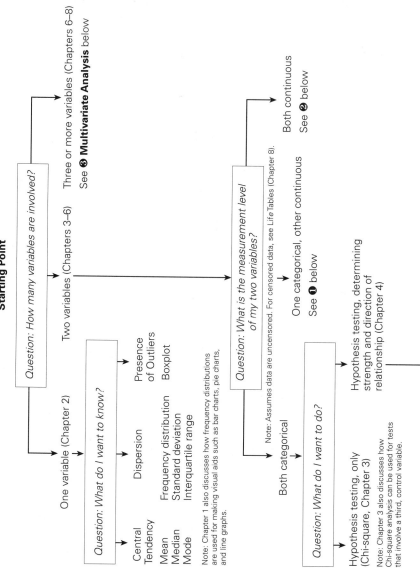

Starting Point

Question: How many variables are involved?

One variable (Chapter 2)   Two variables (Chapters 3–6)   Three or more variables (Chapters 6–8)

See ❸ **Multivariate Analysis** below

Question: What do I want to know?

Central Tendency	Dispersion	Presence of Outliers
Mean	Frequency distribution	Boxplot
Median	Standard deviation	
Mode	Interquartile range	

Note: Chapter 1 also discusses how frequency distributions are used for making visual aids such as bar charts, pie charts, and line graphs.

Question: What is the measurement level of my two variables?

Note: Assumes data are uncensored. For censored data, see Life Tables (Chapter 8).

Both categorical   One categorical, other continuous   Both continuous

See ❶ below   See ❷ below

Question: What do I want to do?

Hypothesis testing, only (Chi-square, Chapter 3)

Note: Chapter 3 also discusses how Chi-square analysis can be used for tests that involve a third, control variable.

Hypothesis testing, determining strength and direction of relationship (Chapter 4)

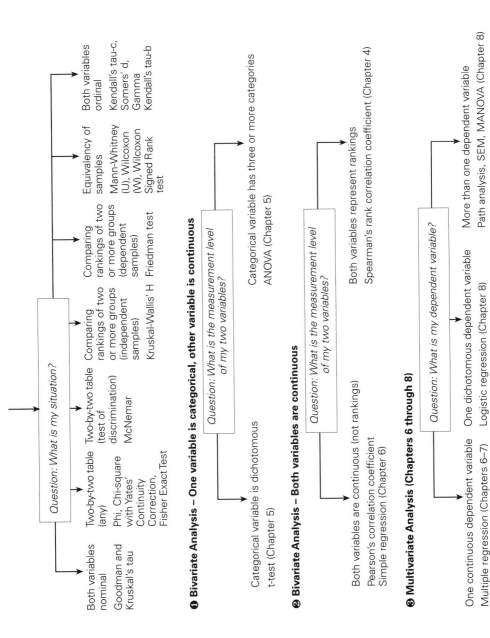

Question: What is my situation?

Both variables nominal	Two-by-two table (any)	Two-by-two table (test of discrimination)	Comparing rankings of two or more groups (independent samples)	Comparing rankings of two or more groups (dependent samples)	Equivalency of samples	Both variables ordinal
Goodman and Kruskal's tau	Phi, Chi-square with Yates' Continuity Correction, Fisher Exact Test	McNemar	Kruskal-Wallis' H	Friedman test	Mann-Whitney (U), Wilcoxon (W), Wilcoxon Signed Rank test	Kendall's tau-c, Somers' d, Gamma Kendall's tau-b

❶ Bivariate Analysis – One variable is categorical, other variable is continuous

Question: What is the measurement level of my two variables?

Categorical variable is dichotomous
t-test (Chapter 5)

Categorical variable has three or more categories
ANOVA (Chapter 5)

❷ Bivariate Analysis – Both variables are continuous

Question: What is the measurement level of my two variables?

Both variables are continuous (not rankings)
Pearson's correlation coefficient
Simple regression (Chapter 6)

Both variables represent rankings
Spearman's rank correlation coefficient (Chapter 4)

❸ Multivariate Analysis (Chapters 6 through 8)

Question: What is my dependent variable?

One continuous dependent variable
Multiple regression (Chapters 6–7)

One dichotomous dependent variable
Logistic regression (Chapter 8)

More than one dependent variable
Path analysis, SEM, MANOVA (Chapter 8)

Note: When data are censored, use Cox regression (Chapter 8).

INTRODUCTION

For many professionals and students, past experiences with statistics often have been less than fully satisfying—perhaps nightmares best forgotten. This is both unfortunate and increasingly unnecessary. This book and accompanying materials are guided by the underlying philosophy that statistics is an enterprise that is both *practical and easy.* Modern advances in computers and software have reduced the importance of hand calculations, allowing students to work readily with real-life applications. Conceptual understanding and application are central to statistics, not arithmetic and cumbersome calculations.

For public managers and analysts, this book shows how to apply the principles and practices of statistics to problems of public management and analysis. Whether through program evaluation; policy analysis; performance measurement; or program client, citizen, or employee surveys, statistics offers public managers and policy analysts ample opportunities for "speaking truth to power."[1] In doing so, these professionals inform public discourse and add value to democratic processes at all levels of government. The ability to analyze data will enhance the students' skills and can help to further their careers.

This book is part of a set that consists of
- A textbook: *Essential Statistics for Public Managers and Policy Analysts*
- A workbook: *Exercising Essential Statistics,* which includes
  - exercises with applications in public management and analysis
  - a CD-ROM with data sets and presentations in various formats.

All of the above materials include various features that make it easier to understand statistics and to benefit from its application. The textbook is written in an accessible, direct, and economical style. A flow chart located in the front of the book, called the "Statistics Road Map," is a quick reference tool that will help guide readers to choose the correct statistical method for their research. From there, a series of eight chapters build upon each other, taking the reader from the very fundamentals of research design all the way through advanced statistics. Each chapter begins with a list of learning objectives—the skills and concepts students can expect to know when they have finished reading. Key terms are shown in bold italics and are listed at the end of each chapter for easy reference.

De-emphasizing the role of sometimes intimidating calculations, this book favors conceptual understanding. Computers do all but the most basic calculations, and I encourage their use. The handful of included manual calculations will enhance conceptual understanding of some of the basic fundamentals of statistics. The exercises and applications reflect practical problems of managers, drawn from problems that many have shared.

The workbook extends conceptual understanding through further application of statistics principles. It is an integral part of this set. Chapters 1 through 8 of the workbook correspond to the equivalent chapters in the textbook and are organized in five parts: "Q & A" reinforces key learning points and assists in test preparation; "Critical Thinking" stimulates insight into statistics principles; "Data-Based Exercises" emphasizes hands-on skill-building and additional applications; "Research in Practice" shows completed applications that reflect professional norms and illustrates appropriate write-ups in public management and policy analysis; and "Suggested Readings" recommends books for further study in areas of interest.

The data sets in the CD-ROM are largely based on real-life data and include employee and citizen surveys. They also cover topics of environmental, welfare, and public safety interest and are relevant to all levels of government. Complete documentation, including survey instruments that can be tailored to students' own situations, is found in Chapter 11 of the workbook. Data are provided in SPSS and other formats for use in other software packages. The workbook also includes a tutorial for using SPSS (Chapter 9). Chapter 10 of the workbook examines the use of spreadsheets for analysis, with examples drawn from spreadsheets that also are on the CD-ROM (in Microsoft Excel).

The workbook, together with these data sets, teaches students how to apply statistics to practical problems in the real world. Students will also discover the principles that allow them to go beyond these examples to specific problems they encounter in the workplace. After using this learning package, readers will see not only how practical and easy statistics can be but also how the effective use of statistics can help them.

I'd like to hear from you. The textbook, the workbook, and the CD-ROM reflect decades of feedback from other professionals and students. Don't be shy. Let me know what features you like and what should be improved on. Now, let's get started!

Evan M. Berman
Florida, USA
berman@mail.ucf.edu

Note

1. This phrase is borrowed from the classic work of Aaron Wildavsky, *Speaking Truth to Power* (Boston: Little, Brown, 1979).

CHAPTER 1

Why Research? An Introduction

CHAPTER OBJECTIVES

After reading this chapter, you should able to:
- Describe the six steps of conducting program evaluation
- Distinguish between descriptive and relational analysis
- Operationalize outcomes in measurable ways
- Understand the importance of rival hypotheses
- Describe general guidelines for conducting scientific surveys
- Evaluate the appropriateness of alternative methods of data collection

Why research? The ethos of public management is to "go out and make a difference," not to sit behind a desk and crunch numbers. Public managers often join agencies because they seek to serve and help their communities and country. Not surprisingly, managers are sometimes puzzled by the suggestion of practicing research and statistics: research appears boring in comparison with developing and implementing new programs, and statistics seems, well, impossibly challenging with little payoff in sight.

In fact, analytical techniques involving research and statistics are increasingly in demand. Legislatures and citizens want to know what return they are getting from their tax dollars. Most grant applications increasingly require public managers to be accountable for program outcomes. Public managers must demonstrate that their programs are producing effective outcomes and that they are doing so in cost-effective ways. This demand for outcome evaluation and monitoring far exceeds any requirement of proper funds management. A related demand is that public managers are expected to know what their citizens and clients want from them. Systematic surveys can provide valid and objective assessments of citizen and client needs, priorities, and perceptions of programs and services. Systematic surveys of citizens and clients are increasingly used and are often part of outcome evaluation.

This chapter provides an overview of conducting program evaluations and scientific surveys. It discusses major concepts relating to these activities. Program evaluation and scientific surveys produce data that are analyzed using procedures described in subsequent chapters of this book. Of course, data are also obtained through other ways than program evaluations and surveys. Although this book mainly focuses on data analysis, this chapter sets the stage. **Readers who are interested in the analysis of data, and not the collection of data, may wish to skip this chapter.**

How difficult can it be to document program outcomes? There usually is more to program evaluations than meets the eye. Consider the following example. In response to growing concerns about teen violence, many communities and states have created after-school programs. The idea, according to elected officials, and supported by the public, is to get teenagers off the streets and into supervised environments. As a public manager, your job is to implement such a program. Funding guidelines require that you document the success of the program.

Among your first tasks is to figure out what the program is expected to accomplish. You might be surprised to learn that sometimes little thought has gone into specifying specific outcomes for this program, or that some elected officials and experts have different views. Some advocates only want teenagers off the streets, but others expect them to learn something as well. Still others feel that anger management should be taught. Even if you are responsible only for program evaluation, oftentimes you will find yourself formulating program outcomes.

Next, assume that you and others agree that anger management is one of several appropriate activities for the after-school program. Specifically, the after-school program will teach students to recognize and deal with anger in appropriate ways. You might even try to target "high risk" students. How will you measure the success of your anger management efforts? Should you ask students whether they feel less angry? Should you ask their parents and teachers as well? Should you ask teachers to record the number of classroom incidents, such as student outbursts? Should you do all of this? If so, in what way?

Suppose you decide to ask teachers to track classroom incidents. Which incidents should be tracked? Is it appropriate to compare different classroom incidents across schools or classes? Should you develop baseline data and, if so, which? Also, how accurate do you think the teachers will be in their reporting and tracking? Are their responses likely to be biased in any way? Or suppose you decide to send a survey to parents. Do you need to send your survey to all parents? How many questions should you ask? What response rate is appropriate? How do you avoid biased questions?

Finally, consider the possibility that the number of classroom incidents drops during the course of your anger management program. How do you know that the drop is due to the anger management course? Could teachers and parents have become more involved in anger management themselves? What if some students who are known to be angry and violent were trans-ferred out of the school? In short, how sure can you be that any changes are due to the after-school program?

These questions are hardly academic. Elected officials and senior managers expect others to have answers to such questions, regardless of whether they concern after-school programs, prison overcrowding, environ-mental protection, or national security. Determining which outcomes ought to be measured and measuring their attainment in credible ways are activi-ties germane to all public programs and polices. Public departments need people with skills to assess program outcomes, and many new, analytically oriented jobs have been created in recent years. The purpose of this chapter is to provide an overview of research methods, focusing on program evalua-tion, including survey research, which often is part of evaluation.

The first part of this chapter addresses different strategies for designing your research. The second part examines measurement and sampling, and the third part discusses some specific data collection strategies. Collectively, the material in this chapter is also called *research methodology*—the science of methods for finding things out. Research methods have wide-ranging applications in disciplines such as economics, political science, sociology, and public administration. Research methodology has its own jargon for referencing phenomena and issues that everyday language cannot describe well. In some instances, alternative terminology has come into circulation, which, in this book, is shown in parentheses adjacent to its first-time use.[1]

RESEARCH DESIGN

Six Steps

Although program evaluation is sometimes regarded as a purely analytical activity (something that one can do alone behind a desk), a strong case can be made that research in public management involves both analysis and consensus building. If program evaluation is to be used rather than just gather dust on a shelf, then its conclusions and recommendations must be embraced by those who have the power to affect change. Study conclusions must be seen as credible and consistent with opportunities for change. Program managers and other officials often want to have input into what and how programs are evaluated. Managers want to know that evaluators are measuring things in ways that are consistent with the managers' understanding and priorities, and that evaluators provide information that is relevant to their management of the program. They want to have input. As the saying goes, "people do not resist their own ideas."

At the same time, evaluation must also be objective and scientifically valid. Evaluation findings must stand up under the light of public scrutiny. They must reflect objectivity and a broad perspective on agency mission and public needs—not merely parochial, departmental interests. The way in which outcomes are assessed must, indeed, be thorough and consistent with the standards of science. It does no manager much good to receive a study that others view as being biased and lacking in credibility.

The following *six steps of program evaluation* provide a strategic road map that combines these dual needs—to be both responsive and objective.

1. *Define the activity and goals that are to be evaluated.* What are the key objectives and constraints according to key decision makers? What are the main objectives and concerns according to program staff? How do clients and others outside the program view it?
2. *Identify which key relationships will be studied.* Which program outcomes does the evaluation measure? Which factors are hypothesized to affect these program outcomes? Which counter-explanations are considered?
3. *Determine the research design that will be used.* Will a control or comparison group be used? Is there a need for benchmarking or developing a baseline of current performance? Are periodic or follow-up measurements foreseen and, if so, over what time period?
4. *Define and measure study concepts.* Which study concepts require detail in measurement? Which concepts require little detail? Will existing data be used, and how accurate are they? Will new data be gathered through, for example, a survey or focus group? If so, who will undertake such a project, and how long will it take? What statistical requirements must the data meet for subsequent analysis? What resources and expertise are needed for data collection and program evaluation? What suggestions do key decision makers and others have for improving measurement?
5. *Collect and analyze the data.* Which statistical techniques will be used for data analysis? What type of conclusions are researchers seeking from the data? Do the data meet the requirements of different statistical techniques?

6. *Present study findings.* How, and to whom, will conclusions be presented? Can presentations be part of other consensus and decision-making processes? Can preliminary feedback about tentative findings be obtained from key decision makers and others? Who requires a detailed analysis and presentation? Who requires only a brief overview of main findings? What should the final report look like, and to whom should it be sent?

In the opening part of this chapter, we already discussed the need to determine program goals. Building on that, a distinction often is made between short-term and long-term outcomes. This distinction is helpful in public management because many public programs and policies have an outlook of three, five, or even twenty years. Managers cannot afford to wait that long in order to determine whether their programs are working or on track to being successful. ***Short-term outcomes*** are the immediate outcomes of program activities that support long-term outcomes (or goals). For example, although many factors affect high school violence (a long-term outcome), anger management education can contribute to lower classroom violence only if it helps students to better recognize and deal with their anger. The extent to which students achieve this understanding is an important short-term outcome that supports the long-term outcome of reduced violence. ***Long-term outcomes*** are measures of the extent to which the ultimate objectives of a program (or goals) are achieved, such as the reduction of school violence. Assessments of new programs sometimes focus on short-term outcomes because long-term outcomes have yet to occur, and analysts are usually involved in processes of clarifying both short-term and long-term program outcomes. In any event, analysts often interview those who have a stake in the program, such as key decision makers, clients, citizens, and program staff, about program outcomes and activities. Doing so can help ensure that the importance of various short-term and long-term outcomes is correctly identified.

Relationships

Evaluation usually involves both *descriptive analysis* and the study of *relationships*. Descriptive analysis provides information about the state of things—such as whether a teenage violence problem exists. Descriptive analysis is used to determine the *level* of outcomes, such as the extent of high school violence, the nature of its perpetrators, and the geographic areas in which it most often occurs, as well as the extent to which teenage violence is perceived as a problem. Descriptive analysis is very useful in public management and policy because managers need to know the state of the world that they are trying to shape. They need to know, for example, the number of teenagers who have been hurt by others at school. This simply is a number—such as 5 percent.

Managers also want to know the causes of problems and the effectiveness of their interventions. This involves examining **relationships,** that is, specifying which things are related to each other and the ways in which they are related to each other. For example, we might examine whether students who participate in after-school programs describe themselves as being less angry or prone to "acting out" against others. Specifically, we want to know whether participation in after-school programs decreases the extent of acting out by students. We might also examine the effect of drugs and gangs on teenage violence. By knowing how policies and programs shape outcomes, managers can recommend and pursue alternative courses of action. Most studies involve both descriptive analysis and examination of relationships.

Variables are key to descriptive analysis and relationships. Simply, **variables** are empirically observable phenomena that vary (hence, the name *variable*). This is best illustrated by a few examples. "High school violence" is a variable because it varies across schools. Variables have attributes that define what is measured. For example, high school violence can be measured as being absent, sporadic, occurring from time-to-time, or ongoing. Another example is the variable "gender." Gender varies in the population, and the attributes of gender are male and female. We can examine, for example, whether a relationship exists between gender and high school violence, such as whether females are less likely to commit such acts. The variable "race" often has more than two attributes (Caucasian, African-American, Native American, and so forth), whereas the variable "income" can have few or a nearly indefinite number of attributes. The term *attribute* is sometimes also called *value,* and these terms are used interchangeably: the phrases "the variable 'gender' has two attributes" and "the variable 'gender' has two values" are synonymous. It might also be noted that in a study of only female drug offenders the variable "gender" does not vary and is therefore called a **constant.** Many people are well familiar with variables. In surveys, often each survey item is treated as a separate variable, and the response categories of each question are its attributes. For example, the question "What is your gender?" is considered as a variable, and the response categories "male" and "female" are the attributes belonging to this variable.

Relationships are further distinguished as being either *causal* or *associational.* **Causal relations** show cause and effect, such as the impact of anger management programs on high school violence, or the impact of employee compensation on workplace productivity, or the impact of certain environmental policies on water quality. Among causal relations, we further distinguish between *independent variables* and *dependent variables.* **Dependent variables** are variables that are affected by other variables (hence, they are dependent on them). **Independent variables** are variables that cause an effect in other variables but are not themselves shaped by other variables (hence, they are independent). For example, in a study of the impact of anger management on high school violence, anger management is the independent variable that affects high school violence, which is the dependent variable. It is common to think of each causal relationship in the following manner:

Independent Variable(s) → Dependent Variable

An important step in any research is specifying the dependent and independent variables. Doing so provides clarity and direction to the research. Although many studies examine several relationships, most evaluations focus on explaining only a few dependent variables. In our case, we might want to focus on high school violence.

Independent Variable		*Dependent Variable*
Anger Management	→	High School Violence

Of course, our evaluation needn't be limited to only studying this relationship, but specifying it in this manner helps concentrate our evaluation on (1) accurately determining the level of high school violence and (2) examining whether anger management is associated with it. We might also study the effect of gun control laws (independent variable) on this dependent variable, or other relationships such as the effect of homework assistance (independent variable) on academic performance (dependent variable).

It is often the intent of program evaluation to stake a claim of *causation.* In the above case, managers might want to say anger management has caused the decline of high school violence. Many people have heard the expression "correlation does not prove causation." This is true. Causation requires both (1) *empirical (that is, statistical) correlation* and (2) *a plausible cause-and-effect argument.* These two **criteria for causality** must be present. Statistical analysis tests whether two variables are correlated, but causality also requires a persuasive argument (also called theory) about how one variable could directly affect another. In regard to the impact of anger management on high school violence a plausible theory might readily be written up. Anger management training teaches how to identify anger and release it in ways that are nonviolent toward others. Thus, both statistical correlation and a persuasive theoretical argument are required to stake a claim of causation.

How difficult can it be to make a theoretical argument of cause and effect? Examining, say, the relationship between gender and high school violence, we have yet to make a plausible cause-and-effect argument. If we lack specific evidence (especially evidence that might persuade a skeptical audience) that gender, defined by reproductive organs and hormones, causes violence, then we best regard this relationship as a mere correlation, that is, an **association.** Empirical correlations remain mere associations until analysts have argued, in exacting detail, how one variable can plausibly cause another.[2]

Finally, relationships that have not yet been empirically tested are called **hypotheses.** For example, a study hypothesis might be that, on average, female teenagers are less prone to violence than males. Then, subsequent empirical data prove the hypothesis to be either true or false for the population from which these data are drawn. Subsequent chapters in this book discuss how to analyze data and draw conclusions about hypotheses. Academic research studies are usually quite explicit about which hypotheses are being tested and why they are relevant.

Rival Hypotheses and Limitations of Experimental Study Designs

The purpose of research design is to help ascertain that changes, such as improved anger management or a decline in classroom incidents, are in fact occurring and that they are plausibly related to the program—not other factors. But what if, parallel to anger management, another program aims to reduce student access to weapons? Then, it is conceivable that any reduction in school violence might be in part or in whole ascribed to this other program. Such other explanations that threaten the credibility of study conclusions are called **rival hypotheses.** Variables that are used to measure them are called **control variables.** Control variables are empirical, just as dependent and independent variables are, but get their name from their research role: to test whether relationships between independent and dependent variables hold up under the presence of alternative, rival explanations. Thus, in our example, the presence of a weapons access policy is certainly a control variable that the manager will want to take into account. Indeed, the credibility of research findings often rests on the extent that pertinent rival hypotheses have been identified and incorporated into study designs.

Two ways of dealing with control variables are through experimental design and statistical analysis. **Experimental designs** address rival hypotheses through the use of control groups, which are similar to the study group in all aspects except that members of the control group do not participate in the intervention. Many managers are familiar with control groups through the medical literature in regard to testing the effectiveness of medical treatments. In **classic, randomized experiments** participants are randomly assigned to either a control or experimental (or study) group. The assignments are random to ensure that any observed differences between these two groups are due only to the drug and not to any other factor. Random assignment ensures that the two groups are similar, and baseline data are used to further rule out any chance differences of respective starting conditions. Further, neither the participants of the control and study groups nor their doctors are told whether they are receiving the experimental drug or the ineffective placebo (they both look alike), because doing so might cause patients or their doctors to alter their behavior. In short, everything is done to ensure that the *only* difference between the groups is that one gets the treatment and the other does not. The logical inference, then, is that any difference *must* be due to the experimental drug, not anything else. The research design rules out every other factor.

Programs and policies are the public management equivalent to clinical interventions. Classic, randomized experiments are notoriously difficult to implement in public administration and policy because it is generally legally and ethically impossible to deny citizens or jurisdictions programs and policies. In the above example, we do not envision randomly assigning teenagers to after-school programs. Some parents would be outraged if their children were denied access to the anger management program. They might even sue. Rather, we must make certain allowances in our research design. We could run a pilot anger management program in one school and compare results against another school that has not (yet) provided it. We must wisely choose our comparison school such that the characteristics of it and its students closely match the school in which we implement our anger management program. The rub is that there usually are differences between the two schools. For example, what if teenagers in the comparison group come from homes with higher incomes that enable them to participate in more after-school sports programs that in turn enable them to release their anger? This is an important rival hypothesis.[3]

Comparisons between experimental and comparison groups that do not meet the standard of classic research designs are called **quasi-experimental designs.** They may lack randomization, baseline (or pretest) measurement, or a (valid) comparison group. Clearly, imperfect research designs increase the presence of plausible rival hypotheses. Quasi-experimental designs are shown in Box 1.1. Then, any differences between groups may reflect the effects of programs *and* other factors, such as different incomes discussed earlier. And there may be other problems that vary from situation to situation. For example, some students in the control group might learn about the anger management program in the other group, affecting their behavior. Or, what if a murder occurs in one school but not the other, giving heightened awareness in that school to the problem of school violence?

The fact that we are unable to control fully for rival hypotheses through research design should not cause us to abandon the use of comparison groups and baselines. Comparison groups provide a useful reference, especially when measurement over time shows widening trends between groups.

In Greater Depth...

Box 1.1   Research Designs

Research designs can be characterized using the following notation, where R = randomization, X = intervention, and O = measurement. The following is based on the enduring, classic work of Donald Campbell and Julian Stanley.

A. The classic, randomized design can be graphically depicted as follows. Any significant program impact would be indicated when $(O2-O1) > (O4-O3)$.

	Pretest	Program	Posttest
Group 1:	R O1	X	O2
Group 2:	R O3		O4

B. Quasi-experimental designs vary from this design in several ways:

1. Research design with nonrandomized comparison group:

	Pretest	Program	Posttest
Group 1:	O1	X	O2
Group 2:	O3		O4

2. Research design with no comparison group:

	Pretest	Program	Posttest
Group 1, only:	O1	X	O2

3. Research design with comparison group and posttests, only:

	Pretest	Program	Posttest
Group 1:		X	O2
Group 2:			O4

4. Research design with posttest measure, only:

	Pretest	Program	Posttest
Group 1, only:		X	O2

Source: Donald Campbell and Julian Stanley, Experimental and Quasi-Experimental Designs for Research *(Chicago, Ill.: Rand McNally), 1963.*

Without a baseline, it is harder to persuade others that a program has had an impact. Rather, when rival hypotheses are present, ***statistical techniques*** are commonly used to determine their impact on program outcomes. Generally, statistical techniques are approaches for studying variables quantitatively. In this regard, control variables often are regarded as additional independent variables that affect program outcomes, and Chapters 3 and 6 discuss the evaluation of rival hypotheses. Although this part of the discussion about rival hypotheses is postponed, a few important conclusions should be drawn from the above discussion: research should (1) identify rival hypotheses of concern to stakeholders and others, (2) plan for the collection of data about rival hypotheses along with other data (because we can't or don't want to engage twice in data collection), (3) consider the use of comparison groups (as feasible), and (4) examine the plausibility of rival hypotheses through statistical analysis.

MEASUREMENT AND SAMPLING

Measuring Concepts

The rigor with which study concepts are defined (such as the level of anger or high school violence) enhances the validity of our efforts. ***Measurement validity*** simply means that something measures or reflects what it is intended to. A research task is to be clear about that which is studied. For example, how should we measure high school violence? Or anger?

In this regard, variables are to be distinguished from concepts. Whereas variables belong to the realm of directly observable phenomena, concepts belong to the realm of ideas. ***Concepts*** are abstract ideas that are indirectly observed. Many interesting matters of public management and analysis involve concepts, such as notions of democracy, effectiveness, citizen satisfaction, and, yes, high school violence and anger. The rigor with which these concepts are defined affects study credibility. Typically, ***processes of concept measurement*** have two steps. First, all relevant dimensions of the concept are specified and variables identified (this is called *conceptualization*). Second, each variable is operationalized by identifying ways of measuring it (this is called *operationalization*).

Consider the following example. Suppose we want to measure "student anger" and "high school violence." First, we ask, *What are the different dimensions of these concepts, as relevant to us?* Typically, different managers and analysts will answer this in different ways. For example, we might identify three dimensions to the concept of "anger:" emotions of anger, thoughts (cognition) of anger, and physical rage. Each dimension stands alone and can be measured separately. For example, some students might have thoughts of anger but little emotion associated with it, and vice versa. Some may have rage and emotion but little cognition. Similarly, we can reach a consensus that the most important dimensions of high school violence are those that involve weapons, physical contact (without weapons), and verbal assaults. These are not seen as degrees of violence but as different *types* of violence. The degree of each of these types of violence can be measured separately, as shown in the next step.

Second, we ask, *Which variables are used to measure each of these dimensions?* Any measurement will be incomplete, but we must do our best to be as accurate as possible. Regarding thoughts of anger, we can ask students about the frequency and intensity of such thoughts. We can ask them how often they have thoughts that involve anger, how intense or lasting those thoughts are, and where and when those thoughts typically occur to them. We can similarly ask them about the frequency and intensity of emotions and physical rage. Likewise, we might ask students (perhaps in a confidential survey) to identify instances of physical contact (without weapons) and verbal assaults. Then, we would carefully define our concept of "verbal assault" so that no ambiguity exists (a rival hypothesis!) about that which respondents are in fact responding to.[4]

Conceptualization and operationalization are inexact sciences, at best. Seldom are analysts able to borrow the conceptualizations of past studies; in most instances, they must use their own creativity. The task of the analyst is, then, also to argue that his or her measurement is appropriate, even among the better ways of doing so. Measurement should be comprehensive and unambiguous. In this regard, *no correct number of dimensions or variables exist, only bad or lacking ones.* Analysts may try to improve the validity of their measures by using existing measures (when they exist), or by getting the consensus of experts and stakeholders. Sometimes, analysts try to show that their measures are valid by showing that they correlate with other measures in ways that are to be expected. For example, the measure "physical contact without weapons" might be triangulated by records of the school nurse (treatment of scrapes and bruises) and a student survey. Although such correlation does not prove that the measure is valid, certainly the lack of correlation would raise some eyebrows. Clearly, analysts must determine the appropriate level of rigor of their concept measurement. In practice, the rigor of concept measurement largely depends on the complexity and role of concepts: comprehensive measurement is sometimes reserved for variables of key or critical interest, especially dependent variables, whereas other variables may receive less rigorous measurement.[5]

Measuring Variables: Levels and Scales
Whereas the previous section discussed various issues relating to concepts, we now turn our attention to measuring variables. A scale can be thought of

as the collection of attributes used to measure a specific variable; for example, the variable "gender" is commonly measured on a scale that is defined by the attributes "male" and "female." Scales are important because they affect the type of data we later end up with; for example, we could measure incomes by asking respondents for their exact income or by asking them to identify their income using prespecified income brackets. Scales vary greatly—they are sometimes as unique as the variables they measure, and analysts often must creatively decide how existing scales can be adapted to their needs. It is common practice to distinguish *four* levels of measurement scales: *nominal, ordinal, interval,* and *ratio.* It is also common to refer to a variable that has, for example, an ordinal-level measurement scale as an ordinal-level variable or, simply, as an ordinal variable. The importance of the **measurement level** is threefold: (1) it determines the selection of test statistics (this is highly relevant to subsequent chapters), (2) it affects the amount of information collected about variables, and (3) it affects how survey and other types of questions are phrased.

A nominal-level variable is one whose scale exhibits no ordering among the categories. It provides the least amount of information. For example, the variable "gender" has a nominal scale because "men" are not "more" than "women," regardless of any coding scheme that assigns numbers to these categories. They are nominal categories. "Region" is also a common nominal scale: there is no ordering among the values of North, South, East, and West.

By contrast, ordinal-level variables are those whose scales do provide order among categories (hence, their name *ordinal*), although no exact distances exist among the categories. "Order" means that categories can be compared as being "more" or "less" than one another. For example, assume that we measure teenage anger by asking adolescents whether they feel irritated, aggravated, or raging mad. Clearly, someone feeling "raging mad" is more angry than someone who only feels "aggravated," although someone who has this feeling is more angry than someone who feels "irritated." "Distance" means that we can measure how much more one category is from another. Ordinal scales lack distance. While we can say that "raging mad" is more angry than only feeling "aggravated," we cannot say *how much* more angry "raging mad" is than "aggravated." The most common ordinal scales are *Likert scales;* they are important and widely used in survey research (see Box 1.2).

Consider the example of asking respondents whether they agree that high school violence is an important problem. While we could ask them to answer this on a "yes" or "no" scale, we prefer to ask them the extent to which they feel that it is a problem using one of the scales shown in Box 1.2. Doing so increases the amount of information that we obtain about this variable. Specifically, we might ask them to express their assessment using

In Greater Depth...

Box 1.2 Likert Scales

Likert scales are ordinal scales developed by Professor Rensis Likert in 1932 for the purpose of measuring attitudes. Likert scales are a basic staple of many surveys and often shape how survey questions are asked. Their popularity rests in the fact that they have been widely tested and found to be valid.

Likert scales often have three major variations regarding levels of *agreement, importance,* and *satisfaction,* and each has either 5 or 7 categories (or, points). Five-point scales are identical to seven-point scales except that they omit the categories of "somewhat." Some surveys (for example, political polls) also lack the category "don't know or can't say," thereby forcing respondent answers. Academically, this is objectionable because it fails to measure accurately the responses of those who genuinely "don't know" or "can't say" while overestimating adjacent categories.

Examples are shown below. Please see Chapter 11, "Documentation," in this workbook for alternative formatting and layout.

1. Please state your agreement with the following statements, using the following scale:

   7 = Strongly Agree   3 = Somewhat Disagree
   6 = Agree   2 = Disagree
   5 = Somewhat Agree   1 = Strongly Disagree
   4 = Don't Know / Can't Say

   Students who are violent should be removed from class.   [ ]
   I would like us to have anger management classes.   [ ]
   There should be an after-school homework assistance program.   [ ]

2. How important are the following items to you? Please use the following scale:

   7 = Very Important   3 = Somewhat Unimportant
   6 = Important   2 = Unimportant
   5 = Somewhat Important   1 = Very Unimportant
   4 = Don't Know / Can't Say

   Feeling safe in my neighborhood   [ ]
   Putting those who commit crimes in jail [ ]
   Seeing more guards in school   [ ]

(continued)

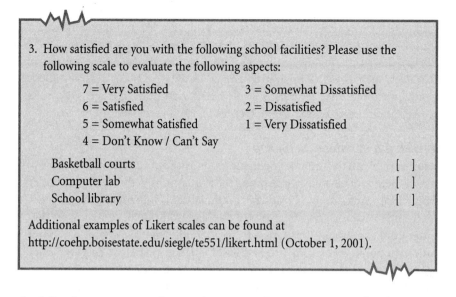

3. How satisfied are you with the following school facilities? Please use the following scale to evaluate the following aspects:

7 = Very Satisfied	3 = Somewhat Dissatisfied
6 = Satisfied	2 = Dissatisfied
5 = Somewhat Satisfied	1 = Very Dissatisfied
4 = Don't Know / Can't Say	

Basketball courts   [   ]
Computer lab   [   ]
School library   [   ]

Additional examples of Likert scales can be found at
http://coehp.boisestate.edu/siegle/te551/likert.html (October 1, 2001).

the following response scale: very important, important, somewhat important, don't know (or, can't say), somewhat unimportant, unimportant, or very unimportant. Collectively, ordinal- and nominal-level variables are often called ***discrete*** or nonmetric.

Interval- and ratio-level variables are those whose scales exhibit both order and distance among categories. We can say that someone who exercises daily does so seven times more often than someone who exercises only weekly. Someone who earns $75,000 per year makes exactly three times that of someone making $25,000. The *only* difference between interval and ratio scales is that the latter have a true "zero" (for example, height can be zero, but not IQ). Because this, generally, has no implication for public administration and policy analysis, we refer to both interval and ratio scales as being ***continuous*** (or metric) scales.[6]

In the above example, we lack any metric scale to measure the extent of the respondents' feelings about the important of high school violence. However, counting instances of high school violence is an example of a metric scale. *In short, we prefer metric scales over ordinal scales, which in turn are preferred over nominal ones.*[7] Scales play an important role in the selection of statistical techniques (discussed in later chapters) and in survey construction.

Finally, we must avoid scales that are *incomplete, ambiguous,* or *overlapping.* An example of an incomplete scale is omitting "zero" as a response category when asking respondents how many fistfights they witnessed. An example of an ambiguous scale is asking respondents to answer a question on the presence of violence "on a scale of 1 to 10" without defining each value. The problem is that respondents may have different definitions of any specific value, such as the value of "6." An example of a scale with overlapping categories is one that has "fistfights" and "scuffles" as separate categories, or one that asks respondents their incomes using overlapping categories.[8] These are obvious problems. Other factors also affect the validity of variables, such as well-known problems of leading (or biased) survey questions, or samples that are biased or restricted. Additional concerns of operationalization are discussed in the section on surveys, below.

Measuring Variables: Sampling

After variables have been defined, questions arise about how information about them will be collected. Among these questions is the matter of target population. Specifically, about which population is information to be gathered, and how many members of the population do we need to reach? The latter implies getting information from a sample, that is, a subset of a population. In public management, samples of citizens, clients, or employees are quite common. Three frequently asked sampling questions are: (1) when is a sample needed? (2) what is the best way to select the sample? (3) how large should the sample be?

First, samples are needed when it is impractical to survey all members of a population. A *census* is a survey or count of the entire population, such as all citizens in a jurisdiction or all program clients. Censuses are practical for small populations, but studies of large populations often use samples. The purpose of a sample is to make *generalizations about the population.* That is, we are interested in knowing how a population, not just the sample, feels about something. In this regard, only representative samples allow for making generalizations about the entire population. A representative sample is one that has characteristics similar to those of the population as a whole. Unrepresentative samples have a biased (or skewed) mix of characteristics (for example, a greater proportion of females) and do not lend themselves to generalization.

Second, *the most accurate way of making representative samples is through random sampling.* **Random sampling** is a process that gives each population member an equal chance of being selected for the study sample. A common approach is to select participants blindly, thereby minimizing any researcher-induced bias. Two popular methods of random sampling are assigning a number to each population member and using computer-generated random numbers to select the sample, and using randomly dialed telephone numbers for selecting participants in phone surveys. Chance selection implies that representative samples are similar but not identical to the population. There will be (slight) differences between the sample and the population with regard to age, gender, income, and so on.

Third, large random samples will more accurately reflect characteristics of the population from which they are drawn. A measure of this accuracy,

Table 1.1———————〜〜〜—Relationships between Sample Size and
Sampling Error

Sample size	Sampling error (%)	Sample size	Sampling error (%)
100	± 9.8	500	± 4.4
200	± 6.9	800	± 3.5
300	± 5.7	1,200	± 2.8
400	± 4.9	2,000	± 2.2

also called the ***sampling error,*** is defined as the range within which results
will vary in 95 of 100 repeated survey efforts. Larger samples better mirror
the population from which they are drawn and thus have smaller sampling
errors. Sampling errors reflect *reliability,* the extent to which repeated measurement produces the same result. By definition, larger samples have better
reliability. The relationship between sample size and sampling error for
samples drawn from populations over 20,000 is shown in Table 1.1. For
populations of this size, *sampling errors are independent of population size.*
The same sampling error applies for a survey of a medium-sized jurisdiction
of 40,000 as for the entire United or the world![9] Another consideration is
that gains in accuracy must be balanced against cost and effort. Accuracy
gains on samples over 1,200 are seldom justified. Most samples range
between 200 and 800. Larger samples are required only when analyses
include many subsets (for example, many districts for which data must be
separately reported).

Decisions on sampling can be aided by some technical considerations.
First, small populations (say, less than 100 or 200) do not require sampling;
rather, a census should be conducted. Second, the list from which a sample is
drawn (called a ***sampling frame***) seldom matches the population exactly.
For example, property tax rolls are biased against renters. Sampling frame
inaccuracies should be identified and acknowledged, but they can seldom be
overcome. In other instances, sampling frames are lacking, such as when
clients are served on a walk-in basis and no record is kept of names. In that
situation, managers randomly select days and times at which anonymous
walk-ins are surveyed. Third, when the population includes subgroups of
small numbers (for example, small minority groupings), ***stratified sampling***
is used. Stratified sampling first divides the sampling frame according to
each subpopulation to be surveyed and then, randomly, samples within each
subgroup. This gives members from small groups a greater chance of participation than members of large groups. Of course, study results must later be
appropriately weighted to ensure unbiased conclusions. Such weighing is
discussed in Chapter 2. Fourth, nonrespondents must be accounted for by

using a greater initial sample. If a 50 percent response rate is expected and 400 completed surveys are desired, then a random sample should be drawn of 800 participants.

Fifth, generalization assumes that nonrespondents answer in the same manner as respondents. ***Nonresponse bias*** (also called nonresponse error) is the extent to which views of nonrespondents differ from respondents, thus affecting generalizability from the sample to the population. Low response rates merit concern about nonresponse bias. This concern is usually dealt with by comparing sample and population demographics. (Chapter 3 discusses these specific tests.) When differences exist (for example, phone surveys sometimes oversample females), researchers can statistically weigh survey responses to account for over- or undersampling and may conclude that the likely, known effect of such oversampling is very minor. In other cases, caveats may be needed in reporting results.

Finally, in recent years, studies of "exemplary practices" have been conducted. Organizations selected for such studies are not randomly selected, but purposively, because of their exemplary practices. ***Purposive sampling*** is used to produce further insight, rather than generalization. Often, these are case studies that are not even generalizable to other exemplary organizations, but the insights of how things are done are of great importance and most useful in improving public management. Likewise, case studies of policy impacts often are very useful to identify unintended outcomes and program innovations that otherwise might not come to light. This type of sampling yields important and useful insights, but the results are not generalizable.

DATA COLLECTION

Administrative Data

Public managers usually generate or have access to considerable amounts of data from the following sources: work orders or service requests, activity logs, staffing levels, absenteeism records, time logs, client requests, client complaints and error logs, inspection and repair reports, inventory management reports, financial reports, program budgets, grants, and many other data of specific public services. Schools often have data about crimes and violence that occur. Data from these sources often are called ***administrative data.*** They are often used for performance measurement, that is, the activity of monitoring agency or program efforts and outcomes over time.[10]

Administrative data often suffer from some inaccuracies that must be acknowledged or overcome. Data are sometimes (1) missing or incomplete; (2) inaccurately reported; (3) subject to definitions that have changed over

Table 1.2 ⎯⎯⎯⎯⎯ⅿⅿ⎯ Comparing Mail, Phone, and In-Person
Surveys

Criterion	Mail	Phone	In-Person
a. Response rate	Variable	Variable	High
b. Amount of data	Highest	Low to Medium	Low or High
c. Data collection	6–8 weeks	2–3 weeks	4–6 weeks
d. Cost per survey	Low to Medium	Medium to High	Very high
e. Interviewer bias	Low	Medium	Medium

time and therefore cannot be compared; (4) not linked to particular events
or clients, or cannot be disaggregated in necessary ways; or (5) confidential
and unavailable for analysis in any form. These problems require that
analysts identify them, then correct or remove inaccurate data, and make
reasonable adjustments to link data across time or cases. The rigor with
which these problems are identified and addressed enhances the validity and
credibility of these administrative data. Some agencies assign responsibility
for data keeping and thereby attempt to minimize these problems.

Agencies or programs with a large number of records may wish to take a
sample of them. For example, agencies in public health or welfare frequently
have a very large number of clients. Then researchers apply the above
sampling procedures to administrative data and draw a random sample for
further analysis.

Surveys

Citizen, client, and employee surveys are common in public management.
Three types of surveys are *mail, phone,* and *in-person surveys.* Each has
somewhat different advantages, and actual experiences may vary according
to the specific conditions (see Table 1.2). *Phone surveys* are increasingly used
for citizen surveys because of cost and speed advantages. Data collection for
phone surveys can often be completed in two to three weeks (unlike mail
surveys, which may require multiple mailings) and are cheaper than mail or
in-person surveys. Random sampling is often achieved through random
digit dialing. This procedure randomly chooses the last four digits of phone
numbers (thus ensuring geographic relevancy by using known area codes
and exchanges). Phone surveys also are used for client surveys, in which case
clients are randomly selected from a list of clients. Although phone surveys
are shorter than mail or in-person surveys, up to eighty different items can
be asked when questions are easy and asked in a similar format. Employee
surveys are frequently conducted by confidential pen-and-paper survey. To

ensure both high response rates and anonymity, employees sometimes are asked to complete the surveys simultaneously and then return them in blank envelopes.

Surveys typically follow the following steps: (1) obtaining permissions and resources for conducting surveys; (2) interviewing stakeholders to fully understand the study context and to specify study objectives; (3) identifying the sampling frame and obtaining a (random) sample of the study population; (4) designing, testing, and improving a pilot survey; (5) implementing the final survey instrument; (6) analyzing and reporting findings.

It is obvious that biased questions and protocols diminish study validity and, hence, must be avoided. To avoid bias, interviewers should follow the exact same script, with no variation among them. Neither the interviewers nor the protocol should introduce bias. Also, questions should be clear (that is, unambiguous and specific) and answerable by respondents, avoiding double-barreled phrasing, avoiding leading (or biased) phrases, and avoiding negative statements.[11] Regardless of the type of survey, a general guideline for developing survey questions is that they should be *as easy as possible* for the respondent to answer while providing researchers with all the information that they need. Questions that deal with the same topic should be grouped together. Likert scales greatly assist in developing surveys because the same response scale can be used for many different items.

Response rates are as much a threat to survey validity as are biased questions. Response rates of general citizen surveys are typically in the 20 to 35 percent range, despite call backs. Phone surveys of program clients have higher response rates, reflecting greater affiliation of respondents with the survey's subject matter. When survey response rates are low, concerns of nonresponse bias, discussed earlier, may need to be addressed. In this regard, some academic studies deal with nonresponse bias in mail surveys by conducting a phone survey of selected items among nonrespondents of the mail survey. The responses of respondents and nonrespondents are then compared.

Finally, many agencies leave **customer comment cards** on reception counters for clients to take and complete voluntarily. Results from these cards are *not* generalizable, because clients completing these cards are self-selected, perhaps skewed toward clients with gripes. Thus, the response sample is unrepresentative. Although these efforts are invalid for the purpose of generalization, these comments often serve other managerial purposes such as providing an early warning of problems that managers may wish to pursue.

Other Data Sources

Four other sources of data are *observers, actors, experts,* and *focus groups.* **Observers** are sometimes used to assess the condition of facilities and infrastructure, such as roads, public facilities, and park grounds. Typically, considerable care is taken to ensure that observers conduct their observations in the same manner, and from time to time reliability checks are conducted for this purpose. *Actors* are observers who are actively involved in what they observe. Role playing is sometimes used to assess frontline services, such as toll collection or welfare application, by observing standards and possible discrimination. *Experts* are used when objective data alone are insufficient for making judgments about program outcomes. For example, landfill maintenance, analysis of medical records, and the quality of higher education programs require a balance of objective facts and subjective opinion. Then, experts are used who either work together or separately in coming to a consensus.

Focus groups are purposive samples that are used for generating insights about program services and goals. For example, a citizen focus group on law enforcement might be asked about perceptions of officers in a jurisdiction, as well as program needs and outcomes. Focus groups often are homogeneous, because different populations have different experiences and may drown each other out. For example, minorities and whites often have very different perceptions about law enforcement personnel. While focus groups are valuable, the small number of focus group participants suggests that generalization is not possible.

PUTTING IT TOGETHER

It should now be clear that many different aspects go into conducting a valid program evaluation. The six steps of program evaluation, discussed earlier in this chapter, provide an organized process for considering the different activities and concerns. Below is a summary proposal, for evaluating an after-school program, integrating many of the above elements. In some ways, we can think of proposals as final reports that lack data analysis or conclusions.

Proposal for Evaluating an After-School Program
In recent years, new after-school programs have been implemented in our region. The purpose of this proposal is to outline a strategy for evaluation. Input has been sought and obtained from many sources, including county management, school administrators, teachers, and a panel of school psychologists. We also conducted two focus groups with school students. A consensus exists that school violence is an important problem and that an after-school program presents an opportunity to reduce it. However, many observers believe that the benefits of after-school programs extend beyond the current issue of school violence, and we were encouraged to evaluate other outcomes, too.

The main after-school activities whose outcomes we will evaluate are the homework assistance and anger management components. Student participation in after-school programs often is voluntary, although many schools have made an effort to ensure that those teenagers participate who they believe are prone to violence, socially isolated, or academically at risk.

To better determine the impact of these after-school programs, we will include after-school programs that vary in their use of anger management and homework assistance. A few after-school programs provide only recreational activities, and we feel that those are an appropriate comparison group for these others programs. Although to date no baseline data has been gathered, we propose to do that as soon as the proposal is approved. Baseline data are important in evaluating the impact of these programs.

We will be focusing our efforts on a variety of well-targeted outcome measures. With regard to anger management, we will focus on students' knowledge of anger management principles, their ability to identify anger in themselves and others, the strategies they use to release anger in nonviolent ways, and their willingness to help others use such strategies. With regard to homework assistance, we will focus on the utilization of this service, the areas in which it is most often used, and perceptions of increased valuation of academics and study discipline. With regard to high school violence, we will assess violence with weapons, physical violence without weapons, and verbal assaults.

While after-school programs could affect violence and improve academic ability, other factors contribute to these outcomes as well. This evaluation acknowledges these other factors and will collect information about the following variables for purposes of statistical control: student access to weapons, student social isolation, peer pressure exerted by violence-prone groups, school enforcement of nonviolence policies, teacher awareness of teenage violence predictors, and teacher and staff commitment to reducing teenage violence. We will also consider student academic performance, composition of student household (number of parents and siblings living with student), gender, and race.

We will collect data from a variety of sources. School records track incidents of physical violence, though such records vary in accuracy regarding that which is recorded. Rather, the primary sources will be students and teachers. On a quarterly basis, teachers will be asked to participate in a survey about violence in their classes, and on the impact of the after-school programs on students that are in their classes. Also, students will be given a test of their knowledge of anger management principles, as well as an assessment of the usefulness and impact of homework assistance. The latter is, of course, administered only to those who participate in such homework assistance. Both the teacher and student surveys include items regarding the other control variables mentioned above.

We intend to survey all teachers and a sample of students participating in these programs. We anticipate surveying about 100 teachers and a sample of 300 students (which has a sampling error of 5.6 percent). Detailed information about the measurements and survey instruments and protocols is provided in the appendix (not shown here).

CONCLUSION

The task of the analyst is twofold: to be true to the meaning and purposes of that which is being measured, and to be cognizant of the concerns that a skeptical audience might raise which threaten to diminish the credibility of evaluations and surveys. Research methods provide an intellectual foundation for dealing with these concerns, thereby improving the quality of evaluations and surveys.

Specifically, research methods suggest that analysts consider careful measurement of their main study concepts. Often, analysts measure several dimensions of their central study concepts. Research methods also suggest that analysts go beyond merely describing the current state of their topic (for example, the degree of school violence) and also examine variables that are correlated with it (for example, anger management classes). Such variables inform managers of factors (or levers) through which they might influence outcomes. Pursuing this line of thought leads to the logical interest in rival hypotheses—other factors that may also affect the efficacy of such levers—and control groups, which are comparison groups (perhaps nearby schools) that are subjected to different conditions that enable comparison of outcomes. Although analysts are responsible for these design decisions, the quality and acceptance of these decisions often is enhanced by consulting with those who have a stake in the outcomes.

This chapter also discussed the technical matters of sampling and conducting scientific surveys. Random sampling is essential for making generalizations about a population. Larger samples have smaller sampling errors (that is, their estimates of population characteristics are more accurate); many samples are between 200 and 800 respondents (for example, program clients), although larger samples are used when study populations have many subpopulations that are analyzed separately. This chapter also discussed the challenge of response rates (the higher the better), and it explored the pros and cons of alternative survey strategies. Finally, we also discussed guidelines for conducting surveys and formulating survey questions.

Analysts who seek detailed criteria and procedures will be disappointed that only broad guidelines are available. Perhaps the diversity of applications makes this almost inevitable. In any event, staying true to the subject matter and addressing concerns of critics (real or imagined) by anticipating them when possible increase the quality of one's work. In other words, the acceptance and use of analysts' work often hinges on the ability of analysts to show that they have been objective, thorough, and responsive.

KEY TERMS

Actors (p. 21)
Administrative data (p. 18)
Causal relationships vs. associations (pp. 6–8)
Census (p. 16)
Classic, randomized experiments (p. 8)
Concept measurement (process of) (p. 11)
Concepts (p. 11)
Continuous (or metric) scales (p. 15)
Control variable (p. 8)
Criteria for causality (p. 7)
Customer comment cards (p. 20)
Dependent variable (pp. 6, 7)
Discrete (or nonmetric) scales (p. 15)
Experimental design (p. 8)
Experts (p. 21)
Focus groups (p. 21)
Hypothesis (p. 8)
Independent variable (pp. 6, 7)

Long-term outcomes (p. 5)
Measurement levels (nominal, ordinal, interval, ratio) (p. 13)
Measurement validity (p. 11)
Nonresponse bias (p. 18)
Observers (p. 20)
Purposive sample (p. 18)
Quasi-experimental design (p. 9)
Random sampling (p. 16)
Research methodology (p. 3)
Rival hypothesis (p. 8)
Sampling error (p. 17)
Sampling frame (p. 17)
Short-term outcomes (p. 5)
Six steps of program evaluation (pp. 4–5)
Statistical techniques (p. 11)
Stratified sampling (p. 17)
Surveys (mail, phone, in-person) (p. 19)
Variables vs. constants (p. 6)

Notes

1. One speculation on the origin of alternative terminology is that it is part of the competitive process of scientific discovery. Different scientists use different terms, at about the same time, to describe novel but similar phenomena or issues. Another explanation is that disciplines often develop in isolation from each other, and each reaches a different consensus about appropriate terminology. Analysts who work in such interdisciplinary fields as public management and policy analysis should be familiar with these varied uses.
2. We also note that relationships in social science usually are *probabilistic* (occurring sometimes), rather than *deterministic* (occurring each time). Relations seldom occur with 100 percent certainty. For example, when we

say that anger management reduces high school violence, we are not implying that this always occurs. Surely, some teenagers will get violently angry. Rather, we mean that *on average,* (that is, probabilistically) incidents of violence will go down. Even though theories of causal relationships are expressed with a measure of theoretical certainty, there are some after-school programs that are less effective than others. We mean only that *on average* programs are effective. (Later, we will use statistics to assess whether these probabilistic statements are warranted.)

3. Another example is this. Suppose we conclude from a study of young children that attending after-school programs is causally related to increased child abuse. Should we infer that such children should be kept at home? Or could it be that some day care centers use inexperienced or untrained providers and that child abuse rates in these centers are much higher than in those employing experienced, well-trained providers?

4. Here's another example. Suppose, for the purpose of assessing or initiating a public health program of some kind, we wish to measure the extent to which a population of adults has a "healthy lifestyle." "Healthy lifestyle" is an abstract idea that is not directly observable. In the first step, we must identify the relevant dimensions of the concept "healthy lifestyle." We conceptualize that two important dimensions are "physical exercise" and "eating habits," although we could identify additional dimensions. In the second step, these two dimensions are operationalized. For example, we might measure "physical exercise" by asking each person the extent to which they walk, bike, swim, play tennis or racquetball, and do other activities. Likewise, we operationalize "eating habits" by asking them about their use of fast foods, restaurants, snacks, and the like.

5. A reinforcing consideration is that data collection efforts must be kept to manageable proportions. Many scientific studies in public administration and public policy use one to five dimensions per concept (thus, some concepts have only one dimension), and operationalization is often limited to five to eight variables per dimension. To help generate possible dimensions and variables, analysts often consult past studies and keep the research purpose and context in mind. A practical consideration is that when working with existing data (also called "secondary data"), analysts often must use whatever variables are available. Conceptualization and operationalization may then be wanting, to say the least. Then, analysts must acknowledge study limitations (caveats) and argue that the analysis adds value and is the best available.

6. Some texts refer to both interval and ratio scales as "interval," which may cause confusion. Texts that refer to both as "metric" often refer to nominal and ordinal variables as nonmetric or discrete. In this context, the term *metric* has no bearing on the metric system of measurement that uses meters to measure distance.

7. For the purposes of statistical testing, metric variables are also assumed to be continuous, defined as having at least five categories. Metric variables with fewer than five categories, then, are often regarded as ordinal. Ordinal variables with five or more categories (including Likert scales) are sometimes analyzed with metric-level statistics. This latter practice is not without its critics, but it is widely done.

8. An example of overlapping income brackets are $20,000–$40,000 and $40,000–$60,000. It is better to use $20,000–$39,999 and $40,000–$59,999.

9. Small populations have smaller sampling errors. For 5 percent sampling errors, populations of 5,000 require samples of 357, populations of 1,000 require samples of 278, populations of 500 require samples of 217, populations of 300 require samples of 168, populations of 200 require samples of 132. Populations of 100 require samples of 79, suggesting that a census would require only a modest amount of additional effort. Numerous Internet sites provide sample size-estimation tables. One such site is http://www.dssresearch.com/sampleSize/sampling_error.asp (June 1, 2001). The sampling errors shown are maximum estimates, which are commonly used. Specifically, they are based on the assumption that the proportion of respondents answering in a specific way is 50 percent.

10. See, for example, Theodore Poister and Gregory Streib, "Performance Measurement in Municipal Government: Assessing the State of the Practice," *Public Administration Review* 59 (July/August 1999): 325–335. Also see the "Suggested Readings" section of the workbook.

11. For example, "Do you feel safe?" is ambiguous for the purpose of evaluating high school violence. A leading question is, "Would you ever hit a classmate?" which implies that it is undesirable or unacceptable to do so. A better question would be, "Have you thought about hitting a classmate during the last seven days?" An example of a double-barreled question is, "Do you feel that guns should be barred from school and that those who bring guns to school should be punished?" These questions should be asked separately. Also, questions should be answerable. Although respondents may have opinions about school safety, they are apt to be unfamiliar about specific options. Thus, "Do you want anger management programs?" may be unknowable to those who are unfamiliar with such programs. It would be best to precede this question with, "How familiar are you with anger management programs?" Some of the very best survey questions follow the K.I.S.S. rule: they Keep It Simple (and) Stupid.

Univariate Analysis: Description

CHAPTER OBJECTIVES

After reading this chapter, you should be able to:
- Understand the use of summary statistics
- Distinguish between measures of central tendency and dispersion
- Identify and be able to derive three types of averages
- Appreciate the importance of "data cleaning"
- Understand the use of boxplots and frequency distributions
- Create histograms, stem-and-leaf plots, and other visual aids for reporting
- Understand the concept of standard deviation

Descriptive information has numerous uses in public management and analysis. Many decisions are based on description alone. For example, knowing how much pollution is occurring, the percentage of citizens favoring improved parks, or the average rate of absenteeism, often is meaningful information that affects public decision making. This descriptive information is also used for subsequent comparison against past performance, the performance of other jurisdictions, and across such respondent or jurisdictional characteristics as gender or area incomes.

This chapter provides techniques for the analysis of single variables (also called **univariate analysis**). Univariate statistics is also called **summary statistics,** that is, statistics that provide information only about certain aspects of our data. Although summary measures do not tell everything about our variables, what they do tell is important. Specifically, there are two basic types (or families) of univariate statistics, which tell us about (1) *central tendency* (also known as "averages") and (2) *dispersion.* If we wanted to fully and completely describe each data set without any missing piece of information, we could fully describe each observation, including each variable's values. This approach, while valid, is an inefficient approach that would provide confusing insights, if any at all.

The summary statistics of univariate analysis can also be used for comparison. For example, we might want to compare the average crime rate in two or more high schools. However, univariate statistics contain no guidelines for determining which differences are "statistically significant." This concept, along with appropriate statistics, is part of **bivariate analysis,** the analysis of two variables. Bivariate statistics will be discussed in Chapter 3. **Multivariate analysis** is the analysis of three or more variables and is discussed later in this book. One task of statistical analysis is choosing the correct, appropriate statistic; the roadmap provided at the beginning of the book can guide you to the correct selection.

As noted in the Introduction, the philosophy of this book is one of hands-on, computer-based application. The quality of your results is only as good as the quality of the data (many of you have heard the expression "garbage in, garbage out"). Prior to any analysis, analysts perform data coding, input, and cleaning, all of which follow data collection. **Data coding** is the process of preparing data (from pen-and-paper surveys or electronic or other sources) for input into statistical software programs. **Data input** is the activity of recording these data in statistical software programs. **Data cleaning** is the process of identifying and removing reporting and recording errors, which is aided by univariate analysis. Without data cleaning, such errors may have a negative (biasing) effect on your results. It is common practice to assume that unexamined data usually contain various errors (such as mistyped values) that must be identified and removed.

Data cleaning usually consists of two steps. First, analysts identify implausible values in their data that they then remove or correct. For example, a variable "age" that has a value of "999" certainly requires further investigation. This might be a coding error or used to indicate a missing value, in which case analysts should ascertain that "999" is defined in their statistical software as a missing value for this variable. Second, analysts attempt to ascertain that their data set is complete and accurate. To this end, the number of observations (records) in the data set is verified against the number of records in the source (paper or electronic), and a random sample of records is selected for detailed comparison. Only *after* the analyst has determined that the data are complete and free from coding and entry errors can data analysis proceed further.[1]

MEASURES OF CENTRAL TENDENCY

The first family of univariate analysis is **measures of central tendency,** which provide information about the most typical or average values of a variable. There are three such measures: the *mean, median,* and *mode.* Analysts frequently report this type of measure when, for example, reporting the mean number of arrests or housing starts or the like. Each of these measures is described below.

The Mean

The **mean** (or arithmetic mean) is what most people call "the average," but analysts should use the word *mean* rather than *average* to avoid confusion with other types of averages. The mean is defined as *the sum of a series of observations, divided by the number of observations in the series.* It is commonly used to describe the central tendency of variables, such as the mean number of crimes, public safety inspections, welfare recipients, abortions, roads under repair, and so on. Mean calculations are essential to most analyses, and are used in almost every report.

The following example shows how to calculate the mean. Although computers and hand calculators are usually used to calculate the mean, you also should know how to do this by hand. For illustration, assume that a sample of eight observations has the following values (or data elements) of a variable that we call "variable x": the values are 20, 20, 67, 70, 71, 80, 90, and 225 ($n = 8$). Then, the mean is calculated as follows:

$$Mean = \sum_i x_i \, / \, n =$$
$$(20 + 20 + 67 + 70 + 71 + 80 + 90 + 225)/8 = 643/8 = 80.38.$$

The notation $\sum_i x_i$ means "the sum of all values of (variable) x," as shown above. In fact, this notation is shorthand for $\sum_{i=1}^{8} x_i$, which specifies adding the first eight values of x, in the order shown. In our example, $x_1 = 20$, $x_2 = 20$, $x_3 = 67$ and so on. Because our variable has only eight values, there is no need for the notation $\sum_{i=1}^{8} x_i$. Also, n is used to indicate that the observations are a sample. If the observations had constituted the entire population, we would have used a different notation: N (or $\sum_i x_i \, / \, N$). This is just a matter of notation, which affects neither the definition nor the calculation of the mean.[2]

Another type of mean is the ***weighted mean,*** which is defined as a mean for which the observations have been given variable weights. Weighted means are commonly used for adjusting over- and undersampling in surveys. For example, when minorities are undersampled, we might want to weigh each of their responses more heavily in calculating the mean. Box 2.1 includes an example of these calculations. By contrast, each of the eight observations discussed above is weighted equally, so using the weighted mean is not necessary.

The Median

A limitation of the mean is that its value is greatly affected when a few very large or very small values are present in the data, relative to other values. In the above example, if x_8 (the eighth observation in the above sequence, which is 225) had been 950, then the above mean would be 171—more than double its initial value! A realistic example of this problem arises when calculating the mean household income in the small hometown of Bill Gates, one of the world's richest people. In that case, the mean is a poor summary statistic of the average household income in that jurisdiction.

The ***median*** is defined as *the middle value in a series (or array) of values.* Its value is, by definition, unaffected by a few very large or small values. *The median should always be used when a few very large or very small values affect estimates of the mean.* Indeed, most summary income statistics of populations report both means and medians because they can be so different. The median is appropriate for both continuous- and ordinal-level variables. The interpretation of the median is that half of the observations lie above the median, and the other half lie below it. To find the median, the data must be ordered from low to high and then the value of the middle observation determined. If the number of observations is uneven, the median is the value of the middle observation. If the number of observations is even, the median is the mean of the two observations that are nearest to the middle location of the array. This location is found through visual inspection or the formula $(n + 1)/2$, where n is the number of observations.

In the above example, variable x has an even (eight) number of observations, which have already been arrayed from low to high. The two middle values are 70 and 71 (at locations 4 and 5) and so the median is 70.50 (at location $[8 + 1]/2 = 4.50$). If a ninth observation is added to variable x, for example, $x_9 = 275$, the median becomes 71. Note that these estimates are unaffected by the values of the highest or lowest values. If $x_9 = 875$, the median is still 71, because the value of this variable does not affect the value of the middle observation in the series. When reporting the median for ordinal-level variables, some analysts avoid fractions and report exact categories values.[3] Note that having few very large or very small values can also

In Greater Depth...

Box 2.1   Weighting Your Data

Weighted means are easily calculated. The formula for weighted means is $\sum_i w_i x_i / \sum_i w_i$, which means: "identify the weights, then multiply each weight with the value of each observation, then add these values and, finally, divide this number by the sum of all weights. Confused? The following example demonstrates this process:

Value	Weight	Weighted Value
2	0.5	1
2	1.0	2
3	2.0	6
3	2.0	6

The unweighted mean is $(10/4) = 2.50$, and the weighted mean is $(15/5.5) = 2.73$. Weighted means have many applications, including in survey research. Nonresponse bias is the bias that occurs because survey samples seldom match the population exactly: Nonrespondents might have answered differently from respondents. Perhaps the best approach is to conduct a separate survey of nonrespondents and compare their responses with those of the initial respondents. But this method often is expensive and complicated. A second best approach, then, is to compare "weighted" responses against the actual responses (called "unweighted" responses). The weighted responses are those that would have been obtained if the sample distribution had perfectly matched that of known population demographics. Typically, census and other sources provide information about age, race, and gender. Consider the following demographics (from the workbook, *Exercising Essential Statistics,* Chapter 1):

Age	Population(%)	Sample(%)
18–45	62.3	62.8
46–65	24.1	26.8
66+	13.6	10.4

Race	Population(%)	Sample(%)
white	81.5	84.3
nonwhite	18.5	15.7

(continued)

Box 2.1 *(continued)*

Gender	Population(%)	Sample(%)
Male	49.0	43.9
Female	51.0	56.1

Clearly, residents over 66 years of age are undersampled: their responses should be weighted by (13.6/10.4) = 1.308. Given the above information, the weight assigned to every white female respondent of age 45–65 years is (81.5/84.3)*(51.0/56.1)*(24.1/26.8) = 0.790. (A few extra decimals are used here in order to avoid introducing bias.) Similarly, weights are assigned for all other groupings. For example, the weight assigned to every nonwhite male respondent over 66 years is (18.5/15.7)*(49.0/43.9)*(13.6/10.4) = 1.720. (While this is a large value, there are few such respondents in the sample.) Then, analysts can compare weighted and unweighted responses to determine the extent of nonresponse bias, if any (see workbook). Keep in mind that weighted means are best-guess estimates, and they should not be used instead of actual survey data.

be caused by data entry errors, for example, coding x_8 as 1,225, when it should be 225. This property of the mean is yet another reason for taking data cleaning seriously.

Examples of the median are common in demographic studies of income, in which a few individuals or households typically have very large incomes. Other examples include studies of average jail time served by inmates (some people serve very long sentences!), average wait times for tax returns or class registration, and average jury awards (some people have received huge sums). A rule of thumb is that when the mean and median are considerably different, analysts should report both. When the mean and median are similar, it suffices to report only the mean. The measure of what constitutes a "considerable difference" is a judgment call informed by the magnitude of the difference and the study's context.

The Mode

The *mode* is defined as *the most frequent* (typical) *value(s) of a variable.* The mode is appropriate for all levels of variable measurement. In the above example, the mode of variable x is the value twenty. Another example is that the mode of people living in households is two. Although this summary statistic is infrequently used, it is most useful when variables have two or more values that are much more frequent than other values. For example,

Table 2.1 ———— ᴧᴧᴧ— Illustration of Grouped Data

Category	Interval of variable x	Frequency	Cumulative frequency
1	1–5	12	12
2	6–10	5	17
3	11–15	18	35
4	16–20	36	71
5	21–25	14	85

suppose that most hospital patients stay either one or five days after a certain type of surgery. Other patients stay other lengths of time, but these lengths are less frequent. Then, we say the modes are one and five. The mode is useful in such cases because both the mean or median would lead us to a single value, which, in this case, is a poor measure of central tendency because of the two values that occur most often.

Using Grouped Data

The above calculations assume that the analyst has data for each observation, such as is typically used in statistical software programs. However, analysts sometimes have published data only in the tabular format, or a similar one. *Grouped data* refers to observations that have already been grouped in different categories. An example is shown in Table 2.1. The column labeled "Interval of variable x" could be almost anything, such as the groupings of city sizes, students' test scores, motorists' speeds through toll booths with electronic collection, or regional water quality ratings. The ranges show the values of each category. Ranges are sometimes shown as footnotes to tables, which then only show categories and frequencies. The "Frequency" column counts occurrences. For example, it indicates that there are twelve cities in category 1, five cities in category 2, and so on. The column *Cumulative frequency* shows the running total of frequencies of each category and may be absent from some grouped data tables.

Calculations of means and medians of grouped data are *best-guess esti-mates* and should *be used only when individual observations are unavailable.* Unfortunately, few computer programs can read tabular formats of grouped data, and so calculations must be done by hand. *Note that the ability to make these calculations does not affect understanding of other material in this book (with the exception of our discussion of quartiles, which immediately follows).*

The *mean of grouped data* is calculated in two steps. First, the mean of the categories is calculated using the formula $\sum_i w_i r_i / \sum_i w_i$, whereby r = row number and w = the number of observations in each row. Applying the above data, we find that the weighted mean of categories is $(12*1) + (5*2) + (18*3) + (36*4) + (14*5)/(12 + 5 + 18 + 36 + 14) = 290/85 = 3.412.$[4]

Second, the *variable value* associated with this group mean value is determined. This requires interpolation in the following manner. The mean of the grouped data, 3.412, lies somewhere between categories 3 and 4. The estimate of the average variable value associated with category 3 is defined as the midpoint of its range, or $(11+ 15)/2 = 13$, and the midpoint of the value associated with category 4 is $(16 + 20)/2 = 18$. Then, the variable value associated with the category location of 3.412 (which is $3.000 + 0.412$) is defined as the midpoint estimate of the range associated with category 3 (that is, 13) *plus* 0.412 of the difference of these category midpoints, or $(18 - 13) = 5$. Hence, the estimated value of the variable mean is $13 + (0.412*5) = 15.06$ (with rounding). An equivalent expression is that 3.412 "lies 41.2 percent from category 3 toward category 4," which is graphically shown below:

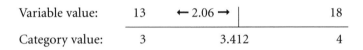

Variable value:	13	← 2.06 →		18
Category value:	3		3.412	4

The *median of grouped data* is estimated in an analogous way. The sample has a total of eighty-five observations, and so the median is defined by the value of the $[(85 + 1)/2] =$ forty-third observation when values are ordered. Examining the cumulative frequencies, we find that the median falls somewhere between the third and fourth categories:

Variable frequency:	12	17	35		43	71	85
Category value:		1	2	3 ← 0.222 →		4	5

The value of the forty-third observation lies $(43 - 35)/(71 - 35) = 0.222$ from category 3 toward category 4, hence, with a category value of 3.222. Using the same method of interpolation as above, the corresponding variable value of category location 3.222 is $[13 + 0.222*(18 - 13)] = 14.11$. Note the difference between the estimated group mean and median. The linear interpolation used for calculating grouped means and medians assumes defined distances between categories, hence, a continuous level of variable measurement.

The *mode of the grouped data* is the most frequent observation. This is category 4, which has a midpoint value of 18. The mode of this grouped data is thus 18.

MEASURES OF DISPERSION

The second family of univariate analysis, *measures of dispersion,* provides information about the distribution of the values of a variable. These measures tell us how widely values are dispersed around their measures of central tendency. This is useful when, for example, we want to know the range of student test scores around the mean or median, specifically, whether most students have scores that cluster closely around the mean, or whether broad variation exists. More generally, measures of dispersion are used to address the following questions regarding variables:

- What is the range of the values (minimum, maximum)?
- What is the distribution of values based on percentiles?
- Are most values closely clustered around the mean and median, or is there great variation?
- Are any values very large or very small that might affect the value of the mean?
- Are any values unusually large or small (referred to as outliers) that affect the estimate of statistics?

These are important questions regarding variables, and public audiences expect analysts to have a ready grasp of them. The latter question also relates to data cleaning; measures of dispersion are often used to aid in that effort. Indeed, tables such as Table 2.1 often are final products that reflect data that has already been cleaned using measures discussed below. Two types of measures of dispersion exist, distinguished by whether they are calculated based on (1) the location or (2) the values of data. These are discussed below.

Boxplots

A *boxplot* is a graphical device that shows various measures of dispersion calculated on the basis of the location of data. (The next section discusses measures of dispersion based on the values of data.) Boxplots are appropriate for both continuous- and ordinal-level variables and are handy devices for showing medians, quartile scores, and outliers. Many computer programs readily provide boxplots for any number of variables, and some

Figure 2.1  Boxplot

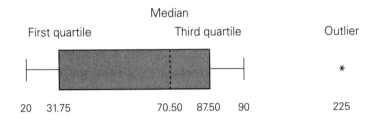

analysts first generate boxplots of each variable to obtain a quick, visual, and preliminary understanding of their data. Based on the data used earlier to calculate the mean and median (see the section "Measures of Central Tendency"), the boxplot shown in Figure 2.1 is obtained. Computers typically calculate these values; the following calculations are shown only for purposes of conceptual understanding. The *median* (defined earlier) is 70.50, calculated in the usual manner (see the section "The Median"). The *first quartile* is simply the lowest quartile score (*it is not a range.*). The location is defined as half the location of the median. As previously discussed, our example has eight values and thus the location of that median is $[(n + 1)/2] = 4.50$, that is, the mean of the values of the fourth and fifth observations, when all observations are ordered from the lowest to the highest values. The *location* of the first quartile, then, is defined as $4.50/2 = 2.25$. The variable value associated with this location (2.25) is defined as the value of the second observation plus one-quarter of the distance between the second and third observations, analogous to the example of the preceding section (see the section "Using Grouped Data"). In our example, that value is calculated as $20 + 0.25*(67 − 20) = 31.75$. The *third quartile* is the third quartile score, or location $4.50 + 2.25 = 6.75$. The value is $80 + 0.75*(90 − 80) = 87.50$. Most computer programs also produce a statistic that is called the *midspread* (or *interquartile range,* IQR). It is defined as the difference between the first quartile and the third quartile, hence, $87.50 − 31.75 = 55.75$. The *range* is simply the difference between the highest and lowest value, or $225 − 20 = 205$. Again, although computers calculate these values, it is important that you have a clear understanding of what these concepts mean.

The boxplot also shows a singular observation with a value of 225 that is labeled "outlier." *Outliers* (or extremes) are analyst-defined observations with unusual values relative to other values in the data. Outliers may be the result of data-coding errors (which should either be fixed or removed) or reflect actual but unusual values in the sample. Such outliers matter because many public decisions are based on average behavior, rather than the unusual behavior of a few.[5] Thus, it makes good sense to distinguish *usual observations from unusual ones.* An important task of data cleaning and preliminary analysis is to identify outliers and to decide whether or not they should be retained. Our position is that observations that are flagged as outliers generally should be retained when they are not coding errors, when they are plausible values of the variable in question, and when they do not greatly affect the value of the mean (of continuous variables). However, when outliers are present in analyses, their effect on final results should be studied. Analysts should also report any observations (outliers) that have been dropped from analysis, along with reasons for doing so.

Boxplots also help analysts to calculate cut-off points beyond which any observations are statistically considered as outliers. These cut-off points are called, respectively, the inner and outer fence. The ***inner fence*** is an imaginary value that lies 1.5 times the midspread below the first quartile. For the above data, the inner fence is $31.75 - (1.5*55.75) = -51.88$. All of our data are greater than the value of the inner fence, and thus our data show no outliers on this lower end. The ***outer fence*** is an imaginary value that lies 1.5 times the midspread above the third quartile. It is calculated as $87.5 + (1.5*55.75) = 171.13$. Our data has one observation that exceeds this value, $x_8 = 225$, which is therefore labeled an "outlier."[6] Analysts might consider omitting x_8 from further analysis. Doing so greatly affects the mean, reducing it from 80.38 to 59.71. As expected, omitting x_8 does not much change the median, which goes from 70.5 to 70.0; the loss of the observation merely redefines the location of the middle observation. As discussed above, the decision to drop an observation from analysis should be based on argument. If the observation is deemed to be representative of the population from which it is drawn, then it should be retained. If it is thought to be unrepresentative, then it should be excluded. Whatever the decision (retention or deletion), the case must be argued and its impact on further analysis noted.

The box further shows two ***whiskers*** extending out from the first and third quartiles. The end points of these whiskers are *the lowest and highest values of the variables that are not outliers.* These differ only from the lowest and highest values of the data when there are outliers. Together with the box (shown as the "area" between the first and third quartiles), analysts obtain a quick visual image of the spread of the data. If the whiskers and box are relatively short, then the variable varies little in the sample. If the whiskers and box are long, there is more variation to talk about.

In short, boxplots are a great tool of preliminary data analysis and are easily produced by computers. They help identify outliers and achieve an understanding of the distribution. Imagine the analyst who rushes headlong

Figure 2.2 ————— ⌇⌇— Stem-and-Leaf Plot

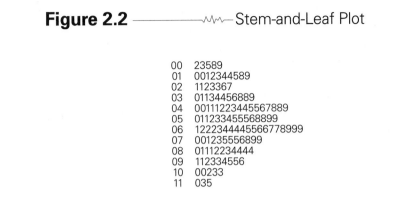

```
00   23589
01   0012344589
02   1123367
03   01134456889
04   00111223445567889
05   011233455568899
06   1222344445566778999
07   001235556899
08   01112234444
09   112334556
10   00233
11   035
```

into producing detailed tables and reports, only to redo this work after outliers (and perhaps other problems, too) have been discovered in the data!

Frequency Distributions

Just as boxplots show measures of dispersion based on data location, *frequency distributions* describe the range and frequency of values of a variable. They are simple to make and often are a prelude for generating various attractive graphics that are shown in this section. Frequency distributions often are shown in reports as a final *product* of univariate analysis. They presume that other analyses have been conducted, especially the identification and removal of outliers and coding errors.

When variables are continuous (or metric), a *stem-and-leaf plot* is a quick visual representation of the frequency distribution of continuous variables. These plots, too, can be used for detecting unusually large values. The categories are computer generated, based on the range and number of observations. The stem-and-leaf plot shown in Figure 2.2 was generated for a continuous variable that has 124 observations. In a stem-and-leaf plot, these observations are shown ordered from low to high. The left column is called the stem, and the right-hand column is called the leaves. The values are found by combining the stem and leaves: the stems are the first figures of any number, and the leaf is the figure that is added onto it. The lowest number of the series is 002 followed by 003, 005, 008, 009, 010, 010, 011, 012, and 013, and so on. The five highest values are 103, 103, 110, 113 and 115. The median is at location [(124 + 1)/2] = 62.50, and is 058. These values can also be shown in a *histogram* in Figure 2.3. A histogram is similar to a stem-and-leaf plot but differs in that it shows the number of observations in each category. Like the stem-and-leaf plot, a histogram is useful because it provides a quick visual of the central tendency, the extent of dispersion, and also whether any unusually large or small observations are

Figure 2.3 ————————〰〰〰—Histogram

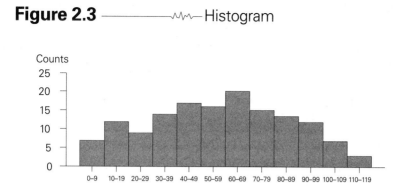

present. Unlike the stem-and-leaf plot, histograms allow analysts to see how many observations are present in each category. Also, the category widths (shown in Figure 2.3 in increments of 10) can be user defined.

Frequency distributions can also be illustrated in tabular form. Tables 2.2 and 2.3 show some examples of frequency distributions for ordinal variables from an employee survey about working conditions and the results by department, respectively. Table 2.1 is also an example of a frequency distribution. It shows the counts for each category and suggests that observations are most frequent in category 4 and less frequent in categories 1 and 2. Table 2.1 shows how interval-level data may be recoded. Although no hard-and-fast rules exist about how wide each category should be, analysts should avoid recoding in ways that mislead. Surely, categories can be created of unequal intervals (such as category 1 with range 1–14, category 2 with range

Table 2.2 ————————〰〰〰— Frequency Distribution: Employee Survey

Statement	Mean[a]	Strongly agree (%)	Agree (%)	Don't know (%)	Disagree (%)	Strongly disagree (%)	N
I am satisfied with my job at Seminole County	3.88	22.8	58.5	5.5	10.7	2.5	969
Seminole County is a good place to work compared with other organizations	3.64	15.4	53.6	14.1	13.1	3.8	969
Each individual is treated with dignity	3.02	8.1	34.2	18.6	29.6	9.5	967

5 = Strongly agree; 4 = Agree; 3 = Don't know; 2 = Disagree; 1 = Strongly disagree.

Table 2.3 ─────── ᐯᐯ─ Frequency Distribution: Results by Department

Statement	Administrative services		Community services		Environmental services	
	Mean	N	Mean	N	Mean	N
I am satisfied with my job at Seminole County	3.59	51	3.36	28	3.84	101
Seminole County is a good place to work compared with other organizations	3.45	51	3.14	29	3.63	101
Each individual is treated with dignity	2.67	51	2.98	28	3.05	101

15–17, and category 3 with range 18–25) that lead to a different conclusion. To avoid perceptions of lying with statistics, a rule of thumb is that categories should be based on *category ranges of equal length,* unless compelling reasons exist that are clearly explained.

Any of the three tables can be used as the basis or "backbone" for generating displays that highlight important conclusions and that are found in the main bodies of written reports and as presentation slides. *Bar charts* are graphs that show the frequency of occurrences through stacks (Figure 2.4). Bar Chart A shows options for 3-D effects and shading. Bar Chart "B" is also called a Pareto Chart, an ordering of categories according to their frequency or importance. This is a visually useful way of drawing attention to that which is important, as well as to the unimportance of other categories that, cumulatively, add very little to our understanding of the problem. Sources 5 through 7 seem barely worth debating.

Pie charts typically are used to focus on equality: who gets most (or least) of what? They, too, can be shown in various ways, here, with a slice that has been pulled out. *Line graphs* are used for continuous data, in part to avoid displaying a very large number of bars. Here, the lines show averaged occurrences each month. The line graph in Figure 2.4 actually shows two variables in a way that highlights important trend differences.

Standard Deviation

When variables are continuous, the question "How widely are the data dispersed around the mean?" has especially high salience because continuous variables often have a large number of values that can be (very) widely dispersed. By contrast, many ordinal-level variables have only a few values

Figure 2.4 ————————∿∿∿—Graphical Displays

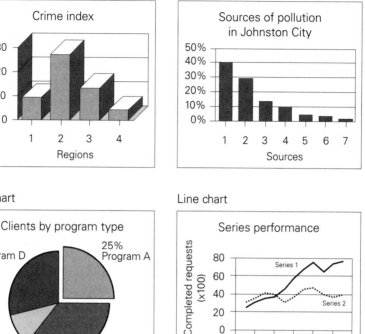

Bar chart A

Bar chart B

Pie chart

Line chart

and thus may have a limited range. The ***standard deviation*** is a measure of dispersion that is calculated based on the values of the data. The standard deviation has the desirable property that, when the data are normally distributed (discussed below), 68.3 percent of the observations lie within ±1 standard deviation from the mean, and 95.4 percent lie ±2 standard deviations from the mean, and 99.7 percent lie ±3 standard deviations from the mean. A key qualifier of the following discussion is *when the data are normally distributed.* The term ***normally distributed*** means that the distribution of a variable resembles a "bell-shaped curve." Many variables are normally distributed, such as student scores, IQ scores, average crop yields, or lightning flashes. This, too, is explained below.

Although the computer calculates the standard deviation, for explanatory purposes we note that the *standard deviation* is defined as:[7]

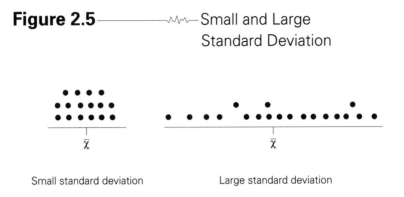

Figure 2.5———————⌁⌁⌁— Small and Large Standard Deviation

Small standard deviation

Large standard deviation

$$s = \sqrt{\frac{\sum (x_i - \bar{x})^2}{n-1}}$$

Thus, when an observation lies far from its mean, $(x_i - \bar{x})^2$ is large, and when an observation lies close to the mean, $(x_i - \bar{x})^2$ is small. Likewise, when *most* observations are scattered widely around the mean, $\Sigma(x_i - \bar{x})^2$ is large, and when *most* observations are scattered narrowly around the mean, $\Sigma(x_i - \bar{x})^2$ is small. Thus, data that are widely spread around the mean will have a larger standard deviation than data that are closely clustered around the mean. This is shown in Figure 2.5.[8] Computers also calculate s^2, called the "variance" of a variable. However, this measure has no particularly important properties and is provided as information only.

For the data shown in the stem-and-leaf plot (Figure 2.2), the computer calculates that the mean is 56.39 and the standard deviation is 27.43. Thus, when the data are normally distributed, about two-thirds of the observations will fall between 28.96 and 83.82. About 95 percent lie between the values of 1.53 and 111.25.

This information is used to calculate **confidence intervals,** which are defined as the range within which a statistic is expected to fall on repeated sampling. The formula for calculating a 95 percent confidence interval (the range within which the mean will fall in 95 of 100 samples) is $\bar{x} \pm 1.96 * s / \sqrt{n}$. (The value of 1.96 is more fully discussed in Chapter 5.) Thus, if the sample is based on 100 observations, we expect the above mean to lie between $(56.39 \pm 1.96 * 27.43 / \sqrt{100}) = 51.01$ and 61.77. The formula for calculating a 99 percent confidence interval is $\bar{x} \pm 2.58 * s / \sqrt{n}$.

Another use of the standard deviation is as an aid in identifying outliers for normally distributed variables. When variables are normally distributed,

Figure 2.6 ——————〜〰〜—Normal Distribution: Bell-Shaped Curve

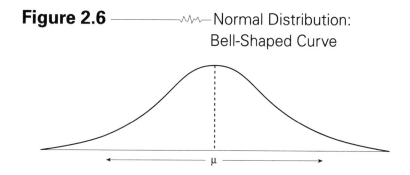

values that lie more than three standard deviations from the mean are often considered outliers. Thus, values greater than [56.39 + (3*27 − 43)] = 138.68 or less than [56.39 − (3*27 − 43)] = −25.90 would be considered outliers. Such observations can often also be identified using boxplots.

As stated, *normally distributed* means that distribution of the data resembles a bell-shaped curve such as that shown in Figure 2.6. In practice, almost no data are exactly normally distributed, but they appear to have something resembling a bell-shaped curve. Many analysts rely on a *visual inspection* to determine this, supplemented with statistics reported below. The sample data are not expected to match a theoretical bell-shaped curve perfectly because, as a sample, deviations due to chance selection should be expected. But if the sample is consistent with a bell-shaped curve and if we had an infinite number of drawings, the sample would eventually look normal.

Computers also calculate two further measures of interest. **Skewness** is a measure of whether the peak is centered in the middle of the distribution. A positive value indicates that the peak is "off" to the left, and a negative value suggests that it is off to the right. **Kurtosis** is a measure of the extent to which data are concentrated in the peak versus the tail. A positive value indicates that data are concentrated in the peak; a negative value indicates that data are concentrated in the tail ("fat tail"). Values of skewness and kurtosis have little inherent meaning, other than that large values indicate greater asymmetry. A rule of thumb is that the ratio (absolute value) of skewness to its standard error, and of kurtosis to its standard error, should be less than two (these statistics are calculated by the computer). Large ratios indicate departure from symmetry. The respective ratios of skewness and kurtosis of our data, as calculated by the computer, are | − 0.06/0.22 | and | − 0.73/0.43 |, which are both well below 2.0. Thus, our data are well centered; the tail is a little fat but not enough to cause us to worry about the normality of our data.[9] Additional statistics of normality are discussed in Chapter 5.

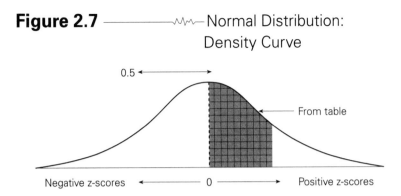

Figure 2.7 ———————Normal Distribution: Density Curve

Many computer programs can superimpose a curve over the histogram to help tell analysts if their data are normally distributed. If this curve looks close to a perfect bell-shaped curve, the data are considered normally distributed. Many statistical tests discussed in Chapter 5 and beyond assume that variables are normally distributed; we will return to this important matter in subsequent chapters.

Finally, based on calculated means and standard deviations, all data are transformable into z-scores (or standardized values) by using the formula $z = (x_i - \bar{x})/s$. Computers can calculate these values for each observation. Variables whose values have been standardized are called ***standardized variables.*** All standardized variables have the property that their means are exactly zero and their standard deviations are exactly 1 (or unity). This property allows us to compare the distribution of variables. It also allows us to answer questions of the following type: What percentage of female welfare clients have more than 2.6 children, assuming that the number of children is normally distributed, the mean number of children is calculated to be 2.20, and the standard deviation is 0.44? Consider the standardized normal curve shown in Figure 2.7. By definition, the area under a standardized, normal (bell-shaped) distribution is 1.00 (A curve in which the area is 1.00 is called a *density curve.*) This means that an observation has a probability of 1.00 of being somewhere under the curve, and the midpoint is, by definition, 0.50. In the Appendix, the table of "Normal Curve Areas" is used to determine the probability density from the 0.50 point (mean). The above information, plugged into the formula leads to a standardized score (also called ***z-score***) of 0.91 (2.60 – 2.20/0.44). The area from 0.50 to 0.91 is 0.3186 (from the appendix). Thus, 50% + 31.86% = 81.86% of cases have a value less than the value that gave rise to this z-score (2.60), and 1 minus 08186, or 18.14%, have a larger value. Note that negative z-scores, for example, −1.25, indicate a probability less than 0.50. The fraction of female welfare clients with less than 1.65 children is 1 – (0.5 + 0.3944) = 0.1056.[10] We will return to further uses of the standard deviation later, in Chapters 5 and 6.

CONCLUSION

Univariate, or summary, statistics is important to public management and analysis, providing descriptive information that affects policy decisions. By immersing themselves in the measures of central tendency (averages) and measures of dispersion (distribution), researchers can see what their data look like and how they behave. The tools of univariate analysis are also the beginning of any solid body of research. Summary statistics familiarize analysts with their data and make them aware of any coding errors, outliers, or other weaknesses in the data. Without thorough use of univariate analysis for data cleaning, research findings become more vulnerable to attack from the critics.

After analysts have ascertained the validity of their data, they then turn to producing descriptive information about their variables. Measures of central tendency include the mean, median, and mode. Although the mean is the most widely used measure of central tendency, the median should be used when a few very large or small values affect the value of the mean. The median is the value below which half of the observations lie. The mode is simply the most frequently occurring observation. Measures of central tendency are widely used in analysis to tell researchers, for example, the mean rate of school violence in a school district in which student behavior is an important concern, or the median income in a population.

Measures of dispersion describe the distribution of variables, that is, how close or far apart observations lie from each other. An important tool when assessing variable distributions, boxplots (median, first and third quartiles, interquartile range) not only tell analysts where their data lie, they also help to identify outliers (unusually small or large values) that can affect later analysis. Frequency distributions also give researchers more information about their data and can provide the basis for colorful presentation tools, such as bar charts, pie charts, and graphs. The standard deviation lets analysts determine if their data are normally distributed. Remember, only after careful double-checking of the data and conclusions for inaccuracies (such as erroneously coded observations) should tables and graphs be developed for final reports and presentations.

KEY TERMS

Bar chart (p. 40)

Bivariate analysis (p. 28)

Boxplot (pp. 35–38)

Confidence interval (p. 42)

Data cleaning (p. 28)

Data coding (p. 28)

Data input (p. 28)

First quartile (p. 36)

Frequency distribution (p. 38)

Grouped data (p. 33)

Histogram (pp. 38–40)

Inner fence (p. 37)

KEY TERMS   *(continued)*

Interquartile range (p. 36)
Kurtosis (p. 43)
Line graph (p. 40)
Mean (p. 29)
Measures of central tendency
  (p. 29)
Measures of dispersion (p. 35)
Median (pp. 30, 36)
Midspread (p. 36)
Mode (p. 32)
Multivariate analysis (p. 28)
Normally distributed (p. 41)
Outer fence (p. 37)
Outliers (pp. 36–38)

Pie chart (p. 40)
Range (p. 36)
Skewness (p. 43)
Standard deviation (pp. 40–44)
Standardized variables (p. 44)
Stem-and-leaf plot (p. 38)
Summary statistics (p. 28)
Third quartile (p. 36)
Univariate analysis (p. 28)
Weighted mean (p. 30)
Whiskers (p. 37)
Z-scores (p. 44)

Notes

1. The workbook, Chapter 2, has data coding, input, and cleaning exercises. The data sets for such exercises are included on the accompanying CD-ROM. The workbook also includes an SPSS user's guide as Chapter 9.

2. Calculations of means usually result in fractions (for example, "the mean number of arrests is 8.52 per officer"). The presence of fractions implies that distances between categories are exactly measured, hence, that variables are measured at the interval or ratio level (see Chapter 1). However, analysts frequently have ordinal variables, such as responses to survey questions that are based on a five- or seven-point Likert scale (see Box 1.2). Some argue that fractions should not be used for reporting the central tendency of ordinal variables because fractions are not defined on ordinal scales. Thus, analysts should avoid writing: "On average, respondents provide stronger support for item A (3.84) than item B (3.23)." Rather, it is better to write: "On average, respondents provide stronger support for item A than item B. For example, whereas 79.8 percent agree or strongly agree that (. . .), only 65.4 percent agree or strongly agree that (. . .)." Despite this caution, fractional reporting of ordinal-level variables is commonplace in analytical reports. The mean is especially inappropriate for nominal-level variables. For example, we cannot say that the average region is 2.45, on a scale of 1 = Northeast, 2 = South, 3 = Midwest, and 4 = West. When working with nominal variables, we should describe response frequencies, such as "23.7 percent of employees live in the Northeast, 19.8 percent live in the West," and so on.

3. For example, assume that on a scale of 5 = Strongly Agree to 1 = Strongly Disagree the median is calculated as 4.20. Rounding off, this is a 4. Then, we write that "half of the respondents agree or strongly agree with this statement, whereas the other half disagree, strongly disagree, or don't know."

4. Often, we report two decimals by default. However, on occasion we may wish to report more or fewer. Here, we report three decimals in order to avoid errors of rounding that would become evident in the following paragraph.

5. For example, decisions about educational programs are based on the mean attainment of students in those programs, expressed as "on average, enrolled students improved their XYZ ability by percent more than students who did not enroll in the programs." Of course, irregular behavior draws attention in its own right, and public laws are often passed to address that. In addition, a lot is learned from case studies of infrequent behavior.

6. Some computer programs, including SPSS, distinguish between outliers and extreme values. Then, outliers are defined as observations that lie 1.5 times the midspread from the first and third quartiles, whereas extreme values are observations that lie 3 times the midspread from the first and third quartiles.

7. For calculating the standard deviation for a population, divide by N.

8. Standard deviations can also be calculated from grouped data, using the following revised formula:

$$s = \sqrt{\frac{\sum w_i (\bar{x}_i - \bar{x})^2}{n-1}}$$

whereby the i's indicate the group categories. Consider the following example. Referring to the data on pages 33–35, we first calculate the estimated group means of each category and then subtract these values from the previously calculated group mean. Respectively, the estimated category means are 3, 8, 13, 18, and 23. Subtracting the value of the overall mean of 15.1, we get −12.1, −7.1, −2.1, 2.9, and 7.9. Then, we take the squared difference of each, which is 146.4, 50.4, 4.4, 8.4, and 62.4, and weight each of these values by the number of observations in each category. Thus, the value for the first category is (12*146.4) = 1,756.8, and subsequent values are 252.0, 79.2, 302.4, and 873.6. We add these numbers, get 3,264, and divide by 85, which is 38.4, and then take the square root, which is 6.2. The estimated standard deviation of the data provided in section 1.4 is 6.2.

9. Another rule of thumb is that both of the following measures should be less than ±1.96: *skewness*/$\sqrt{6/n}$ and *kurtosis*/$\sqrt{24/n}$. In our case, the respective values are –0.27 and 1.66.

10. Standard deviations also underlie the development of control charts, which help managers determine the likelihood that unusually high or low performance is caused by chance. The upper and lower critical limits of control charts are defined as $UCL = \bar{x} + 3(s / \sqrt{n})$ and $LCL = \bar{x} - 3(s / \sqrt{n})$:

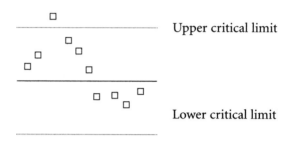

Upper critical limit

Lower critical limit

Hypothesis Testing with Chi-Square

CHAPTER OBJECTIVES

After reading this chapter, you should be able to:
- Construct a contingency table
- Understand the meaning of "statistical significance"
- Test hypotheses using chi-square
- Evaluate chi-square test assumptions
- Determine the "practical significance" of relationships
- Take control variables into account

Descriptive analysis goes only so far. After using descriptive analysis to establish, for example, the level of outcomes, analysts often want to know what factors affect outcomes in order better to influence them. *Bivariate analysis* examines relationships between two variables, such as gender and productivity, or exercise and health. If a relationship exists, we want to describe it so that we can determine how we might use its features for policy and management. For example, if a relationship between education and crime reduction exists that is strong, we might want to encourage more education. If the relationship exists but is weak, we might examine other ways of affecting crime. Through bivariate analysis, we determine whether a relationship exists and, if so, what its nature is.

Many different statistical tests exist for bivariate analysis. The level of measurement of the variables determines which statistical test should be used. As shown in the Statistics Road Map at the beginning of this book:

- When both variables are *categorical,* tests based on contingency tables should be used (Chapters 3 and 4).
- When one variable is *categorical* (for example, gender) and the other is *continuous,* t-test or ANOVA should be used (Chapter 5).
- When both variables are *continuous,* simple regression analysis should be used (Chapter 6).

All tests determine whether a relationship exists, and some tests also provide information about the strength and direction of the relationship. This chapter discusses general procedures for testing whether a relationship exists. This is also called "hypothesis testing," and it is relevant to *all* statistical tests, regardless of measurement level, throughout this book. This chapter applies these general procedures using chi-square, a widely used statistic for testing the existence of a relationship between two categorical variables. Chi-square does not, however, provide information about the strength and direction of relationships. Statistics that provide both hypothesis testing and information about the strength and direction of relationships for categorical variables often are called "measures of association." These are discussed further in Chapter 4.

CONTINGENCY TABLES

A *contingency table* expresses the relationship between two categorical variables. One variable is shown in rows and the other in columns. Each row and column shows the frequency of observations with specific values for both variables. Typically, row and column totals also are present. The placement of the variables in contingency tables depends on the nature of the relationship. When the relationship is assumed to be causal (as determined by the analyst), the dependent variable is shown in the rows and the independent variable in columns. When the relationship is that of an association, no preference exists regarding the location of variables.

Contingency tables, such as those that show the different educational levels attained by different groups of employees, or the utilization of different programs by different groups of agency clients, are ubiquitous in public management. The contingency table shown as Table 3.1 shows the relationship between the year of promotion and the gender of a group of employees. In this example, the relationship is assumed to be causal. Specifically, a

Table 3.1 ⎯⎯⎯⎯⎯ ᰧᰧᰧ⎯ Year of Promotion by Gender

Year	Gender	
	Men	Women
1	14	8
2	16	14
3	7	22
4	6	8
Total	43	52

manager is concerned that employees are promoted at unequal rates based on gender, raising the possibility of gender discrimination in the workplace. Note that the table has a title and (clear) column headings. This is essential. The table is best interpreted when read by row, comparing different columns. For example, it shows that 16 men and 14 women are promoted in the second year. However, because the total number of men and women in the sample is unequal (see "Total" row), it is better to express the numbers as percentages for the purpose of comparison.

Table 3.2 shows that whereas 37.2 percent of men are promoted in the second year, 26.9 percent of women are promoted in that year. It also suggests that, overall, men are promoted faster than women. We conclude this by comparing first-, second-, and third-year rates between men and women, noting that promotion rates are somewhat similar in the fourth year.

CHI-SQUARE

Chi-square (pronounced "ky-square") is a quantitative measure used to determine whether a relationship exists between two categorical variables. Many statistics quantify the relationship between variables. This section

Table 3.2 ⎯⎯⎯⎯⎯ ᰧᰧᰧ⎯ Year of Promotion by Gender: Percentages

Year	Gender		Total
	Men	Women	
1	32.6%	15.4%	23.2%
2	37.2	26.9	31.6
3	16.2	42.3	30.5
4	14.0	15.4	14.7
Total	100.0	100.0	100.0
(n =)	(43)	(52)	(95)

Table 3.3 ———〰〰— Year of Promotion by Gender: Expected Frequencies

	A: Percentages			B: Counts	
	Gender			Gender	
Year	Men	Women	Total	Men	Women
1	23.2%	23.2%	23.2%	10.0	12.1
2	31.6	31.6	31.6	13.6	16.4
3	30.5	30.5	30.5	13.1	15.9
4	14.7	14.7	14.7	6.3	7.6
Total	100.0	100.0	100.0	43.0	52.0
(n =)	(43)	(52)	(95)		

explains the calculation of chi-square, which is used in the following section for hypothesis testing (that is, determining whether a relationship exists). The Greek notation for chi-square is χ^2, which can be used interchangeably with its Latin alphabet spelling, chi-square. *Chi-square* is defined as the difference between the observed (or actual) frequencies (shown in Table 3.2) and the so-called "expected frequencies," which are frequencies that would exist when *no differences* exist in the rate of promotion. When no relationship exists between variables, the column percentages are identical (Table 3.3, part A). The column "Total" in part A shows the distribution of promotion rates as taken from Table 3.2. When no relationship exists between gender and the rate of promotion, then men and women, by definition, do not differ in promotion rates. Thus, the rate of each group is identical to that of the aggregate. For example, part A shows that 30.5 percent of both men and women are promoted in their third year.

Based on the column percentages, the "expected frequencies" can be calculated. For example, when no difference of promotion rates exists between men and women, then 30.5 percent of 43 men, or 13.1 men, would have been promoted in their third year (part B). Similarly, 30.5 percent of 52 women, or 15.9 women, would have been promoted in their third year, and the other expected frequencies are calculated in similar fashion in part B.

It is self-evident that when no relationship exists between these variables in the data, the values of observed and expected frequencies must be identical. It is also true that the greater the relationship, the greater the difference between the observed and expected frequencies. The *chi-square* (χ^2) statistic measures the difference between the expected and observed frequencies and is thus a quantitative measure of this relationship. Chi-square is defined in the following manner:

$$\sum_i \frac{(O_i - E_i)^2}{E_i}$$

whereby O_i is the observed frequency in a cell and E_i is the expected frequency in a cell. As is readily seen, when $E_i = O_i$ the chi-square value for that cell is zero. Using the frequencies shown in Tables 3.1 and 3.3 (part B), we find that the chi-square value of the first cell is $(14 - 10)^2/10 = 4^2/10 = 16/10 = 1.60$. Calculating chi-square for all of the cells yields 8.97, as shown in Table 3.4. *Of course, the value of chi-square is usually calculated by the computer.*[1]

In short, when no relationship exists between the variables, chi-square equals zero. The greater the relationship, the greater the value of chi-square. Finally, note also that chi-square is always positive and that it provides no information about the direction of the relationship (see Box 3.1).

HYPOTHESIS TESTING

We will now use chi-square to determine whether a relationship exists between gender and promotion. This is called "hypothesis testing." In our example, the hypothesis is that a relationship exists between gender and the rate of promotion; a hypothesis is a tentative statement about some relationship or condition that is subject to subsequent verification. The **purpose of hypothesis testing** is, simply, to determine whether a relationship exists. Specifically, we ask, "What is the probability that the above distribution of promotion rates among 95 men and women is consistent with a distribution in which men and women are promoted at *equal* rates?" That is, is a chi-square value of 8.97 sufficiently large to conclude that men are promoted at a faster rate than women? A *key task* in statistics is to determine how large

Table 3.4 ⎯⎯⎯⎯⎯⎯〰⎯ Calculating Chi-square

Year	Men Obs.	Men Exp.	Men χ^2	Women Obs.	Women Exp.	Women χ^2	Total χ^2
1	14	10.0	1.60	8	12.1	1.39	2.99
2	16	13.6	0.42	14	16.4	0.35	0.77
3	7	13.1	2.84	22	15.9	2.34	5.18
4	6	6.3	0.01	8	7.6	0.02	0.03
Total	43	43.0	4.87	52	52.0	4.10	8.97

Note: Obs. = Observed Frequency; Exp. = Expected Frequency

In Greater Depth...

Box 3.1   The Direction of Relationships

Relationships between *ordinal variables* can be characterized as positive or negative. A positive relationship means that large values of one variable are associated with large values of the other variable *and* that small values of one variable are associated with small values of the other variable. A negative relationship implies the opposite: large values of one variable are associated with small values of the other variable *and* vice versa. This matter does not arise in the text example because gender is a nominal variable. It makes no sense to say that the relationship between gender and promotion is positive or negative.

To determine visually whether a relationship is positive or negative, focus on the corner cells of a contingency table. When a relationship is *positive,* the relative frequencies (percentages) of the cells in the upper left and lower right corners in a contingency table should be large, relative to other cells. Conversely, a *negative* relationship suggests that the relative frequencies of cells in upper right and lower left corners should be large. Thus, analysts can try to determine the direction of relationships visually by examining the relative frequencies of the corner cells, as shown in the table.

POSITIVE RELATIONSHIP			NEGATIVE RELATIONSHIP		
	LO	HI		LO	HI
LO	65%	29%	LO	31%	62%
HI	35%	71%	HI	69%	38%

A limitation of the chi-square statistic is that it provides no information about the direction of relationships. Sometimes, visual inspection of large contingency tables is cumbersome and inconclusive. Fortunately, other statistics do provide information about the direction of relationships between ordinal-level variables, so that analysts need not rely on visual inspection. These statistics include Kendall's tau-b and tau-c and are discussed in Chapter 4.

any measure of a relationship must be in order to say that it is "statistically significant." This part of hypothesis testing involves:
- the null hypothesis;
- the concept of statistical significance;
- critical values;
- steps to determine statistical significance.

These issues are relevant to all statistical tests, such as chi-square tests, t-tests, and others that are discussed in this book.

The Null Hypothesis

Since statistics is a careful and cautious discipline, we presume that no relationship between variables exists and that any relationship that is found may have been obtained purely by chance. The *null hypothesis* states that *any observed pattern is solely due to chance* and that, hence, no relationship exists. Thus, the null hypothesis (that is, that no relationship exists) is assumed, and an objective of statistical testing is to examine whether the null hypothesis can be rejected. This idea is similar to the court of justice in which there is a presumption of innocence until proven guilty beyond a reasonable doubt. In the above case, we presume that no relationship exists between gender and the rate of promotion.

In statistics the specific concern is that we may find a relationship in our sample when in fact none exists in the population. This may occur because of a fluke in our random sample. We endeavor to disprove this possibility. Another way of looking at this issue is that if we assume that a relationship does exist we might be guilty of not trying hard enough to prove that it doesn't exist. By assuming that a relationship doesn't exist, we need only satisfy the standard of "reasonable evidence" in order to claim that it does exist. That standard is that it should be *very unlikely to find a relationship among variables* (that is, a test-statistic value such as chi-square) *of a certain (large) magnitude when in fact no relationship exists in the population.*

The null hypothesis is stated as follows:

H_0: No relationship exists between gender and the rate of promotion.
H_A: A relationship exists between gender and the rate of promotion.

"H_0" is the null hypothesis, and "H_A" is called the *alternate hypothesis*. H_0 is also sometimes called the straw man because we endeavor to "strike it down" or disprove it. The *alternate hypothesis* is the logical opposite of the null hypothesis; all possibilities must be accounted for between the null hypothesis and the alternate hypothesis.

In most instances, the null hypothesis is that *no relationship exists* between two variables, and the alternate hypothesis is that *a relationship does exist* between two variables. However, if the researcher has a priori information that a relationship can exist only in one direction (for example, that men can be promoted faster than women but that women cannot be promoted faster than men), then it is appropriate to state the null hypothesis as "men are not promoted faster than women" and the alternate hypothesis as "men are promoted faster than women." However, because, as is often the case, we cannot a priori rule the direction of the relationship (it could be that women are promoted faster than men), we use the customary approach indicating that no relationship exists. If a relationship exists, we later can use the approach described in Box 3.1 to determine its direction.

Many scholars prefer to state the above hypotheses as follows:

H_0: No relationship exists between gender and the rate of promotion in the population.

H_A: A relationship exists between gender and the rate of promotion in the population.

This usage clearly indicates that we are using sample data to draw inferences about relationships in the population. Indeed, we are not interested in our sample, per se. Who cares about the preferences of, say, five hundred citizens? We care about them only to the extent that their opinions *represent* those of the entire population. In the end, we want to know how the population thinks about something, not merely a sample of it. We use a sample to infer conclusions about the population. To distinguish conclusions about the sample from those of the population, Greek letters are also used to refer to the population. Then, the above hypothesis is also written as:

$$H_0: \mu_m = \mu_f$$
$$H_A: \mu_m \neq \mu_f$$

whereby μ is the rate of promotion in the population.

Statistical Significance

The phrase "statistically significant" often carries considerable weight in public discourse. To say that something is "statistically significant" is tantamount to throwing the weight of science behind a statement or fact. But what exactly does the phrase "statistically significant" mean? *Statistical significance* simply means the probability of being wrong about stating that a relationship exists, when in fact it doesn't. The phrase *level of statistical significance* refers to the level of that probability, that is, *how often* we would be wrong to conclude that a relationship exists when in fact none exists. In other words, that we incorrectly reject the null hypothesis when in fact it is true. As stated above, the reason that we might be wrong is that our data are based on a random sample; had we drawn a different sample, we might have concluded otherwise.

The statistical standard for significance is 5 percent; we are willing to tolerate a 1-in-20 chance of being wrong in stating that a relationship exists (that is, concluding that the null hypothesis should be rejected, when in fact it shouldn't). Many researchers also consider a 1-in-100 (1 percent) probability of being wrong as an acceptable standard of significance. The latter is a stricter standard. We are less likely to be wrong stating that a relationship exists (when in fact it doesn't exist) when it is significant at the 1 percent level than when it is significant at only the 5 percent level.

We could set the bar even higher—for example, by choosing a level of significance of one-tenth of 1 percent—but doing so may cause us to conclude that no relationship exists, when in fact it does exist. A standard of less than 1 percent is thus thought to be too risk averse. Why not settle for a 10 percent level of significance? Because we would be accepting a 10 percent chance of wrongfully concluding that a relationship exists, when in fact none exists. Usually, that is thought to be too risky.

By convention, 5 percent is usually thought to be the uppermost limit of risk that we accept. Thus, relationships that are significant at more than 5 percent (say, 6 percent) are said to be *not significant*. Only relationships that are significant at 5 percent or less are considered significant, and relationships that are significant at 1 percent or less are said to be *highly significant*. Another convention is that most relations are reported as being significant only at the 1 percent or the 5 percent level. Thus, a relationship that is statistically significant at the 3 percent level is reported as being "significant at the 5 percent level," but not at the 1 percent level. A relationship that is significant at one-tenth of 1 percent is reported as being "significant at the 1 percent level."

Sometimes the phrase "level of confidence" is also used. This is simply 100 percent minus the level of statistical significance. Thus, a 5 percent level of significance is the same as a 95 percent level of confidence. And a 1 percent level of significance is the same as a 99 percent level of confidence. A 95 percent confidence interval is defined as the values that would be found on repeated sampling, in 95 out of 100 times.

The Five Steps of Hypothesis Testing

Recall the above question: How large should chi-square be in order to conclude that a statistically significant relationship exists between gender and year of promotion or, in other words, to reject the null hypothesis and accept the alternate hypothesis? All statistical tests follow the same *five steps of hypothesis testing*.

1. State the null hypothesis (in Greek letters).
2. Choose a statistical test (see the introduction to this chapter).
3. Calculate the test statistic (t.s.) and evaluate test assumptions.
4. Look up the critical value (c.v.) of the test.
5. Draw conclusion:

If | t.s. | ≤ c.v., do not reject the null hypothesis.

If | t.s. | > c.v., reject the null hypothesis.

We already discussed the first two items on this list, and we have seen how to calculate the chi-square test statistic. Most statistical tests make assumptions about variables: we will address those of the chi-square test statistic very soon. Now we discuss critical values. The *critical value* is the minimum value that a test statistic must be in order to rule out chance as the cause of a relationship. Technically, the critical value is the value above which the test statistic is sufficiently large to reject the null hypothesis at a user-specified level of significance.

The following is for enhancing conceptual understanding only because computers, again, do most of the work. The *critical value* of any test statistic is determined by two parameters: (1) the desired level of statistical significance and (2) the number of degrees of freedom (df). As previously stated, by convention, analysts are interested in rejecting the null hypothesis at the 1 percent and 5 percent levels. The *degrees of freedom* address the practical, statistical problem that the magnitude of most test statistics is affected by the number of observations or categories. For example, the formula for calculating the chi-square test statistic requires us to calculate a value for each cell and then to add them all up. All things being equal, the larger the number of cells, the larger the value of this test statistic. The statistic "degrees of freedom" controls for this problem.[2] (What this also means is that it is generally meaningless to compare the values of different chi-square test statistics based on tables of unequal sizes and, as we will soon see, unequal numbers of observations.)

Each type of statistical test has its own way of calculating degrees of freedom. The degrees of freedom for any chi-square test are defined by the formula $(c-1)(r-1)$, whereby c = the number of columns in a contingency table and r = the number of rows. In Table 3.1, df = $(2-1)*(4-1)$ = 3. If our table had six rows and four columns, the number of degrees of freedom would be $(6-1)*(4-1)$ = 15, and so on.

To determine the critical value of our test, we turn to a table of chi-square critical values (see Appendix). The table shows the levels of significance in columns and the degrees of freedom in rows. Assume that we wish to test whether our previously calculated χ^2 test statistic (8.97) is statistically significant at the 5 percent level. The critical value at this level of significance and three degrees of freedom is shown to be 7.815. Thus, applying the very last step in the method for testing hypotheses, we evaluate the absolute value of 8.97 as indeed larger than the critical value, and so we conclude that *a relationship exists between gender and the rate of promotion at the 5 percent level of significance (or at the 95 percent level of confidence).* Alternatively, you can write that *a statistically significant relationship exists between gender and the rate of promotion* ($\chi^2 = 8.97, p < .05$). This important language is found in most analyses.

But is this relationship also significant at the 1 percent level? The critical value of this chi-square test at the 1 percent level and three degrees of freedom is 11.341. We evaluate that the absolute value of 8.97 is less than the critical value at this level of significance, and so we conclude that the relationship between gender and years of promotion is not significant at the 1 percent level but only at the 5 percent level as just shown.

Note some features of the table of chi-square critical values. First, at any given level of significance, the value of the chi-square critical values increases as the degrees of freedom increase. This is consistent with the problem mentioned above: contingency tables with more rows and columns will have larger test statistics simply as a result of having more cells. The degrees of freedom "compensate" for this fact. Second, at any given number of degrees of freedom, the value of the chi-square critical values increases as the level of significance decreases. This, too, makes sense because a 1 percent level of significance will have a higher threshold than a 5 percent level.

Statistical software programs calculate the test statistics and report the level of statistical significance at which the test statistic is significant. For example, software output might have shown "$p = .029$," which indicates that the test statistic is statistically significant at the 5 percent level but not at the 1 percent level. The probability "$p = .000$" means that the relationship is highly significant, at better than the 1 percent level. The probability "$p = .1233$" or "$p = .9899$" indicates that the relationship is not significant. Software programs do not ordinarily report critical values at the 1 percent and 5 percent levels; rather, they show the level of significance at which test statistics are significant. Looking up critical values is a valuable exercise that increases conceptual understanding but one that you will only sporadically need to do.

Chi-Square Test Assumptions

Nearly all test statistics make *assumptions* about the variables that are used. *Violation of test assumptions invalidates any test result.* There are three **chi-square test assumptions.** First, the variables must be categorical, which our variables are. Second, the observations are independent, as ours are. Independent observations are those that are not necessarily correlated with each other, such as gender and productivity. The concept of dependent samples is more fully discussed in Chapter 4 and involves such experimental situations as before-and-after measurement. Third, all cells must have a minimum of five expected observations. When this condition is not met, it is usually because the contingency table contains a large number of rows and columns relative to the number of observations. That is, the data are spread too thin across too many cells. To correct this problem, simply redefine the data categories (that is, combine adjacent rows or columns) in order to create a smaller number of cells. Examination of Table 3.3 shows that our data meet this second assumption, too. The smallest expected frequency count is 6.34. If our data had violated this assumption, we would have combined rows or columns, recalculated results, and reported the revised conclusions.[3]

Finally, many analyses contain observations that have missing data for one or more variables. Observations with missing data are excluded from analyses in which they occur. This matter is further discussed in Box 3.2.

Statistical Significance and Sample Size

Most statistical tests are also affected by *sample size,* which has implications for the likelihood of finding statistically significant relations. Specifically, it is easier to find statistically significant relations in large data sets than in small ones. This is more than a statistical artifact: rather, it reflects that having more information makes us more confident of our conclusions, and vice versa. The sample size affects the statistical significance of many widely used test statistics, including chi-square.

By example, assume we had a sample of 950 employees, rather than 95 employees, with the same relative distribution as shown in Table 3.2 (see Table 3.5). It is easy to verify that the data in Table 3.5 are distributed in the same exact manner as shown in Table 3.2. But the added observations affect the calculation of the chi-square test statistic. The value of the chi-square test statistic in the first cell is $(O_i - E_i)^2/E_i$, or $(140 - 100)^2/100 = 16$. This is exactly *ten times* that of the previously calculated value. Indeed, each cell value is ten times larger, as is the chi-square test statistic, which now becomes 89.7. Yet, the chi-square critical value is still defined as $(c - 1)(r - 1)$. The critical value for rejecting the null hypothesis at the 1 percent level is still 11.345. Whereas previously we could not reject the null hypothesis at this level, we now succeed in doing so by virtue of *having more observations.* This phenomenon occurs with many other widely used test statistics, too.

Of course, the opposite is also true: if we had tried to test for significance using only, say, twenty observations (instead of ninety-five), we would have failed to reject the null hypotheses at even the 5 percent level. This reflects having too little information in order to be sufficiently confident in our conclusions. By convention, many researchers prefer to test their null hypotheses on sample sizes of fifty to a few hundred (say, 400). This is a rough guideline, only. One implication is that analysts are neither surprised to find statistically significant relations in large samples, nor surprised to

In Greater Depth...

Box 3.2 Dealing with Missing Data

A frequent question is how statistical analysis handles missing data. For example, assume that in our analysis of productivity and gender we have information on someone's gender but not productivity, as shown in the table for observation 221. The problem of missing data is relevant to this chapter, as well as all other chapters in this book. Rather than trying to guess the productivity of observation 221, we exclude the *entire observation* for any analysis that involves the variable with missing data. We do not like to guess data values, because it is difficult to credibly justify such guesses. Note that this problem does not occur for an analysis of gender and award; the values of observation 221 do contribute to this analysis. (Perhaps the only exception to not guessing values concerns time series data, in which missing observations are sometimes estimated as the mean of adjacent ones.)

Observation	Productivity	Gender	Award
218	4.3	1	0
219	4.9	1	1
220	3.9	2	0
221	.	1	1
222	2.8	2	0
223	5.2	1	1
224	3.7	2	1

The incidental exclusion of a few observations from among many observations (say, several hundred or thousands) does not bias the results in any material way. Most analyses have a few missing observations. However, bias may occur when the proportion of observations with missing data is large and a pattern exists among observations with missing data. For example, study results are likely biased when a study has 40 percent of observations missing regarding the variable "attitudes toward abortion," or when most of these occur among a subset of the survey population, such as males. To the extent that men and women have different views on abortion, the pattern of missing observations will affect study results.

What can be done with variables that have *excessive* missing data? First, the best strategy is to avoid having this problem. For example, in surveys, it may be

(continued)

Box 3.2 *(continued)*

possible to follow up with respondents to collect such data. Second, it may be that the reason for missing data is uncertainty about the meaning of some survey question or errors in the way the data have been gathered. In that case the missing data indicate an underlying problem of lack of validity, and it may be best to ignore the variable. Third, in other instances, analysts may be compelled to use the variable but then caveat their results, acknowledging the problem of large percentages of missing data. They may even be able to estimate the extent of bias arising from missing data.

In short, observations with missing data are excluded from statistical analyses, and awareness is required of any biasing effect that this *might* have.

---

find the lack of statistical significance in small samples. Another implication is that, when working with large samples, minute differences between groups can be found to be statistically significant, even when they have very little practical relevance. Bigger samples are not necessarily better: they merely increase the importance of questions about the practical significance of findings, discussed further.

A Useful Digression: The Goodness-of-Fit Test

The chi-square test can also be used to test whether the frequency distribution of one variable is consistently that of a prespecified distribution or norm. This is called a *goodness-of-fit test.* For example, we may want to test whether a distribution of male promotion rates such as shown in Table 3.2 is consistent with one in which 28 percent of men are promoted within the

Table 3.5 ⎯⎯⎯⎯⎯⎯⎯⎯∿∿⎯ Year of Promotion by Gender: Observed and Expected Counts

| | A: Observed counts | | | B: Expected counts | |
| | Gender | | | Gender | |
Year	Men	Women	Total	Men	Women
1	140	80	220	100	121
2	160	140	300	136	164
3	70	220	290	131	159
4	60	80	140	63	76
Total	430	520	950	430	520

Table 3.6 ⎯⎯⎯⎯⎯∿∿⎯ U.S. Census Response by Age Groups

Age	U.S. Census (%)	Survey sample (%)
18–45	62.3	62.8
46–65	24.1	26.8
66+	13.6	10.4

first year. Or, we might want to know whether in an inspection of automobiles a 6 percent failure rate is consistent with a prespecified norm of, say, 8 percent. We can also test the hypothesis that the distribution of a variable is equal across all categories (for example, that the promotion rate of men is not affected by their length of employment). In each instance, the chi-square test is adapted as follows. First, one variable represents the actual (observed) observations, and the other variable represents the expected distribution against which the actual observations are tested. Second, the chi-square test statistic is calculated for categories of actual observations, only.

We illustrate this in the following way. Assume that we just completed a citizen survey yielding 1,034 valid responses. We next want to know whether the age distribution of these respondents is consistent with that of the U.S. Census for that area. The lack of consistency may suggest problems of under- or oversampling and, hence, possible bias that we might want to know about. Consider the results shown in Table 3.6. Here, the Census population frequencies are the expected frequencies, and the sample frequencies are the observed frequencies. With 1,034 completed survey responses, the expected frequency of the 18–45 age category is (1,034*0.623) = 644. The expected frequencies of the two other categories are, respectively, (1,034*0.241) = 249 and (1,034*0.136) = 141; similarly, the observed (actual) frequencies are 649, 277, and 108. When using the usual formula $(O_i - E_i)^2/E_i$, the chi-square value for the first category (age 18–45) is $(649 - 644)^2/644 = 0.039$. The values for the second and third categories similarly are calculated and are, respectively, 3.149 and 7.723. Thus, the chi-square test statistic is 10.91 (with rounding). The number of degrees of freedom for the goodness-of-fit test is defined as (number of categories minus 1) or, here, 2. The critical value at the 5 percent level of significance with df = 2 is 5.991 (see Appendix), and thus we conclude that the sample *is significantly different* from the population. Specifically, the above data suggest that the researchers undersampled older respondents and that they thus may want to re-weight their findings (see Box 2.1) to examine what effect this has on their conclusions, if any. Note that if the sample had consisted of only 300 completed responses, then the chi-square would have been 3.16, which is not significant.

This example is readily adapted to other situations. For example, assume we test 400 cars and find a 6 percent failure rate. Is that any different from a norm of 8 percent? We calculate that the actual frequencies are $(0.06*400) =$ 24 failed cars and $(0.94*400) = 376$ passed cars. The expected frequencies are $(0.08*400) = 32$ failed cars and 368 passed cars. The chi-square test statistic for the failed category is $(24 - 32)^2/32 = 2.000$, and for the passed category $(376 - 368)^2/368 = 0.174$. Thus, the chi-square test statistic is 2.174. The critical value at the 5 percent level and df = 1 is 3.841 (see Appendix), and thus we conclude that the failure rate is *not different* from the prespecified norm of 8 percent.

THE PRACTICAL SIGNIFICANCE OF RELATIONSHIPS

Statistical significance is important but in many ways insufficient for making management and policy decisions. Hypothesis testing merely establishes whether a relationship is present, and we have just seen that in large data sets such testing is quite easy to do. Hypothesis testing, however, is but the first step. When the presence of a relationship is established, we want to ask more questions about the **practical significance** of a relationship.

- What is the *direction* of the relationship, specifically, is it a positive or negative relationship? As one variable increases, does the other increase or decrease? This, obviously, is of basic concern to policy and management. (The direction of relationships is discussed in Box 3.1.)
- By *how much* does one variable increase or decrease as a result of changes in the other? This is called the *practical significance* of a relationship. For example, by how much are men more likely to be promoted than women in the first year? The greater the practical significance, the greater its relevance for management and policy.
- What is the *strength* of the relationship? That is, with how much certainty can we predict one variable as a result of knowing the other? For example, if we know an employee's gender, with how much certainty can we predict his or her year of promotion? We can be very certain or not very certain about the increase or decrease (that is, practical significance) that occurs.

Contingency tables are useful in determining the *practical significance* of relations. We know that men are promoted "statistically significantly" faster than women, but by how much? A lot or a little faster? We apply the descriptive techniques of Chapter 2. One way to express a sense of difference is to ask how much longer it takes women to get promoted than men. The mean promotion rate of men is 2.12 years, and for women it is 2.58 years. So, we can say that, on average, men are promoted 0.46 years faster than women, or that, on average, it takes women $(2.58 - 2.12)/2.12 = 21.6$ percent longer to be promoted than men.

Figure 3.1 ———————⌇⌇—Promotion Rates

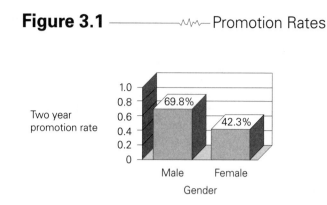

We can flesh this out a little more. For example, comparing medians, we find that half of the men are promoted within two years, as compared with three years. We can also examine percentile distribution. Then we find that whereas 25 percent of men are promoted within one year, the same number of women are promoted in two years. Or, using cumulative frequencies, we can say that whereas 69.8 percent of men are promoted within two years, only 42.3 percent are promoted after two years, as shown in Figure 3.1.

Whether or not these differences are "practically significant" ultimately rests with managers and elected officials. But we do want to go beyond merely saying that something is statistically significant. It is probably important whether men are promoted 4 percent faster, or 40 percent faster, and in what year these differences most often occur. Of course, in searching for practical significance, analysts must remain true to their data. Ethics do matter. The task of analysts is to inform, not to bias. The same data can be presented as "while the difference is statistically significant, the differences are minute in the fourth year: 14 percent of men are promoted in the second year, as are 15 percent of women." Of course, this ignores the huge differences that occur in many preceding years. When data on those years are provided too, managers won't be caught off guard later when the differences come to light. This latter information is best added to the discussion of Figure 3.1 to fully illuminate the nature of the differences.

As noted earlier, chi-square provides no information about the direction or strength of relationships. Box 3.1 discusses how the direction of relationships is determined through a visual inspection of contingency tables. This has little meaning in our example, in which one variable is nominal. However, additional statistics have been developed to better deal with the direction and strength of relationships involving ordinal data, and these are discussed in Chapter 4.

Table 3.7 ——————〜〜〜— Year of Promotion by Gender: Controlling for Productivity

| | Low productivity | | High productivity | |
| | Gender | | Gender | |
Year	Men (%)	Women (%)	Men (%)	Women (%)
1–2 Years	47	22	85	52
3+ Years	53	78	15	47
Total	100	100	100	100
(n =)	(17)	(18)	(26)	(34)

RIVAL HYPOTHESES: ADDING A CONTROL VARIABLE

Finally, we extend our discussion to deal with *rival hypotheses.* The following is but one approach, and we will provide many other approaches in subsequent chapters. Rival hypotheses were first mentioned in Chapter 1. They are alternative, plausible explanations of findings. Previously, we established that men are indeed promoted faster than women. Suppose that we wish to entertain the rival hypothesis that the promotion rate is different because men are more productive than women. That is, that there is no gender discrimination per se. Regardless of your purposes, you will want to examine this possibility: either to show that productivity differences (if any) do not explain gender discrimination (hence, gender discrimination really does exist), or to show that the alleged gender discrimination is but an artifact of productivity differences.

Assume that we somehow measured productivity. Variables associated with rival hypotheses are called control variables. The control variable "productivity" is added to our data set. To examine the above hypothesis, we divide the sample into two (or more) groups, namely, employees with high productivity and those with low productivity. For each of these groups, we make a contingency table analysis by gender. If it is true that productivity, and not gender, determines the rate of promotion, then we expect to find no differences in the rate of promotion within the *same* level of productivity (high or low) because the differences exist across levels of productivity, and not by gender. Next, we construct a table (see Table 3.7). Note how the control variable "goes on top." We still have a total of 95 employees, 43 of which are men, and 52 of which are women. For simplicity, and in order to avoid violating chi-square test assumptions (we must maintain a minimum of five expected frequencies in each cell), the variable "year of promotion" has been grouped, although this needn't be done in other instances. The relevant hypotheses are now:

H1$_0$: No relationship exists between gender and rate of promotion among employees with high productivity.

H1$_A$: A relationship exists between gender and rate of promotion among employees with high productivity.

H2$_0$: No relationship exists between gender and rate of promotion among employees with low productivity.

H2$_A$: A relationship exists between gender and rate of promotion among employees with low productivity.

Chi-square test statistics are calculated for *each* of the two different productivity groups. We could find that one or both relationships are now statistically significant. When both relationships are not statistically significant, the result is called an **explanation** of the initial findings; that is, the statistically significant result has been explained away. Sometimes it is said that the previous relationship has proven to be "spurious." When both relationships are statistically significant, the result is called a **replication** of the initial findings. When only one of the relationships is statistically significant, the result is called a **specification** of the initial findings. We would want to further examine the relationship that is not explained away. Finally, rarely does using a control variable result in uncovering statistically significant relationships that are otherwise insignificant. When this occurs, the result is called a **suppressor effect.** That is, the existing relationship is suppressed in the absence of the control variable.

Through our data, we obtain the following results. The chi-square test statistic for the relationship between gender and year of promotion among employees with low productivity is 2.39, which is not statistically significant ($p = .117$). Thus, we conclude that gender does *not* discriminate in the rate of promotion among employees with low levels of productivity. But the chi-square test statistic for the relationship between gender and year of promotion among employees with high productivity is 6.65, which is statistically significant at the 1 percent level ($p = .010$). Gender differences continue to explain differences in the rate of promotion among employees with high levels of productivity. This type of finding is called a *specification.*[4]

CONCLUSION

When researchers assess the existence and the nature of relationships between two variables, hypothesis testing and chi-square applications are invaluable tools. Hypothesis testing is an important step in data analysis because it establishes whether or not a relationship between two variables exists in the population, that is, whether a relationship is "statistically significant." Processes of hypothesis testing involve:

1. Stating the null hypothesis
2. Choosing the appropriate test statistics
3. Ensuring that data meet the assumption of test statistics
4. Calculating test statistic values
5. Comparing the test statistic values against critical values and determining at what level a relationship is significant (or, relying on the computer to calculate test statistics and state the level at which they are statistically significant).

When one is confronted with two categorical variables, which can also be used to make a contingency table, chi-square is a widely used test for establishing whether a relationship exists (see Statistics Roadmap at the beginning of the book). Chi-square has three test assumptions: that variables are categorical, that observations are independent, and that no cells have fewer than five expected frequency counts. Remember, violation of test assumptions invalidates any test result. Chi-square can also be used for testing whether the distribution of a variable is consistent with a prespecified distribution or norm (called a goodness-of-fit test).

Once analysts have determined that a statistically significant relationship exists through hypothesis testing, they then need to assess the practical significance of their findings. Remember, large data sets easily allow for findings of statistical significance. Practical significance deals with the relevance of statistical differences for managers; it addresses whether statistically significant relationships have meaningful policy implications. Specifically, managers need to know the direction of relationships, the strength of relationships, and by how much an increase in one variable affects the other variable in order to determine, for example, by how much a school anger management program reduces school violence. The analysis of practical significance requires univariate analysis and is aided by statistics that are discussed in the next chapter. Finally, managers also often want to know whether these findings are robust in the face of rival hypotheses, that is, alternative explanations that affect the strength of relationships. For example, is the effectiveness of anger management programs affected by the socioeconomic background of students? Chi-square can be used for addressing the effect of rival hypotheses, too. In short, chi-square is a valuable tool for managers to establish the effectiveness of their programs, although managers will need additional analysis to deal with questions about the practical relevance.

KEY TERMS

Alternate hypothesis (p. 55)

Chi-square (pp. 52–53)

Chi-square test assumptions (p. 59)

Contingency table (p. 30)

Critical value (p. 58)

Degrees of freedom (p. 58)

Explanation (p. 67)

Five steps of hypothesis testing
 (pp. 57–59)

Goodness-of-fit test (pp. 62–64)

Level of statistical significance (p. 56)

Null hypothesisz (p. 55)

Practical significance (pp. 64–66)

Purpose of hypothesis testing
 (pp. 53–54)

Replication (p. 67)

Rival hypotheses (p. 66)

Sample size (and hypothesis
 testing) (pp. 60–61)

Specification (p. 67)

Statistical significance (pp. 56–57)

Suppressor effect (p. 67)

Notes

1. The computer-calculated value of chi-square is slightly higher, 9.043, due to rounding errors in calculating the expected frequency counts. This same result is achieved when using expected frequency counts with three decimals. The expected frequency counts are then, for men: 9.976, 13.588, 13.115, and 6.321; for women: 12.064, 16.432, 15.860, and 7.644. Of course, maintaining three decimals is more labor-intensive for this illustrative, manually calculated example in the text, which retains only one decimal in calculating the expected frequencies.

2. The concept of degrees of freedom is not easy to explain. Some texts explain it as the number of calculations that are not predetermined after others have already occurred. Succinctly, if an array (or column) has four data elements, and the sum total is also known, then after choosing the first three elements, the fourth element is predetermined: hence, we are free to choose only three elements, and the array is said to have three degrees of freedom, or $c - 1$.

3. The rationale is to ensure that chi-square calculations are not unduly affected by small differences in cells with low counts: note that the expected frequency is in the denominator of the chi-square formula. Some analysts feel that the standard of no cells with expected frequencies below five is too strict. They feel that (1) all cells should have greater expected frequency counts than 1.00 and (2) that no more than 20 percent of cells have expected frequency counts lower than 5. The stan-

dard adopted in the text is more conservative. The point is, of course, that test statistics should not be affected by a few sparse cells.

4. This approach is rather inefficient: note how we had to combine categories in order to preserve an adequate number of observations in each cell. In subsequent chapters, we will examine approaches that are both more efficient and conclusive. Of course, when productivity is found to cause explanation or specification, you subsequently want to report on the bivariate relationship between the rate of promotion and productivity. That, of course, is a different relationship from the one discussed in this section.

Measures of Association

CHAPTER OBJECTIVES

After reading this chapter, you should be able to:
- Understand the concept of "proportional reduction in error"
- Determine the strength and direction of relationships
- Know why Kendall's tau-c is increasingly used for tests involving two ordinal variables
- Test for relationships involving very small samples
- Test whether two or more evaluators agree in their rankings
- Evaluate differences between "before" and "after" test scores

This chapter presents a broad, almost encyclopedic range of statistics that are used for testing the association of two categorical variables. Many of these statistics supplement the chi-square test discussed in Chapter 3. Although chi-square is widely used for testing the statistical significance of relationships (that is, establishing whether a relationship exists), it provides no information about the direction and strength of those relationships. By contrast, many statistics discussed here provide both and are based on the concept of *proportional reduction in error* (PRE). Analysts are increasingly using PRE-based statistics because they reveal more information about relationships than chi-square.

In addition, this chapter discusses statistics for some rather special situations. These include statistical tests that are uniquely developed for analyzing very small samples, tests that are designed for assessing differences between before and after test scores, and tests to determine the compatibility of rankings and samples. Many of these tests are referred to as *nonparametric statistics*. This name is derived from the fact that these test statistics involve very few test assumptions.

This chapter greatly differs from Chapter 3 in that it covers a very broad range of statistics. Analysts and managers will want to become familiar with the type of situations for which these statistics are used so that they can refer to these statistics as these situations arise. It is quite probable that managers will focus on those statistics that relate to problems that they most frequently encounter.

PROPORTIONAL REDUCTION IN ERROR

Proportional reduction in error (PRE) *is defined as the improvement, expressed as a fraction, in predicting a dependent variable due to knowledge of the independent variable.* Frequently, analysts want to know with how much certainty knowledge of one variable can be used to predict another. For example, we may know that receiving welfare is statistically associated with having a low income, but to what extent is having a low income a good predictor of also receiving welfare? When low incomes are a good predictor of receiving welfare, we say that the relationship between these two variables is *strong;* when low incomes are a poor (but a statistically significant) predictor of receiving welfare, we say that the relationship between these two variables is *weak*. PRE is used as a measure of the **strength of a relationship** between two variables, that is, the extent to which one variable is a good predictor of the other.

Calculating PRE

The following is one of several ways that a PRE fraction may be calculated. Slight variations exist on that which follows and are also discussed in this chapter. In practice, computers are used to calculate PRE fractions, and what follows is thus for illustrative purposes only. Assume that in a sample of 160 people, 90 people are not on welfare and 70 are on welfare (see Table 4.1). If we guessed every time that people are *not* on welfare, we would be wrong 70 times. The mode (the most frequent category) is our best guess, because if we guessed that they are on welfare, there would be 90 wrong guesses, which is (slightly) worse. The best guess is that people in the sample are not receiv-

Table 4.1 ────〜〜〜── Welfare and Income

Receiving Welfare	Income		Total
	Low	High	
No	40	50	90
Yes	60	10	70
Total	100	60	160

ing welfare. However, *when the level of income is also known,* as well as the number of welfare recipients in each level of income, then even fewer wrong guesses (or errors) are made. To illustrate, consider Table 4.1. When we know that subjects (for example, program participants) have low income, then we make 40 errors when guessing that they are on welfare. Likewise, when they have high income, we make 10 wrong guesses when guessing that they are not on welfare. Thus, the total number of mistakes when taking income into account is now 50, slightly less than the earlier 70 wrong guesses. The proportional reduction in errors (wrong guesses) can be defined as:

$$\frac{\text{Errors without knowledge of the independent variable} - \text{Errors with knowledge of the independent variable}}{\text{Errors without knowledge of the independent variable}}$$

Here, that is $(70 - 50/70) = 0.2857$, or 28.6 percent, with rounding. That is, as a result of knowing respondents' incomes, we are able to improve our guesses of their welfare situation by 28.6 percent.

PRE fractions range from 0.00 (no association or improvement in prediction) to 1.00 (perfect association or prediction). While there are no absolute standards for PRE scores, many analysts regard scores of less than 0.25 as indicating a weak association, scores between 0.25 and 0.50 as moderate association, and scores above 0.50 as strong association. Thus, the above value of 28.6 percent is said to indicate a *moderate* association between these two variables.[1]

Paired Cases

Although some statistics with a PRE interpretation (or "PRE statistics") are calculated in the above manner, others use a different method based on the concept of **paired cases.** This method distinguishes among similar, dissimilar, and tied pairs and is used to determine the direction of relationships. *Similar pairs* are pairs of observations that rank similarly low (or high) on both variables: both observations score high or low on both variables. *Dissimilar pairs* are pairs of observations that have reverse ranking on two variables—one observation scores high and the other low, and vice versa, on both variables. *Tied pairs* are those that rank similar on one variable and dissimilar on the other variable. The *direction of relationships* is either positive or negative, and knowing this often is of great importance to analysts. For example, public managers may want to know whether student participation in anger management classes increases or decreases classroom violence. Teachers may hope that the relationship is statistically significant and negative, that is, that increased participation decreases violence (but then, who knows what students learn and apply?). Statistics that provide this information greatly simplify the task of analysts because they need not rely on the visual method for determining the direction of relationships described in Chapter 3.

In Table 4.1 the number of similar pairs is calculated as 40*10 = 400. The number of dissimilar pairs is 50*60 = 3,000. The number of tied pairs on Welfare is (40*50 + 60*10) = 2,600, and the number of tied pairs on Income is (40*60 + 50*10) = 2,900. When the table is organized to show causal relations, then the number of tied pairs on Welfare is also called the number of tied pairs on the dependent variable (y), and the number of tied pairs on Income is called the number of tied pairs on the independent variable (x). The calculations for larger tables follow the same logic but are more complex.[2]

Different statistics, discussed below, make different uses of similar, dissimilar, and tied pairs. However, all have in the numerator the expression: number of similar pairs – number of dissimilar pairs. Therefore, a positive value indicates a positive relationship between the variables, and a negative value indicates a negative relationship between the variables (see Box 3.1). PRE statistics based on paired cases have a range of −1.00 to +1.00, which also provides information about the strength of the relationship. For example, a PRE test statistic based on paired cases with a value of −0.57 indicates a strong, negative relationship between two variables.

STATISTICS FOR TWO NOMINAL VARIABLES

Examples of analysis involving nominal variables abound in public management and analysis. For example, we might examine how the probability of getting parole varies by race or gender, or how attributes or type of employment varies by gender—the range of possible applications with two nominal variables is endless.

Choosing the right statistical test for nominal data is based on two considerations: the number of observations and whether the data are derived from independent or dependent samples. When analysts have many observations, a broad range of statistics is available. But when few observa-

Table 4.2 ———⟋⋏⟍— Job Applied For by Skills of Recipient

Job	Skills of Welfare Recipient			
	Word processing skills	Public speaking	Spread-sheets	Total
Clerk	14	5	10	29
Office assistant	15	10	20	45
Messenger	5	5	5	15
Total	34	20	35	89

tions are available, variable categories often are combined to construct two-by-two tables (that is, tables with two rows and two columns). Some special statistics have been developed for analyzing these tables. The following paragraphs discuss statistics for situations when analysts have many observations and for situations when they have few (say, less than thirty).

Two Nominal Variables

When analysts have two nominal variables with ample independent observations, the type of table illustrated in Table 4.2 can be constructed. The statistical question is whether these variables are associated, that is, whether skill type affects job type, and vice versa. Two useful statistics are *chi-square* and **Goodman and Kruskal's tau** (τ_{yx}). Chi-square is discussed in Chapter 3 and requires that no cell have fewer than five expected observations. Goodman and Kruskal's tau is a statistic with a PRE interpretation and is thus preferred over chi-square. Goodman and Kruskal's tau is used to determine the level of significance and the strength of a relationship. It is calculated in a similar but not identical manner to that described above. See Box 4.1 for the calculation of Goodman and Kruskal's tau.

Statistical software packages produce two measures of Goodman and Kruskal's tau that vary according to which variable is designated as the dependent variable. These are called **directional measures** and are appropriate for studying causal relationships. Some of these packages include a third type of measure, called a **symmetrical measure,** which is the average of the two directional measures and is appropriate for studying associations.[3] It should be noted that statistical packages routinely provide other statistics for nominal-level variables, as well. One such measure is **lambda** (λ), which is infrequently used because of a computational problem, as discussed in Box 4.1. In practice, analysts often find chi-square and Goodman and Kruskal's tau sufficient for testing their relationships between nominal-level variables. In Table 4.2, Goodman and Kruskal's tau is 0.016 ($p = .579 > .05$) when "Job Applied For" is the dependent variable, and it is 0.016 ($p = .584 > .05$) when Skills is the dependent variable. Thus, the relationship between these two

In Greater Depth...

Box 4.1   Calculating Goodman and Kruskal's Tau
(and a Note on Lambda)

For an example of calculating Goodman and Kruskal's tau, consider Table 4.1, a simple two-by-two table (we will treat those variables as if they are nominal). The number of errors without knowledge of the independent variable income is determined by trying to predict the dependent variable Welfare, given a total of 160 subjects. In trying to allocate 160 subjects over the 90 who do not receive welfare 70/160*90, errors are made because 70/160 is the proportion of subjects who receive welfare and are thus wrongfully classified in the No Welfare category. Similarly, 90/160*70 errors are made predicting those who do receive welfare. The total number of errors without knowledge of the independent variable is 78.75.

With knowledge of the independent variable, we first calculate the number of errors of subjects with low income. Among those, 60/100*40 errors are made predicting that subjects do not receive welfare, and 40/100*60 errors are made predicting that they do. Hence, a total of 48.00 errors are made. Then, we calculate the number of errors predicting welfare among subjects with high income. The number of errors is 50/60*10 + 10/60*50 = 16.67. Hence, the total number of errors with knowledge of the independent variable is 64.67. The PRE is then (78.75 − 64.67)/78.75 = 0.17, suggesting a modest reduction. As previously stated, the computer calculates this value and determines the level of significance (here, $p < .01$).

This modified approach is better than the straightforward approach discussed in the text because a computational quirk occurs when all of the category modes of the independent variable occur on the same category as the dependent variable. Lambda ("lam-da," or λ) is calculated in this manner and suffers from the following problem. Assume that among high-income subjects, 10 are not on welfare and 50 are on welfare (that is, a reversal of the High Income column counts). Then, the total number of errors without knowledge of the independent variable is (160 − 110) = 50. The number of errors with knowledge of the independent variable is 40 + 10 = 50. Hence, the PRE is then calculated as (50 − 50)/50 = 0; yet, clearly, some association is occurring. Goodman and Kruskal's tau does not suffer from this problem and is thus preferred to lambda. Indeed, the Goodman and Kruskal's tau statistic for this latter scenario is 0.059 ($p < .01$), not zero.

(Note: The calculations in this box are for illustrative purposes only, as the computer calculates Goodman and Kruskal's tau and the level at which it is statistically significant.)

variables is not significant.[4] Although Goodman and Kruskal's tau can be used with ordinal data, this test provides no information about the direction of relationships (which is meaningless for nominal-level variables) and should therefore not be used with such data.

The Problem of Dependent Samples

The above statistics are appropriate for independent samples, not for dependent samples. Until now, we have only considered independent samples in this text. *Independent samples* are samples in which there is no necessary association between respondents or their responses. For example, in a citizen survey of randomly selected citizens, there is no necessary relationship between respondents; indeed, they have been randomly selected. Neither do answers to one question necessarily restrict how other questions might be answered that are relevant to respondents (for example, a respondent can be Catholic without this necessarily determining his or her view on abortion). However, *dependent samples* occur whenever two or more variables of each respondent (or observation) are *necessarily* associated with each other, or whenever the variables of two or more respondents are *necessarily* associated with each other. By convention, the following three situations constitute dependent samples: (1) the before and after test scores of subjects in (quasi-) experimental situations (including other repeated measures of subjects), (2) subjects who have been matched (that is, chosen as having similar characteristics), and (3) the ratings of evaluators. "After" scores are viewed as necessarily correlated with "before" scores because the final level of improvement is dependent on initial starting conditions. Paired subjects have similar scores (compared with those who are unpaired), and individual evaluators tend to be consistent in their ratings. Generally, *samples are assumed to be independent, except when the above scenarios are present, or other reasons of necessary correlation are offered.*[5]

The following scenario involves a dependent sample with two nominal variables. For example, we might ask, at different points in time (say, every month), the same group of program clients whether they currently participate in a program or activity, or are experiencing a certain event. This is an example of a repeated measures scenario. A second example is whether the same number of welfare recipients participate in different counseling activities, when each is required to participate in *at least two activities.* The sample is dependent because participation in one activity clearly affects other choices. The test statistic for these data is *Cochran's Q,* a nonparametric test that measures the extent to which different "occasions" (or, activities) experience the same mean number of "events" (or participants): the number of participants in each activity could be either the same participants or different participants. Cochran's Q assumes dichotomous responses; thus all

Table 4.3 ——————～ Dichotomous Event Coding

Participant	Activity 1	Activity 2	Activity 3	Activity 4
1	1	1	0	1
2	0	1	1	1
3	0	0	1	1
4	1	1	0	1
5	1	1	0	1
Mean	0.60	0.80	0.40	1.00

entries are either 1's or 0's. The null hypothesis is that all occasions have the same *mean number of events*, or $\mu_1 = \mu_2 = \mu_3 = \ldots$. The alternate hypothesis is that at least one occasion (or counseling event) has a different mean number of participants. The data shown in Table 4.3 is used for this test. The test statistic, Cochran's Q, is 3.75 for these data, as calculated by the computer.[6] This statistic has a chi-square distribution, which means that the test statistic can be compared with chi-square critical values to determine the level of statistical significance. The above test statistic has three degrees of freedom and is insignificant at $p = .290 > .05$. Thus, there is *no difference* in the participation rates of these four activities: the differences between 0.60, 0.80, 0.40, and 1.0 are not statistically significant. However, Cochran's Q is affected by the small sample size. For a sample of twenty rather than five, with the above values replicated by the additional fifteen participants, Cochran's Q is 15.00 with df = 3, $p = .002 < .01$.

As previously stated, samples are generally assumed to be independent, unless the above scenarios are present or other reasons of necessary correlation are offered. The examples reflect scenarios that few analysts would frequently encounter.

Small Sample Tests for Two-by-Two Tables

As we have just seen, the above tests for independent observations often fail to reject the null hypothesis when sample sizes are small. Small samples abound in public administration and analysis, for example, in analyses of instances of discrimination, serious accidents, or adverse actions involving employees in a single department or unit. Few employees experience these events. Analysts frequently combine their categories to maximize the number of observed frequencies in each cell, hence increasing information. This may result in two-by-two tables, for which additional statistics have been developed. These statistics are also appropriate for nominal data because these statistics merely distinguish between categories regardless of any order (high, low) that might also exist.

Although chi-square and Goodman and Kruskal's tau can be used for two-by-two tables with independent observations, the following measures may also be considered. **Phi** (ϕ) is defined as $\sqrt{\chi^2/n}$, and ranges from 0 to 1 for two-by-k tables ($k \geq 2$). Phi squared (ϕ^2) has a "variance-explained" interpretation; for example, a ϕ^2 value of 0.35 (or, $\phi = 0.59$) means that 35 percent of the variance in one variable is explained by the other. Some argue that when analysts have small samples they should use *chi-square with the Yates' continuity correction.* Small samples (that is, small frequency counts) bias the expected frequencies slightly upward; this bias is "corrected" by subtracting 0.50 from the difference of expected and observed frequencies, thus producing a more conservative test statistic. However, others argue that this correction overcorrects.[7] The *Fisher exact test* also is used for small samples. It compares the observed table with all other possible tables that have the same marginal counts (that is, row and column totals). Based on this comparison, it calculates the probability that the two variables are related. *Yule's Q* is a measure of association with a PRE interpretation but without a test of statistical significance.[8]

For dependent samples, the *McNemar test* is used. This test is frequently used in discrimination cases and is appropriate for small samples. For example, assume that we wish to examine discrimination in employment interviews through a matched sample of job seekers. We send one majority and one minority tester, along with other job candidates, to the job interview. The two testers have equivalent qualifications and backgrounds, and they provide similar responses to questions. Their main difference is race. The McNemar test determines the level at which *dissimilar outcomes* are statistically significant. For example, consider Table 4.4, in which each count compares the employment outcomes of the testers. The McNemar test compares whether the eight instances in which a white but not minority applicant received a job are significantly different from the one instance in which the minority candidate received the job but not the white applicant. The test for the above data is significant ($p = .039 < .05$), which means that this disparate outcome cannot be attributed to chance alone. The McNemar test ignores similar outcomes; thus, the same test result is obtained by examining only the nine dissimilar outcomes. It also ignores similar outcomes in which both testers are hired, such as when employers hire multiple candidates through the same interview process.[9]

Table 4.4 ⎯⎯⎯⎯⎯∿∿⎯ Employment Discrimination Test

Minority Applicants	White applicants		Total
	Hired	Not hired	
Hired	0	1	1
Not hired	8	2	10
Total	8	3	11

Table 4.5 ——— ⌁⌁⌁ Ratings of Three Programs

Group	Rating	Rank	Group	Rating	Rank	Group	Rating	Rank
1	2.5	3	2	3.4	7.5	3	4.8	13
1	2.9	4	2	3.3	6	3	5.0	14.5
1	4.0	10.5	2	4.0	10.5	3	5.0	14.5
1	3.2	5	2	3.9	9	3	3.4	7.5
1	1.2	1	2	2.1	2	3	4.2	12
Mean		4.7			7.0			12.3

STATISTICS FOR MIXED ORDINAL-NOMINAL DATA

Sometimes managers and analysts want to know whether programs or policies vary in their ratings; some may be more popular or perceived as being more effective. This problem involves one nominal variable, which identifies each of the different programs, and one ordinal variable, which is used to rate each program or policy. A different problem arises when analysts want to know whether two or more evaluators agree in their ratings of the *same* program. Then, the nominal variable identifies each of the evaluators and the ordinal variable again rates the program. Both of these problems involve one ordinal and one nominal variable.

Evaluating Rankings

Evaluators often are used to assess program or agency performance by providing qualitative judgments. ***Kruskal-Wallis' H*** assesses whether programs differ in their ratings. Assume that fifteen evaluators are each asked to evaluate one of three programs, and an index score is constructed of their evaluations. This is a test for *independent samples;* each evaluator evaluates only one program. The null hypothesis is that, on average, each program receives the same average ranking. The data are shown in Table 4.5 (for presentation, the variables are in separate columns; these data are entered in statistical software programs as one table with fifteen observations and two variables). The group variable identifies the program. Note that the rating variable is shown as a continuous variable. Kruskal-Wallis' H assigns ranks to the rating variable, thus creating an ordinal variable from the continuous variable. Specifically, it does so by ranking the collective observations of all groups from high to low and then testing whether the means of the ranks of the groups are significantly different. Kruskal-Wallis' H has a chi-square distribution. The H test statistic for the data in Table 4.5 is 7.636 (df = 2, $p = .022 < .05$).[10] That is, the three programs vary in their mean ranking of evaluation scores. Information provided with this result shows that the mean rankings are, respectively, 4.70, 7.00, and 12.30.

Eta squared (η^2) is a measure of association indicating the percentage of variance explained and is defined as $H/(n-1)$. Here, $\eta^2 = (7.636/15 - 1) = 0.545$; hence, 54.5 percent of the variance in ratings is explained by the grouping of programs. It should be noted that the Kruskal-Wallis' H test is a nonparametric version of the Analysis of Variance (ANOVA) test, which is discussed in Chapter 5. The ANOVA test uses interval-level data, rather than assigned ranks, and makes stringent assumptions about the continuous variable, such as whether it is normally distributed; the Kruskal-Wallis' H test is a useful alternative to ANOVA when these test assumptions are not met. By contrast, the Kruskal-Wallis' H test is nonparametric and makes no assumptions about the distribution of the data.

Samples that involve evaluators often are dependent, however. Typically, a few evaluators assess different program items, and we want to know whether evaluators agree in their ratings. This occurs in program reviews, as when outside experts visit programs or facilities such as hospitals or parks departments in connection with accreditation. It also occurs in regulatory inspections (do two or more inspectors or assessors agree?) and in the evaluations of trained observers. By convention, we assume that ratings are necessarily correlated because some raters consistently give high ratings, whereas others give low ratings. Thus, one rating affects other ratings, and we treat these as dependent. The data must be ordinal. The *Friedman test,* developed by the well-known economist Milton Friedman, uses data in the format shown in Tables 4.6 and 4.7 and has a chi-square distribution. The Friedman test ranks the evaluations of the three raters for each item (5 = highest). Table 4.6 shows that Rater 1 has the highest ranking of Item 1. The relative ranking of Item 1 across the three raters is 3, 1, and 2 (Table 4.7) because Rater 1 gives Item 1 a higher rating than Rater 3, who, in turn, gives Item 1 a higher rating than Rater 2. The ratings for Item 2 are tied between the second and third raters. The ranked ratings for Item 2 are 3.00, $[(1+2)/2] = 1.50$, and 1.50. The ranked ratings for Item 3 are 2.00, 2.00, and 2.00 (they are all tied), and so on. Based on these rankings, the mean ranked ratings for each evaluator are determined, as shown in Table 4.6. The Friedman test statistic for the above data is 0.545 (df = 2, $p = .761 > .05$). Thus,

Table 4.6 ———〰— Actual Ratings of Three Evaluators

Item	Rater 1	Rater 2	Rater 3
1	5	3	4
2	4	2	2
3	3	3	3
4	2	4	3
5	1	1	1

Table 4.7 ——— ⌇⌇ Relative Ratings of Three Evaluators

Item	Rater 1	Rater 2	Rater 3
1	3	1	2
2	3	1.5	1.5
3	2	2	2
4	1	3	2
5	2	2	2
Mean rank	2.2	1.9	1.9

we conclude that the ratings of the evaluators are not different; *the evaluators agree with each other.* When columns and rows are reversed, the Friedman test assesses whether differences exist among the mean rankings of items. This test can also be used to examine test score changes in before-and-after situations. Then, the rows are subjects and the columns are the subjects' before-and-after scores. (The Friedman test is quite sensitive to the number of items. It is best to have at least ten rows.)

When evaluators agree with each other, we often wish to have a measure of the strength of their agreement. That is, is the agreement among the raters about their ratings of different items strong, moderate, or weak? The measure of such agreement among raters (also called **inter-rater agreement**) is the average Spearman rank order correlation ($\bar{r}_s$). The **Spearman rank order correlation coefficient** (ρ, pronounced "rho") is defined as the correlation between two variables when both are measured as rankings. Rho has a PRE interpretation. The Spearman rank order correlation assigns ranks to variables and tests whether two rankings are correlated with each other (the null hypothesis is that they are not associated, hence, that the rankings differ). The average Spearman correlation coefficient is simply the average of all Spearman correlation coefficients for all pairs of variables. The easiest way to calculate $\bar{r}_s$ is through the formula $\bar{r}_s = (kW - 1)/(k - 1)$, where $k =$ the number of evaluators and W is the **Kendall's coefficient of concordance.** W is a normalization of the Friedman statistic (it is bounded by zero and one) and is produced by many statistical software packages. Kendall's coefficient of concordance measures the variation that exists across the average ratings of each item. When inter-rater agreement is high, raters agree on which items rank high and which items rank low, thus producing considerable variation and resulting in a high W coefficient. Conversely, when inter-rater agreement is low, the average ratings of items vary little and W is low. To calculate W the column totals represent the average item ratings; therefore, Table 4.6 is inverted (the rows represent raters and the columns represent items). The W statistic for Table 4.6 is then calculated by the computer as 0.695, and $\bar{r}_s$ 0.542, indicating strong agreement among raters.[11]

Equivalency of Two Samples

The above tests are also used to examine whether samples come from the same population. When two samples are found to come from different populations, the implication may be that a policy has differential impact. For example, when samples of male and female drug offenders are found to come from different populations, it may be that men and women are responding to drug treatments or incarceration practices in different ways. Differences between two samples may stem from different central tendencies or any other feature relating to their distributions. A finding that two samples come from different populations usually requires further inquiry to determine the exact nature of the difference.

Although numerous tests exist for determining whether two samples come from the same population, two widely used tests, the **Mann-Whitney (U)** and **Wilcoxon (W)** tests, are simplifications of the more general Kruskal-Wallis' H test, previously discussed. The Mann-Whitney (U) and Wilcoxon (W) tests are equivalent and are thus jointly discussed. To test whether two samples can be said to come from the same population, analysts compare two variables—one from each sample. Each variable measures the same concept. Then, the U and W tests assign ranks to these variables in the exact manner as shown in Table 4.5, but using only two groups. The sum of the ranks of each group is computed, as shown in Table 4.8. Then a test is performed of the statistical significance of the difference between the sums, 22.5 and 32.5. Although the U and W test statistics are calculated differently, they both have the same level of statistical significance: $p = .295$. This insignificance implies that Groups 1 and 2 can be regarded as coming from the same population. By contrast, the p value for comparing Groups 1 and 3 in Table 4.5 is .016. We may note that using the Kruskal-Wallis' H test for these two groups yields the exact same level of significance.[12]

The **Wilcoxon Signed Rank test** is equivalent to these tests but calculates the difference between the before and after scores of subjects. This test can be used for testing all manner of before-and-after test situations, such as involving student test scores and crime rates in different neighborhoods

Table 4.8 〰️ Rankings of Two Groups

Group	Rating	Rank	Group	Rating	Rank
1	2.5	3	2	3.4	7
1	2.9	4	2	3.3	6
1	4.0	9.5	2	4.0	9.5
1	3.2	5	2	3.9	8
1	1.2	1	2	2.1	2
Sum		22.5	Sum		32.5

Table 4.9 ──────〜〜〜 Wilcoxon Signed Rank Test

Before	After	Difference	Signed rank
3.2	4.3	1.1	8.5
4.0	3.8	−0.2	−2.0
2.4	3.5	1.1	8.5
3.0	3.3	0.3	3.0
4.0	4.4	0.4	4.5
4.3	4.2	−0.1	−1.0
3.8	3.3	−0.5	−6.0
2.9	3.9	1.0	7.0
3.8	4.2	0.4	4.5
2.5	3.8	1.3	10.0

before and after a policy change. This is, by definition, a test for dependent samples. This test assigns ranks based on the absolute values of these differences (Table 4.9). The signs of the differences are retained (thus, some values are positive, and others are negative). The Wilcoxon Signed Rank test is based on the sums of all the ranks; a small summed value indicates that the before and after test scores are not significantly different, whereas a large (positive or negative) summed value indicates differences between the two scores. The test statistic is normally distributed. Thus, the sum of the negative ranks is 9, and the sum of the positive ranks is 46. The Wilcoxon test statistic, Z, for a difference between these values is 1.89 ($p = .059 > .05$). Hence, we conclude that there is no difference between the before and after test scores. (However, a doubling of the data shows a significant difference between the before and after scores, $Z = 2.694$, $p = .007$.)

A broad range of equivalency tests exists. Although they serve the same purposes, their methods of testing for equivalency are different. Some of these tests are discussed in Box 4.2.

STATISTICS FOR TWO ORDINAL VARIABLES

In practice, data analysis often involves two ordinal variables. Many citizen and client survey questions are based on five- or seven-point Likert scales. When both variables are ordinal, chi-square can be used as well as PRE measures that are calculated using the concept of paired cases. As before, we prefer PRE measures over chi-square because PRE measures provide additional information about the direction and strength of relationships. These statistics can also be used when analyzing one ordinal and one dichotomous variable (the latter is then treated as an ordinal variable with two values).

Four frequently used PRE statistics are **gamma** (γ), **Somer's d**, **Kendall's tau-b** (τ_b), and **Kendall's tau-c** (τ_c). These PRE statistics differ chiefly in the

In Greater Depth...

Box 4.2   Some More Tests for the Equivalency of Samples

Kolmogorov-Smirnov two-sample test statistic (also called the K–S$_2$ test) compares the cumulative frequency distribution of two independent samples with the same response categories. Specifically, it calculates the differences of the cumulative frequency distributions for each response category and tests the probability of obtaining the largest (also called most extreme) difference if the two samples come from the same population. Comparing Groups 1 and 2 in Table 4.5, we find that the *p* value is .329 > .05; hence, we conclude that Groups 1 and 2 come from the same population.

The *Wald-Wolfowitz runs test* (or simply "runs test") is an independent samples test and examines patterns of dispersion. It assigns ranks to two samples in the same manner as shown in Table 4.8. The order of ranks is 1, 2, 1, 1, 1, 2, 2, 2, —, —, where the numbers indicate group membership (the last two observations are tied). Similar samples have a random sequence, whereas dissimilar samples show clustering, such as 1, 1, 1, 1, 2, 1, 2, 2, 2, 2. A z-score is calculated. In this example, z = –0.335, *p* = .357, and thus we conclude that the samples come from the same population. But the insignificance is largely due to the small sample size; doubling of the number of observations (with the same values) produces a z value of –2.527, *p* = .004.

The *Sign test* is a paired samples test that compares the direction of rank differences. For example, each observation is an evaluator who evaluates two different programs. Ranks are assigned to two samples in the same manner as the Kruskal-Wallis' H test, and then the sign of differences is determined. Using the ranks for Groups 1 and 2 as determined above (runs test), the rank differences are (3 – 7.5) = –4.5, (4 – 6) = –2, (10.5 – 10.5) = 0, (5 – 9) = –4, and (1 – 2) = –1. The Sign test examines the probability that the pattern of positive and negative differences can be ascribed to chance alone, that is —, —, 0, —, —. The *p* value for this test is .125. Again, the insignificance is largely due to the small sample size. Doubling of the number of observations (with the same values) produces *p* = .008, hence indicating that the difference is statistically significant.

Finally, nonparametric statistics are also available for testing whether a variable is consistent with a specific distribution. This is univariate, rather than bivariate, analysis. The *Kolmogorov-Smirnov one-sample test* is commonly used for testing whether variables are normally distributed. The null hypothesis is that the variable is normally distributed. This test is more fully discussed in Chapter 5. The one-sample chi-square test tests whether the distribution of a variable is consistent with a prespecified distribution; this was discussed in Chapter 3 (goodness-of-fit test).

manner in which ties are taken into account. Gamma, for example, is defined as $(Ns - Nd)/(Ns + Nd)$, where Ns is the number of similar pairs, and Nd is the number of dissimilar pairs. Gamma does not take tied pairs into account. By contrast, Somer's d is defined as $(Ns - Nd)/(Ns + Nd + Ty)$, where Ty represents ties on the dependent variable. Because Ty is in the denominator, the value of Somer's d is less than γ, and thus Somer's d is a more conservative estimate of the PRE. Also, the value of Somer's d depends on which variable is identified as the dependent variable. It is a directional measure, and statistical software programs compute test statistics by alternating which variable is specified as dependent.

Tau-b is defined as $(Ns - Nd)/\sqrt{(Ns + Nd + Ty)(Ns + Nd + Tx)}$. It is symmetrical and is even more conservative than Somer's d. However, τ_b is appropriate only for square tables, which is an important limitation. Tau-c overcomes this limitation and can be used for tables of all sizes. Tau-c is defined differently, as $2m(Ns - Nd)/N^2(m - 1)$, where m represents the smaller number of rows or columns, and N is the sample size. Of all of the above tests, τ_c *is considered the most conservative in estimating PRE and is therefore widely used.*

Consider the following examples of these PRE measures. A human resources manager wants to know whether perceptions of the county as an employer are associated with feelings of fairness, especially in the area of work rewards. An employee survey is administered. The lead-in question is: "Please evaluate the following statements by indicating whether you strongly agree, agree, disagree, or strongly disagree with the following statements. You may also state that you don't know." Two items are "I am satisfied with my job in Seminole County" and "The people who get promoted are the best qualified for the job." The results are shown in Table 4.10.

The results show that job satisfaction is quite strongly, and positively, associated with this measure of fairness. Table 4.10 also shows that τ_c has indeed the smallest PRE value and that all statistics are evaluated at the same level of statistical significance. The contingency table can also be examined to determine the practical significance (not shown here). Among employees who agree or strongly agree that the best people get promoted, 93.3 percent also agree or strongly agree that they are satisfied with their job; by comparison, only 69.1 percent of employees who disagree or strongly disagree that the best people get promoted also agree that they are satisfied with their job. Although this difference may appear significant but small, disagreeing that the best people get promoted greatly increases job *dis*satisfaction: 35.4 percent of employees who disagree or strongly disagree that the best people get promoted are dissatisfied with their job, as compared with only 3.2 percent of employees who agree or strongly agree that the best people get promoted. Thus, perceptions of unfairness in job rewards greatly add to job dissatisfaction.[13]

Table 4.10 ———— Comparing Ordinal-Ordinal PRE Measures of Association

Statistic		Value	Approx. Sig.
Chi-square		253.17	0.000
Somer's d	Symmetric	0.323	0.000
	Dep = job satisf.	0.285	0.000
	Dep = promoted	0.372	0.000
Gamma		0.470	0.000
Kendall's tau-b		0.326	0.000
Kendall's tau-c		0.275	0.000

Note: Dep = dependent variables; sig. = significance.

CONCLUSION

Analysts are frequently confronted with categorical data. For example, many surveys (of employees, citizens, or program clients) involve categorical data, such as gender or income (when measured in brackets). Surveys also involve ordinal assessments, such as the extent to which respondents agree or disagree with certain statements. To analyze the extent and manner in which two variables are related to each other, analysts often use the PRE and nonparametric statistics discussed here. PRE-based statistics provide information about the statistical significance of relationships, as well as their strength and direction and are thus preferred to chi-square for testing relationships of categorical variables. Nonparametric statistics are used for rather special situations, such as comparing the ratings of two evaluators, significance testing that involves very small samples, and dependent samples (samples in which observations are correlated).

A plethora of PRE and nonparametric statistics exists. It would be a true challenge to memorize all of the statistics discussed in this chapter. Rather, the task is to be familiar with the types of problems they address. Recognizing the particular situations and problems will help analysts to know when to use each different test. As bewildering as the array of tests might seem, clearly, the tests themselves are not particularly difficult to use. Indeed, they are rather straightforward:

- When both variables are ordinal, Kendall's tau-c is a commonly used PRE statistic for testing the significance, strength, and direction of the relationship between these two variables.
- When both variables are nominal, Goodman and Kruskal's tau is a PRE statistic used for testing the significance and strength of the relationship.
- When the sample is very small, statistics that are specifically designed for that purpose are used, such as the Fisher exact test.

- When a test of discrimination is needed, the McNemar test is used.
- When one variable is ordinal and the other is nominal, the scenario may involve a comparison of evaluators' rankings. Then, Kruskal-Wallis' H is used for independent samples, and the Friedman test is used for dependent samples.

This short list is an important resource for you as you learn to identify each particular situation that warrants the use of a specific test.

KEY TERMS

Chi-square with Yates' continuity
   correction (p. 79)
Cochran's Q (p. 77)
Dependent samples (p. 77)
Direction of relationships (p. 74)
Directional measures (p. 75)
Dissimilar pairs (p. 73)
Eta squared (p. 81)
Fisher exact test (p. 79)
Friedman test (p. 81)
Gamma (p. 84)
Goodman and Kruskal's tau (p. 75)
Independent samples (p. 77)
Inter-rater agreement (p. 82)
Kendall's coefficient
   of concordance (p. 82)
Kendall's tau-b (p. 84)
Kendall's tau-c (p. 84)

Kruskal-Wallis' H (p. 80)
Lambda (p. 75)
Mann-Whitney U test (p. 83)
McNemar test (p. 79)
Paired cases (p. 73)
Phi (p. 79)
Proportional reduction in error
   (PRE) (p. 72)
Similar pairs (p. 73)
Somer's d (p. 84)
Spearman rank order correlation
   coefficient (p. 82)
Strength of relationships (p. 72)
Symmetrical measures (p. 75)
Tied pairs (p. 74)
Wilcoxon Signed Rank test (p. 83)
Wilcoxon W test (p. 83)
Yule's Q (p. 79)

Notes

1. Some authors suggest that values below 0.20 indicate weak relationships; between 0.20 and 0.40, moderate relationships; between 0.40 and 0.60, strong relationships; and above 0.60, very strong relationships. We suggest erring on the side of caution and thus using a higher standard.
2. For example, see Chava Frankfort-Nachmias, *Social Statistics for a Diverse Society,* 2d ed. (Thousand Oaks, Calif.: Pine Forge Press, 1999), chap. 7. Many books provide similar calculations. The example is provided for conceptual understanding only; the computer calculates test statistics.

3. Statistics for Table 4.2 are chi-square = 2.89 (df = 4, p = .576 > .005), lambda (symmetric) = 0.041 (p = .492 > .05), lambda (job = dependent) = 0.000, lambda (skills = dependent) = 0.074 (p = .492 > .05), Goodman and Kruskal's tau (job = dependent) = 0.016 (p = .579 > .05), and Goodman and Kruskal's tau (skills = dependent) = 0.016 (p = .584 > .05). Thus, note that this table also suffers from the computational lambda quirk.

4. The following statistics are also produced by SPSS as output and are provided for completeness only. *Cramer's V* is a chi-square-based measure that is corrected for the problem that χ^2 increases with sample size the number of cells. Cramer's V ranges from 0 (no association) to 1 (perfect association) and is defined as

$$\sqrt{\frac{\chi^2}{n*\min(rows-1,columns-1)}}.$$

Although not calculated as a PRE statistic, values below 0.25 are considered to indicate weak relations, values between 0.25 and 0.50 are moderate relations, and values over 0.50 are strong relations. Many computer programs also produce the *contingency coefficient, C* (also called Pearson's coefficient of contingency), which is calculated as

$$\sqrt{\chi^2/(\chi^2+n)}$$

C is calculated similar to V but has the disadvantage that its maximum value can be less than 1.0. Cramer's V overcomes this problem and is thus preferred. The *uncertainty coefficient, U*, is a measure that is quite similar to lambda and does not offer many advantages in this context. For a formula of this statistic, see R. A. Cooper and A. J. Weeks, *Data, Models, and Statistics Analysis* (Oxford, UK: Philip Allan, 1983), and other general statistics books.

5. Independent observations are also called independent samples, and dependent samples are also called paired or matched observations. The concept of paired observations should *not be* confused with that of paired cases, discussed earlier as part of PRE.

6. Cochran's Q is defined as

$$Q=\frac{(k-1)k(\sum C_k^2-T^2)}{kT-\sum R_i^2},$$

where k = the number of values of the columns, $\sum C_k^2$ = the sum of squared values of each column, $\sum R_i^2$ = the sum of squared values of each row, T = total values of all cases.

7. The chi-square statistic with Yates' continuity correction is defined as

$$\sum_i \frac{(|O_i - E_i| - 0.5)^2}{E_i}$$

8. Yule's Q is defined as follows. Assume the following two-by-two table:

A	B
C	D

Then, Yule's Q is $\dfrac{(AD) - (BC)}{(AD) + (BC)}$.

9. The McNemar test statistic is defined as $\chi^2_{McNemar} = (|f_{0,1} - f_{1,0}|)^2/(f_{0,1} + f_{1,0})$. It has a chi-square distribution, with df = 1. Many statistical software programs also calculate the relative risks and odds ratio for two-by-two tables (paired or independent samples). From Table 4.4, the *relative risk* (or chance) of a minority applicant being hired when also a majority (white) applicant is hired is 0/8 = 0 percent. Likewise, the relative risk (or chance) of a minority applicant being hired when a majority (white) applicant is not hired is ½ = 50.0 percent. The *odds ratio* is 0%/50.0% = 0, which is an indication of how much better the chances for minorities are of being hired when a white applicant is also hired. Although most software program computers calculate these statistics only for two-by-two tables, risks can be manually calculated for larger tables, as well.

10. The formula for H is

$$\frac{12}{n(n+1)}\left(\frac{T_1^2}{n_1} + \frac{T_2^2}{n_2} + \ldots\right) - 3(n+1),$$

where T_i is the sum of ranks in Group 1, and so on.

11. *Kappa* is another measure of inter-rater agreement. Values of kappa below 0.40 are said to indicate poor agreement, values between 0.40 and 0.75 indicate fair to good agreement, and above 0.75 indicate excellent agreement. A limitation of kappa, however, is that both evaluators must use the exact same values (or categories) in their evaluations. By example, kappa cannot be used to evaluate inter-rater agreement among Raters 1 and 2 in Table 4.6 because the ratings of the second evaluator do not include the value "5." Kappa can be used to evaluate inter-rater agreement between the second and third evaluators: kappa = 0.444 (p = .094 > .05), indicating a fair level of agreement. (Kappa is insignificant

due to the small sample. When the sample size is doubled from five to ten, kappa = 0.444 with p = .018). Kendall's W is preferred over kappa because W allows for comparing multiple raters, and does not require that all have the same value.

12. The formula for calculating the Mann-Whitney U test is

$$n_1 n_2 + \frac{n_1(n_1 + 1)}{2} - T_1,$$

where T_1 is the sum of ranks for Group 1, n_1 is the number of observations in Sample 1, and n_2 is the number of observations in Sample 2. The relationship between U and W is that

$$U + W = \frac{m(m + 2n + 1)}{2}$$

whereby m = the number of observations in the group that has the smaller number of observations, and n = the number of observations in the group that has the larger number of observations.

13. In addition to the statistics discussed here, many computer programs will produce additional measures of chi-square, but these often have little utility. The linear-by-linear association is the square of the Pearson correlation coefficient (Chapter 6), multiplied by the sample size, minus one. The Likelihood Ratio is used for n-way tables, in which a third variable is added to the contingency table. See B. G. Tabachnick and L. S. Fidell, *Using Multivariate Statistics*, 3d ed. (New York: HarperCollins), chap. 7.

T-Tests and ANOVA

CHAPTER OBJECTIVES

After this chapter you should be able to:
- Construct index variables
- Test whether two or more groups have different means of a continuous variable
- Assess whether the mean is consistent with a specified value
- Determine whether variables meet test assumptions
- Understand the role of variable transformations
- Know how post-hoc tests are used with ANOVA

When analysts need to compare the means of a continuous variable across different groups, they have two valuable tools at their disposal—t-tests and Analysis of Variance (ANOVA). T-tests are used for testing whether two groups have different means of a continuous (metric) variable, such as when we want to know whether mean incomes vary between men and women. If we want to know whether mean incomes vary across more than two groups, then ANOVA is used. If we want to study whether mean incomes differ by region (a nominal variable) or according to the political orientations of individuals (measured as a categorical variable), then ANOVA is our tool of choice.

This chapter differs from Chapters 3 and 4 in that one of the variables is continuous and the other variable is categorical. Many variables are continuous, such as income, age, height, counts of fish in pond (when there are many), case loads, and service calls. Recoding continuous variables as categorical variables is discouraged because that results in a loss of information. Continuous variables provide valuable information about distances between categories and often have a broader range of values than ordinal variables. We should not recode continuous variables just to use the techniques of the previous chapters.

Also, in Chapter 1, we saw how conceptualization results in measuring several related variables. For example, we might measure the concept "high school violence" by measuring the number of incidents that involve weapons, physical contact, and verbal assaults. We might also measure perceptions of school (un)safety. In this chapter, we show how such related variables can be combined into a single index variable that measures the underlying concept. Index variables often are very useful to researchers because they increase measurement validity by using a range of variables that represent a broad study concept. Usually, index variables are continuous, and hence t-tests and ANOVA can be used for analyzing whether mean index scores differ across different groups. For example, if we want to know whether high school violence (as measured by a continuous index variable) differs across age groups or school districts, we use a t-test or ANOVA. Thus, we begin our discussion showing how index variables are constructed for later use in t-tests and ANOVA.

CREATING INDEX VARIABLES

Making index variables is quite easy—an ***index variable*** is simply the sum of the measurement variables. The hard work is up front, specifying the conceptual dimensions and gathering data for variables that measure them. If we measure "high school violence" by measuring the number of incidents that involve weapons, physical contact, and verbal abuse, as well as perceptions of school safety, then the index variable is simply the sum of each value of the measurement variables. The logic of index variable construction is simple: when respondents score low on measurement variables, then the resulting index score is low, too, and vice versa.[1] Table 5.1 shows how an index variable is created by simply adding up the values of the measurement variables that constitute the dimension or concept. Thus, when respondents score high on measurement variables, the resulting index score is high. When one or more of the measurement variables are missing from an obser-

Table 5.1 ———————〰〰— Creating an Index Variable

Observation	Measure 1	Measure 2	Measure 3	Measure 4	Index
567	1	2	2	4	9
568	4	1	1	1	7
569	4	2	2	4	12
570	5	5	5	5	20
571	1	2	—	1	—
572	1	1	1	1	4

vation, the value of the index variables for that observation is missing, too, as shown for observation 571. Note that whereas measurement variables might be ordinal (for example, measured on a five-point Likert scale), the resulting index variable often is continuous. In the example of Table 5.1, the index variable can range from a minimum of 4 to a maximum of 20.

Although index variables are easy to make, analysts must demonstrate that they are valid measures of the underlying concepts or dimension. Analysts are not expected to use all or even most of the following approaches, but they are expected to justify their index variable in some way. *Measurement validity,* in this context, means that index variables must really measure what they are being said to measure. The most important form of validation is theoretical—a persuasive argument that the measures make sense. One argument is that the measures are reasonable, commonsense ways of measuring the underlying concept. This is called *face validity.* Another argument is that measurement variables should encompass a broad range of aspects. For example, variables measuring "physical exercise" should not be skewed in some biasing way, perhaps underemphasizing individual sports in favor of team sports. This form of validity is called *content validity.*

Empirical evidence can also be mustered in three ways. First, descriptive analysis is used to show that the range of values of the index variable is appropriate. If most values of the index variable are "high," then little will be known about those who score "low." This situation is sometimes caused by summing variables with unequal scales. It is therefore good practice to rescale variables to a common scale before creating an index variable, in order to ensure that all variables contribute equally to the index variable. Also, analysts should examine whether observations with missing values in their index variables create a pattern of bias, perhaps systematically excluding some group(s) of observations.

Second, variables that are used to measure a concept should be strongly associated (or correlated) with each other. This is because each index variable measures different but related dimensions. When variables are not highly related, analysts should consider whether, perhaps, the variables measure different concepts (the index variable is then said to lack unidimensionality). The correlation of measurement variables is called **internal reliability** (or internal consistency), and **Cronbach alpha** (also, *alpha* or *measure alpha*) is an empirical measure of the correlation of measurement variables that is readily computed by most statistical software programs. Alpha ranges from zero to one, where one indicates perfect correlation and a zero indicates the (perfect) lack of any correlation. Values between 0.80 and 1.00 are desired and indicate high reliability. Values between 0.70 and 0.80 indicate moderate (but acceptable) reliability. Alpha values below 0.70 are poor and should cause analysts to consider a different mix of variables. Index variables with alpha scores below 0.70 should be avoided, although values between 0.60 and 0.70 are sometimes used when analysts lack a better mix. Analysts usually collect a few more variables than are minimally needed because they cannot know prior to reliability analysis which variable mix will have a sufficiently high alpha score to lend empirical support for the index measure.

Third, index variables can be validated by comparing them with other measures or sources. For example, if we have access to the medical records of respondents, we might hypothesize that those who indicate high levels of physical exercise have, on average, lower blood pressure or body fact content than those who indicate low levels of exercise. Comparison with external sources is sometimes called **criterion** *(or external)* **validity.** When the index variable correlates as expected, then additional validity is provided. We might also ask respondents on the same survey about their blood pressure and compare that with other responses, such as frequency of exercise. Such comparison against internal sources is called **construct** *(or internal)* **validity** (not to be confused with internal *reliability,* above). Although this does not provide absolute proof (respondents may not accurately know their blood pressure, which is also affected by other factors than exercise), it may provide some reassurance and, hence, a measure of validity. Certainly, the lack of correlation would detract from validity and require further inquiry and explanation.

In sum, a plethora of strategies exists for evaluating the validity of index variables. Again, analysts are not expected to use all of the above approaches, but they should use some to justify their measures. In research, this usually requires some up-front consideration because, after data have been collected, it may be too late to go back for more observations as needed for validation.

T-TESTS

T-tests are used to test whether the means of a continuous (metric) variable differ across two different groups. For example, do men and women differ in their level of physical exercise, as measured by the index variable above?

Figure 5.1 ⎯⎯⎯⎯ᵂᵂ⎯The T-Test:
Mean Incomes by Gender

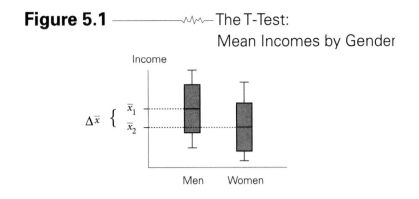

Does crime vary between two parts of town? Do rich people live longer than poor people? Do "high performing" students commit fewer acts of violence than "low performing'" students? The t-test approach is shown graphically in Figure 5.1, which illustrates the incomes of men and women as boxplots (the lines in the middle of the boxes indicate the means rather than the medians).[2] Sometimes, the continuous variable is called a "test variable" and the dichotomous variable is called a "grouping variable." The t-test tests whether the *difference of the means* ($\Delta \bar{x}$, or $\bar{x}_1 - \bar{x}_2$) *is significantly different from zero,* that is, whether men and women have different incomes. The following hypotheses are posited:

H_0: Men and women do not have different mean incomes (in the population).
H_A: Men and women do have different mean incomes (in the population).

Or, using a Greek letter for referring to differences in the population, H_0: $\mu_m = \mu_f$, and H_A: $\mu_m \neq \mu_f$. The formula for calculating the t-test test statistic (a tongue twister?) is

$$t = \frac{\bar{x}_1 - \bar{x}_2}{\sqrt{s_p^2 \left(\frac{1}{n_1} + \frac{1}{n_2} \right)}}$$

As always, the computer calculates the test statistic and reports at what level it is significant. Such calculations are seldom done by hand. To further conceptual understanding of this formula, it is useful to relate it to the discussion of hypothesis testing in Chapter 3. First, note that the difference of means, $\bar{x}_1 - \bar{x}_2$, appears in the numerator: the larger the difference of means, the larger the t-test test statistic, and the more likely we might reject the null hypothesis. Second, s_p is the pooled variance of the two groups, that is, the weighted average of the variances of each group.[3] Increases in the standard deviation decrease the test statistic. Thus, it is easier to reject the null hypotheses when two populations are narrowly clustered around their means than when they are widely spread around them. Finally, more observations (that is, increased information or larger n_1 and n_2) increase the size of the test statistic, hence making it easier to reject the null hypothesis.

The test statistics of a t-test can be positive or negative, although this merely depends on which group has the larger mean; the sign of the test statistic has no substantive interpretation. *Critical values* (see Chapter 3 for a discussion of this concept) of the t-test are shown in the Appendix as **(Student's) t-distribution**.[4] For this test, the *degrees of freedom* are defined as $n - 1$, where n is the total number of observations for both groups. The critical value decreases as the number of observations increase, making it easier to reject the null hypothesis. The t-distribution shows one- and two-tailed tests. *Two-tailed t-tests* should be used when analysts do not have prior knowledge about which group has a larger mean; *one-tailed t-tests* are used when analysts do have such prior knowledge. This choice is dictated by the research situation, not any statistical criterion. In practice, two-tailed tests are most often used, unless compelling a priori knowledge exists or it is known that one group cannot have a larger mean than the other. Two-tailed testing is more conservative than one-tailed testing because the critical values of two-tailed tests are larger, thus requiring larger t-test test statistics in order to reject the null hypothesis. Many statistical packages provide only two-tailed testing. The above null hypothesis (men and women do not have different mean incomes in the population) requires a two-tailed test because we do not know which gender has the larger income. Finally, note that the t-test distribution approximates the normal distribution for large samples: the critical values of 1.96 (5 percent significance) and 2.58 (1 percent significance), for large degrees of freedom (∞), are identical to those of the normal distribution.

T-Test Assumptions

Like other tests, the t-test has various *test assumptions* that must be met to ensure test validity. Statistical testing always begins by determining whether test assumptions are met before examining the main research hypotheses. This section discusses these tests, as well as ways in which tests and variables are (often creatively) adapted to meet test assumptions. Typically, statistical tests involving continuous variables tend to have many more test assumptions than those discussed in preceding chapters. In practice, most variables can be made to meet t-test assumptions. A real-life data example is provided. (Note that the Mann-Whitney (U) test, discussed in Chapter 4, is a nonparametric alternative to t-tests, which can be used when variables, despite best efforts, fail to meet t-test assumptions.)

There are *four t-test test assumptions* that must be met to ensure test validity:
- One variable is continuous, the other variable is dichotomous
- The two distributions have equal variances
- Observations are independent
- The two distributions are normally distributed

The *first assumption,* that one variable is continuous and the other dichotomous, usually does not present much of a problem. Some analysts use t-tests with ordinal rather than continuous data for the testing variable. This is theoretically controversial because the distances among ordinal categories are undefined. This situation is easily avoided by using other tests discussed in Chapters 3 and 4. Also, when the grouping variable is not dichotomous, analysts need to make it so in order to perform a t-test. Many statistical software packages allow dichotomous variables to be created from other types of variables. Thus, ordinal or continuous variables can be recoded as dichotomous, grouping variables. Of course, this reduces information and should be used only when a dichotomous test is desired. Otherwise, ANOVA (discussed below) or regression (Chapter 6) should be considered.

The *second assumption* is that the variances of the two distributions are equal. This is called *homogeneity* (of variances). The use of pooled variances in the above formula is justified only when the variances of the two groups are equal. When variances are unequal (called *heterogeneity*), revised formulas are used to calculate t-test test statistics and degrees of freedom.[5] Although we needn't be concerned with the precise differences in these calculation methods, all t-tests *first* test whether variances are equal in order to know which t-test test statistic is to be used for *subsequent* hypothesis testing. Thus, every t-test involves a (somewhat tricky) two-step procedure. Graphically, the difference between homogeneity and heterogeneity is shown in Figure 5.2. A common test for the equality of variances is the *Levene's test.* The null hypothesis of this test is that variances are equal. Many statistical software programs provide the Levene's test along with the t-test, so that users know which t-test to use—the t-test for equal variances or that for unequal variances. An example of this two-step process involving the Levene's test is shown in the next section.

The term *robust* is used, generally, to describe the extent to which test conclusions are unaffected by departures from test assumptions. T-tests are relatively robust for (hence, unaffected by) departures from assumptions of homogeneity and normality (below) when groups are of approximately equal size. When groups are of about equal size, test conclusions about any difference between their means will be unaffected by heterogeneity.

Figure 5.2 ——————⁓⋀⋁⋀⁓—Equal and Unequal Variances

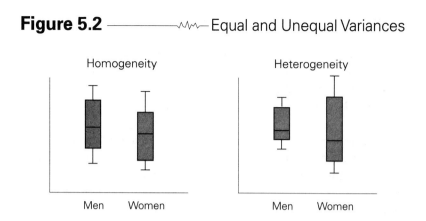

The *third assumption* is that observations are independent. (Quasi-) experimental research designs violate this assumption, as discussed in Chapter 4. The formula for the t-test test statistic, then, is modified to test whether the *difference* between before and after measurement is zero. This is called a ***paired t-test*** (discussed in Box 5.1). In paired tests, degrees of freedom are defined as $n - 1$ (where n is the number of *pairs* or, equivalently, difference scores). Statistical software packages allow users to specify both independent samples t-tests (those previously discussed) and paired t-tests.

The *fourth assumption* is that the distributions are normally distributed. Although normality is an important test assumption, an important reason for the popularity of the t-test is that t-test conclusions often are robust against considerable violations of normality assumptions that are *not caused by outliers.* Outliers can affect the values of means, and are thus of concern. Two tests of normality are the ***Kolmogorov-Smirnov test*** (K-S test) for samples with more than fifty observations and the ***Shapiro-Wilk test*** for samples with fewer than fifty observations. The ***null hypothesis of normality*** is that the variable *is* normally distributed: thus, we *do not* want to reject H_0. A problem with statistical tests of normality is that they are *very sensitive* to small samples and minor deviations from normality. The extreme sensitivity of these tests implies the following: whereas failure to reject the null hypothesis indicates normal distribution of a variable, rejecting the null hypothesis does not indicate that the variable is not normally distributed. Instead, a combination of visual inspection and statistical tests is always used to determine the normality of variables. It is acceptable to consider variables as being normally distributed when they visually appear to be so, even when the null hypothesis of normality is rejected by normality tests. Of course, variables are preferred that are supported by both visual inspection and normality tests.

Remedies exist for correcting substantial departures from normality, but these remedies may make matters worse when departures from normality are minimal. The first course of action is to identify and remove any outliers. Outliers are problematic because they greatly affect the mean of each group and may cause nonnormality. Whether outliers are removed or retained (for example, because they are considered plausible and representative values), test conclusions should be tested for robustness (the impact on conclusions that arise from removing or retaining outliers). The second course of action is *variable transformation,* which is transforming the variable, often by taking $\log(x)$, $\sqrt{x}$ or x^2 and then testing the transformed variable for normality. Variable transformation may address excessive skewness by adjusting the measurement scale, thereby helping variables to better approximate normality.[6] Substantively, we strongly prefer to make conclusions that satisfy test assumptions, regardless of which measurement scale is chosen.[7] Again, it is useful to note that t-test conclusions often are robust for considerable departures from normality that are not caused by outliers.

Typically, analysts have different ways to address test violations. Seldom is there only one way to address test assumptions; different approaches may be successful. Analysts should rely on the weight of *robust, converging results* to support their final conclusion. Analysts should not merely go by the result of one approach that supports their case, ignoring others that perhaps do not.

A Working Example

The U.S. Environmental Protection Agency (EPA) collects information about the water quality of watersheds, including information about the sources and nature of pollution. One such measure is the percentage of samples that exceed pollution limits for ammonia, dissolved oxygen, phosphorus, and pH.[8] A manager wants to know whether watersheds in the Northeast and Southeast have higher levels of pollution than those located elsewhere.

An index variable of pollution is constructed. The index variable is called Pollution, and the first step is to examine it for test assumptions. Analysis indicates that the range of this variable has a low value of 0.00 percent and a high value of 59.17 percent. These are plausible values (any value above 100.00 percent is implausible). A boxplot (not shown) identifies that the variable has four values greater than 50.00 percent that are indicated as outliers. However, the histogram shown in Figure 5.3 does not suggest that these are unusually large values but, rather, that the peak is located off to the left.[9] Testing for normality, we find that the Kolmogorov-Smirnov statistic (discussed above; see Assumption 4) is 0.90, $p = .036 < .05$. Whether this is considered normal depends on one's chosen level of significance. Although we could argue for using this variable in its untransformed state,

Figure 5.3 ———————⋎⋎⋎— Pollutant Samples Exceeding Limit (percent)

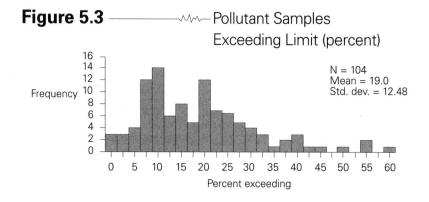

we try further improvement first. Using the above three transformations, we find that only one, the square root, dramatically reduces the level at which the new Kolmogorov-Smirnov test statistic is significant: $p > .05$. (The new test statistic is 0.67. We state this fact for completeness because the K-S statistic has no substantive interpretation.) The transformed variable now has the distribution shown in Figure 5.4. The values of the x-axis reflect the transformed measurement scale. Visual inspection confirms that the transformed variable better approximates the normal distribution. We can also confirm through subsequent visual and statistical analyses that this variable is also normally distributed for each of the two subsets (see Assumption 4). We could have argued for using the untransformed variable, but the transformed variable is to be preferred.

Next, we get down to testing other assumptions and whether watersheds in the Northeast and Southeast vary in the above form of pollution compared with those located elsewhere. The variable Pollution meets other assumptions of being continuous (see Assumption 1), and the observations are independent (they are not matched; see Assumption 3). What we don't

Figure 5.4 ———————⋎⋎⋎— Pollutant Samples: Transformed Variable

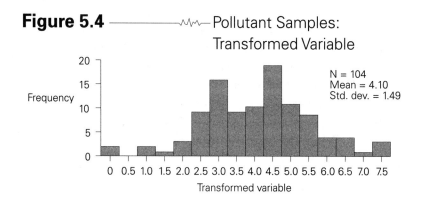

yet know is whether variances are equal or unequal across the two groups of regions (see Assumption 2). We run the t-test on the transformed variable and obtain the results shown in Table 5.2. The results are interpreted as follows. The above means reflect transformed variables. The means of the untransformed values (obtained separately) indicate that 16.38 percent of samples in the Northeast and Southeast violate standards, as do 20.57 percent of samples elsewhere. The question is whether this difference is statistically significant. To answer this, we first determine (Step 1) whether *variances* are equal, which is done using the *Levene's test for the equality of variances*. The test statistic is an F-test, of which the levels of significance are interpreted in the usual manner. The F-test is easy to apply. *The null hypothesis is that variances are equal:* our results show that we fail to reject this null hypothesis at the 5 percent level of significance ($p = .061 > .05$). The variable Pollution thus has equal variances across these two groups.

Now we are ready to test for *equality of means* (Step 2). In the first row (Equal variances assumed), the t-test statistic is 1.252, which we fail to reject ($p = .213 > .05$). Thus, we conclude that the difference is not significant: watersheds in the Northeast and Southeast do not vary in the percentage of samples that exceed standards compared with watersheds elsewhere in the nation. (Note that if we had concluded that variances were unequal, we would have reached the same conclusion.)

This conclusion is consistent for a wide range of root variable transformations that result in a normal distribution (for example, using $x^{.35}$, not

Table 5.2 ⎯⎯⎯⎯〜〜⎯ T-Test Output

Group Statistics

Region	N	Mean	SD
East	39	3.864	1.220
Elsewhere	65	4.241	1.619

T-Test (Independent Samples)

	Step 1: Levene's test for equality of variances			Step 2: T-test for the equality of means		
Variable	F	p		t	df	p (2–tailed)
Pollution	3.576	0.061	Equal variances assumed	1.252	102.000	0.213
			Equal variances not assumed	1.343	96.668	0.182

Note: SD = standard deviation.

shown, rather than the root variable $\sqrt{x}$, that is, $x^{.50}$). Also, we would have reached the same conclusion using the untransformed variable, but with $p = .066$ (not shown). Thus, we conclude that our finding of insignificant differences is indeed *robust*.

We note that Table 5.2 shows a two-tailed t-test of the significance level. As discussed earlier, this reflects that we do not have a priori knowledge about which region has a higher level of pollution. If we did have such knowledge, a one-tailed test should have been used. Critical values for a one-tailed t-test are shown in the Appendix. With df = 102 at the 5 percent level of significance, the critical value is about 1.66. Two-tailed critical values are always greater than one-tailed values, thus two-tailed ones are shown in software output. Two-tailed critical values are equivalent to those that are shown at half the level of significance as one-tailed tests. Hence, the critical value for a two-tailed t-test at the 5 percent level of significance is about 1.99.

Software output may also include the 95 percent confidence interval for estimates of the difference. When t-tests are insignificant, the interval will include the value zero, indicating that no difference between the means can be ruled out. When t-tests are significant, the interval will not include the value zero.

Finally, t-tests can be adapted to test whether the mean of a single group is different from a prespecified value. For example, assume that we want to know whether the percentage of water samples among watersheds in the East that exceed pollution standards is greater than, say, 10 percent, which might reflect some standard. This is called a *one sample t-test*. Statistical software packages require analysts simply to specify the test value. Because only one group is involved, the assumption of equal variances does not come into play. Using as test value $\sqrt{10} = 3.162$ (we apply the square root because the variable has been transformed in that way), we find t = 3.60, $p < .01$. Thus, we conclude that the 16.38 percent of samples in the East that exceed standards is significantly different from a norm of 10.00 percent. The same conclusion is obtained using the untransformed variable (t = 4.46; $p < .01$).

This example shows the use of a t-test for an independent sample. When samples are dependent, a paired test should be used (see Assumption 3). Box 5.1 shows an example of a paired test, which is quite analogous to the one-sample t-test.

ANALYSIS OF VARIANCE

Whereas the t-test is used for testing differences of a continuous variable between two groups, *ANOVA* (Analysis Of Variance) is used for testing means of a continuous variable across more than two groups. For example, we may wish to test whether income levels differ among three or more differ-

In Greater Depth...

Box 5.1   Paired T-Test: An Example

The paired t-test often is used when dealing with before-and-after tests in order to assess student or client progress. Paired t-tests are used when analysts have a dependent rather than an independent sample (see t-test Assumption 3 in the text). The paired-test tests the null hypothesis that the mean difference between the before and after test score is zero. Consider the following data from Table 4.9:

Before	After	Difference
3.2	4.3	1.1
4.0	3.8	−0.2
2.4	3.5	1.1
3.0	3.3	0.3
4.0	4.4	0.4
4.3	4.2	−0.1
3.8	3.3	−0.5
2.9	3.9	1.0
3.8	4.2	0.4
2.5	3.8	1.3

The paired t-test tests the above null hypothesis by testing whether the mean-of-difference variable (Difference) is zero. The paired t-test test statistic is calculated as

$$t = \frac{\overline{D}}{s_D / \sqrt{n}},$$

where D = the difference between before and after measurements, and s_D is the standard deviation of these differences. When the mean of the difference is not zero, then a difference exists between the before and after scores. Because this test involves only one variable, the issue of heterogeneity is absent, and no Levene's test statistics are produced. We do test, however, for normality and find that the difference variable is normally distributed (Shapiro-Wilk = .929, p = .447). This is further confirmed through visual inspection.

The paired t-test yields a t-test test statistic of 2.43, which is significant at the 5 percent level (p = .038). By definition, this result is also obtained using a one-sample t-test when testing that the mean is zero. The mean difference (or

(continued)

Box 5.1 *(continued)*

extent of improvement) between the before and after scores is 0.48; the mean "before" score is 3.39, and the mean "after" score is 3.87.

By comparison, the Wilcoxon Signed Rank test discussed in Chapter 4 shows *no significant* differences between the means of the before and after test scores ($z = 1.88, p = .59$). Why do these two tests disagree? They disagree because nonparametric tests are less powerful than these tests; they require more information (more observations) to reach the same conclusions as other tests, including t-tests. Thus, the ease-of-use of nonparametric tests (they have few if any test assumptions) comes at a price. We may be forced to use these less powerful nonparametric tests when regular test assumptions are not met (for example, when difference variables show excessive nonnormality). Generally, however, t-tests (and other tests discussed in the following chapter) are preferred over nonparametric tests.

ent ethnic groups, or whether the counts of fish vary across three or more lakes. We can also test whether acts of violence vary across three or more groups of students. The F-test statistic compares the variances within each group against those that exist between each group and the overall mean:

$$F = \frac{s_b^2}{s_w^2}.$$

The logic of this approach is graphically shown in Figure 5.5. The overall group mean is $\bar{\bar{x}}$ (the mean of means). The boxplots represent the scores of observations within each group. (As before, the horizontal lines indicate means, $\bar{x}$, rather than medians.) Recall that variance is a measure of dispersion. In both parts of the figure, w is the within-group variance, and b is the between-group variance. Each graph has three within-group variances, and three between-group variances, although only one of each is shown. Note in part A that the between-group variances are larger than the within-group variances, which results in a large F-test statistic using the above formula, making it easier to reject the null hypothesis. Conversely, in part B the within-group variances are larger than the between-group variances, causing a smaller F-test statistic and making it more difficult to reject the null hypothesis. The null hypothesis is:

H_0: No differences between any of the group means exist in the population.
H_A: At least one difference between group means exists in the population.

Figure 5.5 —————ᴡᴡᴡ—ANOVA: Significant and Insignificant Differences

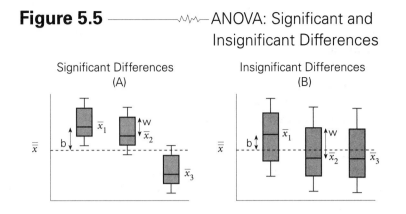

Note how the alternate hypothesis is phrased, because the logical opposite of "no differences between any of the group means" is that at least one pair of means differs. H_0 is also called the **global F-test** because it tests for differences among any means.

The formulas for calculating the between-group variances and within-group variances are quite cumbersome for all but the simplest of designs.[10] In any event, *the computer calculates the F-test statistic and reports at what level it is significant.*[11]

When the above null hypothesis is rejected, analysts will also want to know which differences are significant. For example, analysts will want to know which pairs of differences of watershed pollution are significant across regions. Although one thought might be to use the t-test approach for sequentially testing each pair of differences, this should not be done. Not only would that be most tedious, but it also inadvertently and adversely affects the level of significance; the chance of finding a significant pair by chance alone increases as more pairs are examined. Specifically, the probability of rejecting the null hypothesis in one of two tests is $(1 - 0.95^2) = .098$, the probability of rejecting it in one of three tests is $(1 - 0.95^3) = .143$, and so forth. Thus, sequential testing of differences does not reflect the true level of significance for such tests and should not be used.

Post-hoc tests is the name given to tests that test all possible group differences and yet maintain the true level of significance. Post-hoc tests vary in their method of calculating test statistics and holding experiment-wide error rates constant. Three popular post-hoc tests are Tukey, Bonferroni, and Scheffe. The Scheffe test is the most conservative, the Tukey test is best when many comparisons are made (when there are many groups), and the Bonferroni test is preferred when few comparisons are made. Often, these post-hoc tests will support the same conclusions.

Eta-squared (η^2) is a measure of association for mixed nominal-interval variables and is appropriate for ANOVA. It ranges from zero to one and is interpreted as the percentage of variation explained. It is a directional measure, and computer programs produce two statistics, alternating specification of the dependent variable.

Finally, ANOVA can also be used for testing interval-ordinal relationships. We can ask whether the change in means follows a linear pattern that is either increasing or decreasing. For example, assume we want to know whether incomes increase according to the political orientation of respondents, when measured on a seven-point Likert scale that ranges from very liberal to very conservative. If a linear pattern of increase exists, then a linear relationship is said to exist between these variables. Most statistical software packages can test for a variety of progressive relationships.

ANOVA Assumptions

The assumptions of ANOVA are essentially the same as those of the t-test: (1) one variable is continuous; the other variable is ordinal or nominal; (2) the group distributions have equal variances; (3) observations are independent; and (4) the variable is normally distributed in each of the groups. The assumptions are tested in a similar manner.

Relative to the t-test, a little more concern is needed regarding the assumptions of normality and homogeneity. First, like t-tests, ANOVA is *not robust* for the presence of outliers, and analysts examine the presence of outliers for each group. Also, ANOVA appears to be less robust for deviations from normality than t-tests. Second, unlike the t-test, ANOVA does not provide alternative test statistics when variances are heterogeneous. Our main concern with homogeneity is that there are no *substantial* differences in the amount of variance across the groups. However, the test of homogeneity is a strict test, testing for *any* departure from equal variances. In practice, groups may have neither equal variances nor substantial differences in the amount of variances. In these instances, a visual finding of no substantial differences suffices. Other strategies for dealing with heterogeneity are variable transformations and the removal of outliers, which increase variance, especially in small groups. Such outliers are detected by examining boxplots for each group, separately.

A Working Example

The EPA measured the percentage of wetland loss in watersheds between 1982 and 1992, the most recent period for which data are available (government statistics are sometimes a little old). An analyst wants to know whether watersheds with large surrounding populations have suffered greater wetland loss than watersheds with smaller surrounding populations.

Most watersheds have suffered no or only very modest losses (less than 3 percent during the above decade), and few watersheds have suffered more than 4 percent. The distribution is thus heavily skewed toward watersheds with little wetland losses (that is, to the left), and is clearly not normally distributed.[12] To increase normality, the variable is transformed by twice taking the square root, $x^{.25}$. The transformed variable is then normally distributed: the Kolmogorov-Smirnov statistic is 0.07 ($p = .10 > .05$). The variable also appears visually normal for each of the population subgroups. There are four population groups, designed to ensure an adequate number of observations in each.

Boxplot analysis of the transformed variable indicates four large and three small outliers (not shown). Examination suggests that these are plausible and representative values, which, therefore, are retained. Later, however, we will examine the effect of these seven observations on the robustness of statistical results. Descriptive analysis of the variables is shown in Table 5.3. Generally, large populations tend to have larger average wetland losses, but the standard deviations are large relative to (the difference between) these means, raising considerable question as to whether these differences are indeed statistically significant. Also, the untransformed variable shows that the mean wetland loss is less among watersheds with Medium I than in Small populations (1.77 versus 2.52). The transformed variable shows the opposite order (1.06 versus 0.97). Further investigation shows this to be the effect of the three small outliers and two large outliers on the calculation of the mean of the untransformed variable in the Small group. Variable transformation minimizes this effect. These outliers also increase the standard deviation of the Small group.

Using ANOVA, we find that the transformed variable has unequal variances across the four groups (Levene's statistic = 2.83, $p = .41 < .05$). Visual inspection, shown in Figure 5.6, indicates that differences are not substantial for observations within the group interquartile ranges (IQRs, the areas indicated by the boxes, do not resemble the heterogeneity of Figure 5.2); the differences seem mostly caused by observations located in the whiskers of

Table 5.3 ———⌇⌇⌇— Variable Transformation

Population	N	Untransformed variable		Transformed variable	
		Mean (%)	Standard deviation	Mean (%)	Standard deviation
Small	31	2.52	4.30	0.97	0.50
Medium I	32	1.77	1.68	1.06	0.28
Medium II	30	2.79	6.80	1.07	0.38
Large	27	3.21	3.54	1.26	0.27

Figure 5.6 ———⟋⟍⟋⟍— Group Boxplots

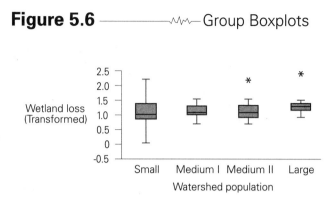

the Small group, which include the five outliers mentioned above. (The two other outliers remain outliers and are shown.) For now, we conclude that *no substantial differences* of variances exist, but we later test the robustness of this conclusion with consideration of these observations (see Figure 5.6).

We now proceed with the ANOVA analysis. First, Table 5.4 shows that the Global F-test statistic is 2.91, $p = .038 < .05$. Thus, at least one pair of means is significantly different. (The term *sum of squares* is explained in note 10.)

Second, which pairs are significantly different? We use the Bonferroni post-hoc test because relatively few comparisons are made (there are only four groups). The results show that the only significant difference concerns the means of the Small and Large groups. This difference $(1.26 - 0.97) = 0.29$ (of transformed values) is significant at the 5 percent level ($p = .028$).[13] The Tukey and Scheffe tests lead to the same conclusion (respectively, $p = .024$ and $.044$). This result is consistent with a visual reexamination of Figure 5.6 which shows that differences between group means are indeed small. The Tukey and Scheffe tests also produce "homogeneous subsets," that is, groups that have statistically identical means. Both the three largest and the three smallest populations have identical means. The Tukey levels of statistical significance are, respectively, 0.73 and 0.17 (both > .05).

Third, is the increase in means a linear increase? This test is an option on many statistical software packages that produces an additional line of output in the ANOVA table, called the "linear term for unweighted sum of squares" with appropriate F-test. Here, that F-test statistic is 7.85, $p = .006 < .01$, and so we conclude that the apparent linear increase is indeed signifi-cant: wetland loss is linearly associated with the increased surrounding population of watersheds.[14]

Fourth, are our findings *robust*? One concern is that the statistical valid-ity is affected by observations that statistically (although not substantively) are outliers. We find that removing the seven outliers identified earlier does

Table 5.4 ─────〰〰── ANOVA Table

	Sum of squares	df	Variance (s^2)	F-test	p
Between groups	1.203	3	0.401	2.907	.038
Within groups	16.002	116	0.138		
Total	17.205	119			

not affect the above conclusions. The resulting variable remains normally distributed, and there are no (new) outliers for any group. The resulting variable has equal variances across the groups (Levene's test = 1.03, $p = .38 >$ .05). The global F-test is 3.44 ($p = .019 < .05$), and the Bonferroni post-hoc test similarly finds that only the differences of the Small and Large group means are significant ($p = .031$). The increase remains linear ($F = 6.74, p = .011 < .05$). Thus, we conclude that the presence of observations with large values does not alter the above conclusions.

We also test the robustness of conclusions for different variable transformations. The extreme skewness of the untransformed variable allows for only a limited range of root transformations that produce normality. Within this range (power 0.222 through 0.275), the above conclusions are fully replicated. Natural log and base-10 log transformations also result in normality and replicate the above results, *except* that the post-hoc tests fail to identify that the means of the Large and Small groups are significantly different. However, the global F-test is (marginally) significant ($F = 2.80, p = .043 < .05$), which suggests that the above difference is too small to detect with this transformation. A single, independent samples t-test for this difference is significant ($t = 2.47, p = .017 < .05$), suggesting that this problem may have been exacerbated by the limited number of observations. In sum, we find converging evidence for the above conclusions. As this example also shows, statistics frequently requires analysts to exercise judgment and to justify their decisions.[15]

Finally, what is the practical significance of this analysis? The wetland loss among watersheds with large surrounding populations is (3.21% − 2.52%/2.52%) = 27.4 percent greater than those surrounded by small populations. It is up to managers and elected officials to determine whether a difference of this magnitude warrants intervention in watersheds with large surrounding populations.[16]

CONCLUSION

This chapter introduced some more tools for researchers to use when comparing their data. Index variables increase measurement validity by using variables that represent a range of study concepts. Index variables are easy to create by simply adding up the values of variables for each observation. This typically results in an interval-level variable, regardless of the measurement levels of the individual variables. Analysts employ various strategies for assessing the theoretical and empirical validity of index variables, such as using Cronbach alpha and establishing criterion validity.

T-tests and ANOVA are used to determine the statistical significance of bivariate relations when one variable is continuous (such as an index variable) and the other is categorical. The basic statistical question of these tests is whether the means of the continuous variable are different for each value of the categorical variable. T-tests and ANOVA can be used to examine, for example, whether area household incomes or crime or accidents vary by gender or race. When the categorical variable involves two groups (the variable has two values), t-tests are used; when the categorical variable involves more than two groups, ANOVA is used.

Although t-tests and ANOVA are widely considered "basic" statistics, analysts must be aware of test assumptions. As most statistical tests, t-tests and ANOVA are valid only when test assumptions are met. The test assumptions of these tests involve (1) the level of measurement, (2) homogeneity, (3) independent samples, and (4) normality. T-test results are relatively robust for violations of assumptions (although not for outliers), but ANOVA is not. When data violate test assumptions, analysts face a range of options that include the removal of outliers and variable transformation. Nonparametric statistics (Chapter 4) include alternative tests, but they are less powerful than those discussed here and are, thus, generally not preferred for the purpose of testing differences among means. The best strategy for strong research is to justify choices that are made during statistical analysis through disclosure ("say what you did and why you did it") and to rely on the weight of converging conclusions to establish the robustness of one's results. By using the procedures described in this chapter, analysts enhance confidence in their conclusions and thus increase their contribution to decision making and policy processes.

KEY TERMS

One-tailed t-test (p. 98)
Paired t-test (p. 100)
Post-hoc test (p. 107)
Robust (p. 99)

Shapiro-Wilk test (p. 100)
T-test (p. 96)
Two-tailed t-test (p. 96)
Variable transformation (p. 101)

Notes

1. Index variables are constructed for each concept. If the concept has several dimensions, then index variables are first constructed for each dimension, and these dimensions are subsequently aggregated to create one index variable of the concept. For example, if the concept "healthy lifestyle" is thought of as having four dimensions— "eating habits," "physical exercise," "work habits," and "leisure"—index variables are first constructed for each of these dimensions, and later these four index variables are conbined to create an index variable of "healthy lifestyle."
2. Boxplots are shown for ease of presentation. It is more appropriate, theoretically, to show two normal distributions, but that clutters the presentation. In any event, continuous data can be presented in boxplots.
3. The formula of the pooled variance is

$$s_p^2 = \frac{(n_1 - 1)s_1^2 + (n_2 - 1)s_2^2}{n_1 + n_2 - 2}.$$

When $s_1 = s_2$, the value of s_p is affected by the relative number of observations in each group, that is, n_1 and n_2. The computer calculates the pooled variance, of course. For more, see David Howell, *Statistical Methods for Psychology*, 3d ed. (Belmont, Calif.: Duxbury Press, 1992), 181–187.
4. The name *Student's t* is derived from W. S. Gossett, who used "Student" as a pseudonym in the early twentieth century to protect his identity. Legend has it that Gossett was concerned that his employer, an agro-industrial company, might want to protect the formula as a trade secret because of competitive advantages: the t-test enables very efficient testing of samples.
5. That is, homogeneity implies that the variances are equal in the population from which the samples are drawn, or, equivalently, the extent to which variances are different cannot be explained by chance alone when using conventional levels of statistical significance. The revised formula for calculating the t-test when variances are unequal is

$$t = \frac{\bar{x}_1 - \bar{x}_2}{\sqrt{\dfrac{s_1^2}{n_1 - 1} + \dfrac{s_2^2}{n_2 - 1}}}.$$

However, see Howell, *Statistical Methods for Psychology,* for the revised formula for calculating degrees of freedom.

6. Students often want to know how they can make variable transformations. In most software packages it is simply a matter of specifying something like: newvar = sqrt(oldvar) or newvar = lg10(oldvar). Students also ask what transformation works best. This is largely unknown. It is a matter of trial and error.

7. Some students initially consider variable transformation as some sort of "playing with the data." However, we need to consider that the ancient development of the common measurement scale (1, 2, 3, 4, 5 . . .) is as arbitrary as any other scale that might have been chosen (such as 1, 4, 9, 16, 25 . . .). The fact that the common measurement scale is frequently useful from the perspective of satisfying test assumptions should not lead us to assign supreme considerations to it or be reluctant to try other measurement scales that work better in other situations. It is far more important to ensure that the variables are normally distributed for the purpose of test validity.

8. For more information about this measure, visit http://www.epa.gov/iwi. See also the accompanying workbook and data set ("Watershed") for replicating the results that follow. The index variable is called "conpolut" on the data set.

9. This is confirmed by the relatively large positive measure of skewness, 1.01. Referring to Chapter 2, note 9, we calculate that the test statistics of skewness and kurtosis of the untransformed variable, respectively, are $(1.01/\sqrt{6/104}) = 4.2$ and $(0.96/\sqrt{24/104}) = 2.00$, indicating asymmetrical skewness and (marginal) kurtosis ($n = 104$). The respective values of skewness and kurtosis of the transformed variable are –0.74 and 0.31, which result in respective test values of $(-0.74/\sqrt{6/104}) = -0.02$ and $(0.31/\sqrt{24/104}) = 0.65$. Both of these absolute values are less than 1.96.

10. The between-group variance (s_b^2) is defined as $\sum_k (\bar{x}_k - \bar{\bar{x}})^2 / k - 1$, where the subscript k identifies groups, $\bar{x}_k =$ each of the group means, $\bar{\bar{x}} =$ the overall group mean (the mean of the means), and $k =$ the number of groups. The within-group variance (s_w^2) is defined as $\sum_k \sum_i (\bar{x}_i - \bar{x}_k)^2 / n - 1$ for each group, where $x_i =$ group observations and $n =$ the total number of observations (across all groups). The terms $\sum(x_i - \bar{x})^2$ are called "sums of squares." See also Table 5.4. Many textbooks provide examples of calculating these values.

11. F-test critical values are defined by two types of degrees of freedom: the degrees of freedom for the numerator is $k - 1$, where $k =$ number of groups. The degrees of freedom for the denominator is $n - k$, where $n =$ number of observations. For example, if there are 4 groups and 76 observations, then df (numerator) = 3, and df (denominator) = 72.

Based on the F distribution (see Appendix), the critical value of $F_{(3,72)}$ = 2.74 at the 5 percent level of significance (estimated based on table).

12. The Kolmogorov-Smirnov test statistic is 0.28, $p = .000 < .01$. Skewness is 5.42, with standard error 0.22. This ratio greatly exceeds two.

13. Statistical software programs report 0.2822. The difference with that reported in the text is due to rounding in Table 5.3.

14. The term *unweighted* simply means that all means are weighted equally, regardless of the number of observations in each group. This reflects our purpose. The weighted linear term, which weights the group means according to the number of observations in each group, should not be used.

15. These results are replicated for the untransformed variable, but only when numerous observations are removed that are identified as outliers for each group. The remaining untransformed variable is not normal for any group, but it does have homogeneous variances. The text findings for the transformed variables strengthen our conclusion that we should regard the stated differences as significant, not as a special case of the nonnormal, untransformed variable.

16. When only "typical" wetland losses are considered (that is, the removal of watersheds that are characterized as outliers in the above analysis), the mean wetland losses of watersheds with small and large surrounding populations are, respectively, 1.73 percent and 2.52 percent, suggesting a 49.2 percent greater wetland loss among watersheds with large populations. The question is whether this categorization of "typical" losses has any traction in public discourse.

Regression I: Estimation

CHAPTER OBJECTIVES

After reading this chapter, you should be able to:
- Use simple regression to test the statistical significance of a bivariate relationship involving one dependent and one independent variable
- Use Pearson's correlation coefficient as a measure of association between two continuous variables
- Understand multiple regression as a full model specification technique
- Interpret standardized and unstandardized regression coefficients of multiple regression
- Know how to use nominal variables in regression as dummy variables
- Understand the importance of the error term plot and the need for testing regression assumptions

This chapter completes our discussion of statistical techniques for analyzing the relationship between two variables and extends it to dealing with situations that involve more than two variables. Regression analysis comes in two forms—simple regression and multiple regression. Simple regression examines the relationships between two *continuous* variables. Simple regression provides information about statistical significance, as well as the direction and strength of relationships. For example, an analyst looking to study the relationship between performance and teamwork, when both variables are continuous, would use simple regression to determine whether these two variables are significantly related, and the direction and strength of their relationship.

However, if an analyst were looking to describe models with two or more independent variables, multiple regression would be the tool of choice. Multiple regression is one of the most widely used multivariate statistical techniques for analyzing three or more variables. The popularity of multiple regression is in large measure due to the ease with which it takes *control variables* (or rival hypotheses) into account. Previously, in Chapter 3, we discussed how contingency tables can be modified for this purpose, but it was a cumbersome and sometimes inconclusive effort. By contrast, multiple regression easily incorporates multiple independent variables. Each independent variable is viewed as a control variable for all of the other independent variables in the model. Another reason for its popularity is that it also takes nominal independent variables into account. Note, however, that multiple regression is no substitute for bivariate analysis. Indeed, a manager or analyst with an interest in a specific bivariate relationship will conduct a bivariate analysis first, before examining whether this relationship is robust in the presence of numerous control variables. Thus, multiple regression is usually one of the last steps of analysis.

The flexibility with which multiple regression takes control variables into account comes at a price, though. Regression, like the t-test, has numerous assumptions. Regression results cannot be assumed to be robust against assumption violations. *Testing of assumptions is always part of multiple regression analysis.* The sequence of practicing multiple regression is (1) model specification (that is, identification of dependent and independent variables); (2) testing of regression assumptions; (3) correcting assumption violations, if any; and (4) reporting the results of the final regression model. These four steps are discussed in two chapters. This chapter discusses essential concepts relating to simple and multiple regression. Chapter 7 discusses assumption violations and corrections, including the use of time series analysis and forecasting. Chapter 7 also discusses non-regression-based forecasting that is used with spreadsheets.

SIMPLE REGRESSION

Simple regression analyzes the relationship between two continuous variables. For example, we might study the relationship between productivity and job satisfaction when both are measured on a continuous scale. Continuous variables assume that the distances between ordered categories are determinable and that, for the purposes of statistical testing, those variables

Figure 6.1 ——————⌇—— Scatterplot

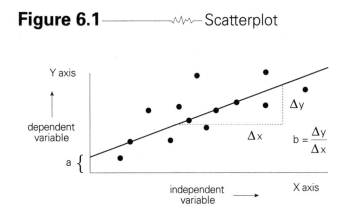

have at least five categories. In simple regression, one variable is defined as the dependent variable, and the other as the independent variable.

Scatterplot

The relationships of two continuous variables can be portrayed in a ***scatterplot***. A scatterplot is merely a plot of the data points of two continuous variables as shown in Figure 6.1 (without the straight line). It is conventional to show the dependent variable on the vertical (or Y) axis, and the independent variable on the horizontal (or X) axis. The relationship between the two variables is estimated as a straight line relationship. The line is defined by the equation $Y = a + bX$, where a is the intercept (or constant), and b is the slope. The slope, b, is defined as $\Delta Y / \Delta X$. The line is mathematically calculated such that the sum of distances from each observation to the line is minimized.[1] By definition, the slope indicates the change in Y as a result of a unit change in X. The straight line is also called the ***regression line***, and the slope (b) is called the ***regression coefficient***.

A positive regression coefficient indicates a positive relationship between the variables, shown by the upward slope in Figure 6.1. A negative regression coefficient indicates a negative relationship between the variables and is indicated by a downward-sloping line.

Test of Significance

The ***test of significance of the regression slope*** is a key test of hypothesis regression analysis that tells us whether the slope (b) is statistically different from zero. When the regression line is horizontal ($b = 0$), no relationship exists between the two variables. The following hypotheses are thus stated:

H_0: $b = 0$, or the two variables are unrelated.
H_A: $b \neq 0$, or the two variables are (positively or negatively) related.

To determine whether the slope equals zero, a t-test is performed. The test statistic is defined as the slope (b) divided by the standard error of the slope [$se(b)$]. The standard error of the slope is a measure of the distribution of the observations around the regression slope:

$$\frac{b}{se(b)}.$$

Thus, a regression line with a small slope is more likely to be statistically significant when observations lie closely around it (that is, the standard error of the observations around the line is also small, resulting in a larger test statistic). By contrast, the same regression line might be statistically insignificant when observations are widely scattered around it. *The computer calculates the slope, intercept, standard error of the slope, and the level at which the slope is statistically significant.*

Consider the following example. A management analyst with the Department of Defense wishes to evaluate the impact of teamwork on the productivity of naval shipyard repair facilities. Although all shipyards are required to use teamwork management strategies, it is assumed that teamwork strategies vary in practice. Coincidentally, a recently implemented employee survey asked about the perceived use and effectiveness of teamwork. These items have been aggregated into a single index variable of teamwork. Employees are also asked questions about perceived performance, as measured by productivity, customer orientation, planning and scheduling, and employee motivation. These items are combined into an index measure of work productivity.[2] Both index measures are continuous variables. The analyst wants to know whether a relationship exists between perceived productivity and teamwork. The printout shown in Table 6.1 is obtained of the results. The printout shows that the slope is 0.223, that the slope coefficient of teamwork is positive, and that the slope is significant at the 1 percent level. Thus, perceptions of teamwork are positively associated with productivity. The t-test statistic 5.053 is calculated as 0.223/0.044 (rounding errors explain the difference from the printed value of t). Other statistics of Table 6.1 are discussed below. The appropriate notation for this relationship is (t-test in parentheses):

$$\text{PRODUCTIVITY} = 4.026 + 0.223**\text{TEAMWORK}$$
$$(5.05)$$
$$** \ p < .01; * \ p < .05$$

It is important to indicate the t-test in parentheses because sometimes researchers identify the standard error in parentheses. Either is acceptable practice, but it is necessary to state which is being used.

Table 6.1 ———— ᴧᴧᴧ— Simple Regression Output

Model Fit

R	R-square	SEE
0.272	0.074	0.825

Dependent variable: Productivity (Empleval on CD)

Coefficients

Model	Unstandardized coefficients		t	Sig.
	b	SE		
Constant	4.026	0.213	18.894	0.000
Teamwork	0.223	0.044	5.053	0.000

Note: SEE = standard error of the estimate; SE = standard error; Sig. = significance.

The primary purpose of regression analysis is hypothesis testing, not prediction. That is, we use the regression model to test the hypothesis that teamwork is related to productivity. However, if the analyst did want to predict Productivity, then the printout also shows the SEE, or the **standard error of the estimate.** This is a measure of the spread of *Y* values around the regression line as calculated *for the mean value of the independent variable, only, and assuming a large sample.* The standard error of the estimate has an interpretation in terms of the normal curve, that is, 68 percent of *Y* values lie within one standard error from the calculated value of *Y,* as calculated for the *mean* value of *X* using the above regression model. Thus, if the *mean* index value of the variable Teamwork is 5.0, then the calculated (or predicted) value of Productivity is (4.026 + 0.223*5) = 5.141. Because SEE = 0.825, it follows that 68 percent of productivity values will lie ± 0.825 from 5.141 when Teamwork = 5. Predictions of *Y* for other values of *X* have larger standard errors.[3]

Goodness of Fit: Correlation Coefficient

The measure of association (or *goodness of fit*) in regression is called the **correlation coefficient,** shown as *R* in Table 6.1. The correlation coefficient, *R,* indicates the extent to which the observations lie closely or loosely clustered around the regression line. *R* ranges from −1 to +1. The sign indicates the direction of the relationship, which, in simple regression, is always the same as the slope coefficient. A '−1' indicates a perfect negative relationship, that is, that all observations lie exactly on a downward-sloping regression line; a '+1' indicates a perfect positive relationship, whereby all observations lie exactly on an upward-sloping regression line. It is, of course, quite uncommon to obtain such values in practice as observations seldom lie

Figure 6.2———————⌇⌇—Three Examples of *R*

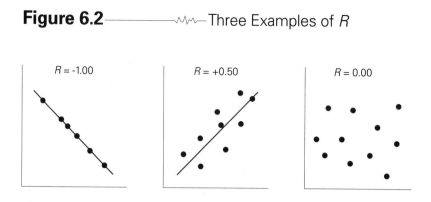

exactly on a line. $R = 0$ indicates that observations are so widely scattered that it is impossible to draw a line. Figure 6.2 illustrates some values of R.

The similarity between R and b (the slope) sometimes causes confusion. The key point is that R does not indicate the regression slope but the extent to which observations lie close to it. A steep regression line (large b) can have observations that lie either loosely or closely scattered around it, as can a shallow (more horizontal) regression line.

Of great interest is R^2, called the *coefficient of determination.* The value of R^2 is interpreted as *the percentage of variation in the dependent variable that is explained by the independent variable.* R^2 varies from 0 to 1, and it has a PRE interpretation. In the above example, teamwork explains only 7.4 percent of the variation in productivity. Although teamwork is significantly associated with productivity, it is quite likely that other factors also affect it. It is conceivable that other factors might be more strongly associated with productivity t and that, when controlled for other factors, teamwork is no longer significant. Typically, values of R^2 below 0.20 are considered weak, those between 0.20 and 0.40 are moderate, and those above 0.40 are considered strong. Values of R^2 above 0.65 are considered very strong.

Finally, *Pearson's correlation coefficient, r,* measures the association (significance, direction, and strength) between two continuous variables. Pearson's correlation coefficient does not assume a causal relationship, as does simple regression. In simple regression, $r = R$, and it is quite common to report r, rather than R, and r^2 rather than R^2 in simple regression. As in simple regression, values of r^2 below 0.20 are considered weak, those between 0.20 and 0.40 are moderate, and those above 0.40 are considered strong. Values of r^2 above 0.65 are considered very strong. When Pearson's correlation coefficients are calculated, a standard error of r can be determined, which then allows for testing the statistical significance of the bivariate correlation. For bivariate relationships, this is the same level of significance as shown for the slope of the regression coefficient. For the above reported relationship, the statistical significance of r is $p = .000$.

Assumptions and Notation

Simple regression assumes that the relationship between two variables is *linear.* The linearity of bivariate relationships is easily determined through visual inspection as shown in Figure 6.2. When variable relationships are nonlinear (parabolic or otherwise heavily curved), it is not appropriate to use linear regression. Then, one or both variables must be transformed, as discussed in Chapter 5.

Simple regression also assumes that the *linear relationship is constant* over the range of observations. This is violated when the relationship is "broken," for example, having an upward slope for the first half of independent variable values, and a downward slope over the remaining values. Then, analysts should consider using two regression models each for these different, linear relations. The linearity assumption is also violated when no relationship is present in part of the independent variable values. This is particularly problematic because regression analysis will calculate a regression slope based on all observations. Then, analysts may be misled into believing that the linear pattern holds for all observations. Hence, it is a necessary practice always to verify regression results through visual inspection.

Linear regression also assumes that the variables are continuous, defined as being at least ordinal and having a minimum of about five categories. Later, we will see that regression can also be used for nominal and dichotomous independent variables. The dependent variable, however, must be continuous. When the dependent variable is dichotomous, logistic regression should be used (Chapter 8).

Finally, the following notations are commonly used in regression analysis. The predicted value of Y (defined, based on the regression model, as $Y = a + bX$) is of course different from the actual ***observed value of Y*** (unless $r^2 = 1$). The ***predicted value of the dependent variable Y*** is sometimes indicated as $\hat{Y}$ (pronounced "Y-hat"). The difference between Y and $\hat{Y}$ is called the regression *error* or ***error term*** (e). Hence the expressions

$$\hat{Y} = a + b^*X \text{ and}$$
$$Y = a + b^*X + e$$

are equivalent, as is $Y = \hat{Y} + e$. There are certain assumptions about e that are important and which, when violated, may result in incorrect conclusions about the statistical significance of relationships. This very important problem will be discussed in the next section.

MULTIPLE REGRESSION

Multiple regression is a powerful strategy for taking control variables into account. When assumptions are met, it quickly allows analysts to examine the impact of several variables on the dependent variable. Multiple regression is used after analysts have examined the nature and strength of bivariate relationships through simple regression and visual inspection of scatterplots. The role of multiple regression is to test the robustness of bivariate relationships when controlled for other variables.

Model Specification

Multiple regression is an extension of simple regression but differs from it in that it aims for *full model specification.* This means that analysts seek to account for all of the variables that affect the dependent variable. However, philosophically, the phrase "all of the variables" is divided into two parts. In the first part are those variables that are of *most* (theoretical and practical) *relevance* in explaining the dependent variable. In social science, this is called a *nomothetic mode of explanation*—the isolation of the most important factors. Typically, multiple regression models identify five to seven (sometimes more) "most important" variables, which are treated as independent variables.[4] This is consistent with the philosophy to seek complete but parsimonious explanations in science.

The second part is "all other variables" that are not identified (or included) in the model. These variables are, hence, not among the most important factors that affect the dependent variable. The cumulative effect of these other variables is, by definition, contained in the error term, shown below. The *assumption of full model specification* is that these other variables are justifiably omitted *only when* their cumulative effect on the dependent variable is zero. This is plausible because each of these many unknown variables may have a different magnitude, thus enabling the possibility that their effects cancel each other out. The argument, quite clearly, is not that each of these "other factors" has no impact on the dependent variable—but only that their cumulative effect is zero. The validity of multiple regression models centers on examining the behavior of the error term in this regard. If it is concluded that the effect of all other variables is not canceled out, then additional independent variables may have to be considered. The specification of the multiple regression model is as follows:

$$Y = a + b_1X_1 + b_2X_2 + b_3X_3 + b_4X_4 + \ldots + error$$

| Dependent = Variable | Independent Variables in Model ("most important factors") | Variables not in Model ("all other factors") |

The use of a nomothetic strategy implies that a range of plausible models exists—different analysts may identify different sets of "most important" independent variables, and they may operationalize them differently. Thus, the term *full model specification* does not imply that only one model or even a best model exists. Rather, the term refers to a family of plausible models. Multiple regression requires two important tasks: (1) specification of independent variables and (2) testing of the error term (discussed in the next section and in Chapter 7).

An important difference with simple regression is the **interpretation of the regression coefficients in multiple regression** (b_1, b_2, b_3, . . .) in the above multiple regression model. Although multiple regression produces the same basic statistics as shown in Table 6.1, each of the regression coefficients is interpreted as its effect on the dependent variable, *controlled for the effect of all of the other independent variables included in the regression*. This phrase is frequently used when explaining multiple regression results. For example, the regression coefficient b_1 above shows the effect of X_1 on Y, controlled for all other variables that are included in the model. Regression coefficient b_2 shows the effect of X_2 on Y, also controlled for all other variables in the model, including X_1. Hence, multiple regression is an important and simple alternative to the approach discussed in Chapter 3 for analyzing control variables. Note, also, that the above model is very different from "running" separate simple regression models for each of the independent variables. The regression coefficients in simple regression *do not control* for other independent variables, because they are not in the model.

The specification of independent variables is a judicious undertaking. The word *independent* also means that each independent variable should be relatively unaffected by other independent variables in the model. To ensure that independent variables are indeed independent, it is useful to think of the distinctively *different types* (or categories) *of factors* that affect a dependent variable. For example, referring to the example in Chapter 1, we ask: "What types of factors affect high school violence?" Categories of factors are (1) student access to weapons (for example, gun ownership in family), (2) student isolation from others, (3) peer groups that are prone to violence, (4) school lack of enforcement of nonviolence policies, (5) unfamiliarity with warning signals (among teachers and other staff). Perhaps you, the reader, can think of other categories. Then, using the strategies discussed in Chapter 1 (conceptualization and operationalization) and Chapter 5 (index variable construction), you can construct either single variables or index measures as independent variables that measure these different factors.

A statistical reason also exists for ensuring that independent variables are as independent as possible. When two independent variables are highly correlated with each other ($r^2 > 0.60$), it sometimes becomes statistically impossible to distinguish the effect of each independent variable on the dependent variable, controlled for the other. The variables are statistically too similar to discern disparate effects. This problem is called multicollinearity, and is discussed in further detail in Chapter 7. This problem is avoided by choosing independent variables that are not highly correlated with each other.

A Working Example

Previously, the management analyst with the Department of Defense found a statistically significant relationship between teamwork and perceived facility productivity ($p < .01$). The analyst now wishes to examine whether the impact of teamwork on productivity is robust when controlled for other factors that also affect productivity. This interest is heightened by the low R-square (0.074) in Table 6.1, suggesting a weak relationship between teamwork and perceived productivity.

A multiple regression model is specified to include the effects of other factors that affect perceived productivity. Thinking about other categories of variables that could affect productivity, the analyst hypothesizes the following: (1) the extent to which employees have adequate technical knowledge to do their jobs, (2) perceptions of having adequate authority to do one's job well (for example, decision-making flexibility), (3) perceptions that rewards and recognition are fairly distributed (always important for motivation), and (4) the number of sick days. Various items from the survey are used to measure these concepts (as discussed in the workbook documentation of the "Productivity" data set). After including these as additional independent variables, the result shown in Table 6.2 is obtained. Comparison with Table 6.1 shows that teamwork *remains statistically significant ($p < .01$) when controlled for all of the other variables in the model* (ability, authority, inducement, and fairness). The results also show that having adequate knowledge and authority are, statistically, positively associated with productivity (both, $p < .01$). Perceptions of fairness in rewards and recognition are also associated with productivity at the 5 percent level of significance. The number of days being sick is not associated with productivity, when controlled for other variables. It is important to note that the sign of the significantly associated variables is positive, as expected. We would have been piqued if it had been negative. We need not be concerned about the negative slope of days sick because this variable is insignificant (not significantly different from zero).

However, a key question is whether the model is fully specified. If the net effect of all variables excluded from the model on the dependent variable is not zero, then perhaps some other variable should also be included that might affect our findings. The error term is examined to determine this possibility.

Table 6.2 ——————⁓⁓— Multiple Regression Output

Model

R	R-square	Adjusted R^2	SEE
0.524	0.274	0.263	0.735

Dependent variable: Productivity (Empleval on CD)

ANOVA Table

Model	Sum of squares	df	Mean square	F	Sig.
Regression	64.239	5	12.848	23.809	0.000
Residual	169.980	315	0.540		
Total	234.219	320			

Coefficients

Model	Unstandardized coefficients		Standardized coefficients		
	b	SE	Beta	t	Sig.
Constant	2.064	0.301		6.850	0.000
Teamwork	0.166	0.040	0.202	4.166	0.000
Knowledge	0.267	0.050	0.263	5.391	0.000
Authority	0.200	0.035	0.288	5.804	0.000
Days sick	−0.011	0.020	−0.026	−0.543	0.587
Fairness	0.076	0.033	0.113	2.284	0.023

Note: SEE = standard error of the estimate; SE = standard error; Sig. = significance.

Recall that the net effect of all variables that are not included in the model is contained in the error term. When the net effect of such variables on the dependent variable is zero, then *no relationship* exists between the error term and the predicted dependent variable. This relationship will be random, without pattern or shape. It is customary to plot the standardized error term (or residual) against the standardized predicted value of the dependent variable. This is called an **error term plot.** The concept of standardization is discussed in Chapter 2 and involves transformation such that variables have a mean of zero and a standard deviation of one. Then, if no relationship exists between these two variables, the scatterplot should be random and clustered around (0,0) as shown in Figure 6.3[5] (adapted from original). This figure is *prima facie evidence* that the net effect of variables not included in the model is zero. Thus, we conclude that the model is valid (or, more precisely, we fail to find empirical evidence suggesting that it is

Figure 6.3 ——————— Error Term Plot

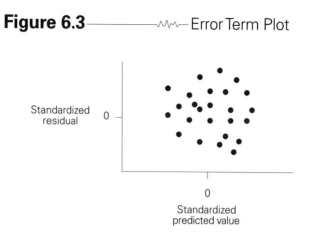

Standardized residual   0 —

0
Standardized predicted value

invalid). In Chapter 7 we examine deviations from the above error term plot (that is, violations of regression assumption), and discuss ways in which violations are identified and overcome. Because the model is valid, the above finding remains that the effect of teamwork on productivity is significant when controlled for other factors in the model. The above model is not the only model that can be constructed but one among a family of plausible models; indeed, from a theoretical perspective, perhaps other variables might have been included, as well. We now turn to discussing the other statistics shown in Table 6.2.

Goodness of Fit for Multiple Regression

The model R^2 is greatly increased over that shown in Table 6.1: R^2 has gone from 0.074 to 0.274. However, a mathematical problem of R^2 is that it has the undesirable property that it increases with the number of independent variables in the model. R^2 increases regardless of whether an additional independent variable adds further explanation of the dependent variable. The *adjusted R^2* (or $\overline{R}^2$) controls for the number of independent variables and is therefore preferred. $\overline{R}^2$ is always equal to or less than R^2. We conclude that the independent variables explain ($\overline{R}^2$) = 26.3 percent of the variation in the dependent variable. An $\overline{R}^2$ of this magnitude indicates a model of moderate strength (explanation). This increase in explanatory power is due to the variables that are identified as statistically significant in Table 6.2.

Standardized Coefficients

The question arises as to which independent variable has the greatest impact on the dependent variable. The slope of the coefficients (b) does not inform us about this because each slope is measured in different units (recall, b =

$\Delta Y / \Delta X$). Comparing different slope coefficients is tantamount to comparing apples and oranges. However, based on the regression coefficient (or slope), it is possible to calculate the **standardized coefficient** (or *beta* [β]). *Beta* is defined as change produced in the dependent variable by a unit of change in the independent variable when both are measured in terms of standard deviation units. Beta is unit-less and thus allows for comparing the impact of different independent variables. Analysts compare the relative values of beta coefficients; there is no inherent meaning to beta. It is appropriate to compare betas across independent variables in the same regression, not across different regressions.

Based on Table 6.2, we conclude that the impact of having adequate authority on productivity is $[(0.288 - 0.202)/0.202] = 42.6$ percent greater than teamwork, and about equal to that of knowledge. The impact of having adequate authority is two-and-a-half times greater than that of perceptions of fair rewards and recognition.

F-test

Table 6.2 also features an ANOVA table. The **global F-test** tests the hypothesis that none of the regression coefficients is statistically significant. The alternate hypothesis is that at least one of the regression coefficients is statistically significant. The F-test test statistic, 23.809, is statistically significant: hence, at least one regression coefficient is statistically significant. Analysts needn't rely on the global F-test for this information: the "significance" column in the table of coefficients shows which coefficients are statistically significant.[6]

As a point of information, the statistics of the ANOVA tables are analogous to Figure 5.5, depicting within-group and between-group sums of squares. The regression sum of squares is analogous to the between-group sum of squares, or, the sum of each $(\hat{y}_i - \bar{y})^2$. The residual sum of squares is analogous to the within-group sum of squares, or the sum of each $(y_i - \hat{y}_i)^2$. These terms are graphically depicted in Figure 6.4 for the single observation y_i; the distance $(\hat{y}_i - \bar{y})$ is the explained variation (shown as length I), and the distance $(y_i - \hat{y}_i)$ is the unexplained variation (or error) shown as length II. Error terms are further discussed in Chapter 7; here, the intent is to understand the rather limited utility of the regression ANOVA table (see n. 6).

Use of Nominal Variables

Multiple regression easily incorporates nominal variables as independent variables. However, a little transformation is required because the assumption of linearity suggests that it is not appropriate to regress a nominal variable against a dependent variable. Consider, for example, a nominal variable such as Region that is coded as West = 1, Northeast = 2, South = 3, and Midwest = 4. Then, it is incorrect to conclude that a predicted Y value

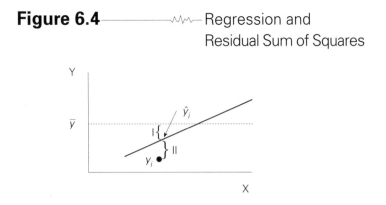

Figure 6.4———————∿∿—Regression and
Residual Sum of Squares

involving Midwest is four times that of West. Clearly, there is no such order-ing among the values of this variable.

This difficulty is overcome by *recoding* the Region variable, creating *separate variables* for each of the response categories (except one, discussed below). Each new variable is dichotomous, having the value of one when it identifies the appropriate group, and zero otherwise. Such variables are called **dummy variables** because they only take on the values of zero and one. The recoding approach is fully shown in Table 6.3. Thus, for example, when Region = 1, the new variable West = 1, and West is zero in all other instances. Similarly, when Region = 2, the new variable Northeast = 1, and this new variable is zero in all other instances. The number of dummy vari-ables is equal to the *number of categories minus 1*. The reason is that the introduction of a variable representing the last category (Midwest), creates a perfect linear relationship among the independent variables: West + North-east + South + Midwest = 1. For mathematical reasons, when such perfect relationships exist among independent variables, it is not possible to calcu-late the regression coefficients.[7]

The implication of not including a variable identifying one of the cate-gories is that results are interpreted as the effect on the dependent vari-able controlled for all independent variables in the model *plus the omitted category.* For example, when the above dummy variables are added to the model of Table 6.3, then, for example, the regression coefficient of West shows its effect on Productivity controlled for all other independent vari-ables, including the effect of the Midwest, which is not entered into the regression.[8]

You may note that this interpretation is similar to considering the effect of gender on productivity, when the variable Gender is coded as 0 = Male and 1 = Female. Then, the regression coefficient of Gender shows the effect of being female on Productivity controlled for all other independent vari-

Table 6.3 Recoding of Variables

Old	New		
Region	West	Northeast	South
1	1	0	0
2	0	1	0
3	0	0	1
4	0	0	0

ables, including the effect of being male. There is no need for adding a separate dummy variable for Male.

Dummy variables can also be used to identify control groups (for example, "exp" = 0) and experimental groups ("exp" = 1). Dummy variables are also useful to identify observations at different time periods, for example, Time = 0 (before intervention) and Time = 1 (after intervention). The use of time series in regression is discussed in the next chapter.

CONCLUSION

Regression analysis is a powerful instrument that analysts can use to reveal all kinds of information in their data. Regression analysis comes in two forms: simple regression and multiple regression. Through simple regression, analysts determine the significance, strength, and direction of a relationship between two continuous (or metric) variables. Simple regression is used for analyzing the relationship between one dependent and one independent variable, by providing an estimate of the relationship (regression line) between the two variables, in addition to the correlation coefficient. When the relationship is an association, only the correlation coefficient is used. A key statistic in the bivariate analysis of two continuous variables is the squared correlation coefficient r^2, which explains the percentage of variance explained and which is used for interpreting the strength of the bivariate relationship. Multiple regression uses two or more independent variables. It is a powerful and very popular technique for taking control variables (rival hypotheses) into account. Multiple regression can also use nominal, independent variables, which are transformed as so-called dummy variables. Analysts will frequently encounter multiple regression in research articles. Multiple regression is a full model specification technique, that is, a technique that seeks to account for all effects on the dependent variable. The popularity of multiple regression is in large part because estimates of the relationships between each independent variable and the dependent variable are controlled for all other independent variables in the model.

Although multiple regression is quite powerful, it does not substitute for developing a thorough understanding of the bivariate relationships in which analysts are interested. Both before and after multiple regression is used, the nature, strength, and practical significance of bivariate relationships should be examined. Indeed, analysts often turn to using multiple regression because they want to learn more about a previously discovered, significant bivariate relationship. They want to know whether a specfic bivariate relationship remains significant when controlled for other variables. Thus, multiple regression usually follows bivariate analysis. Finally, although multiple regression is widely used, it also has various test assumptions that must be met. These are discussed in the following chapter.

KEY TERMS

Adjusted R^2 (p. 128)
Assumption of full model specification (p. 124)
Coefficient of determination (p. 122)
Correlation coefficient (p. 121)
Dummy variable (p. 130)
Error term (p. 123)
Error term plot (p. 127)
Full model specification (p. 124)
Global F-test (p. 129)
Goodness of fit (p. 121, 128)
Interpretation of regression coefficients in multiple regression (p. 125)
Nomothetic mode of explanation (p. 124)

Observed value of the dependent variable (p. 123)
Pearson's correlation coefficient (p. 122)
Predicted value of the dependent variable (p. 123)
Regression coefficient (p. 119)
Regression line (p. 119)
Scatterplot (p. 119)
Standard error of the estimate (p. 121)
Standardized coefficient (beta) (p. 129)
Test of significance of the regression slope (p. 119)

Notes

1. The method of calculating the regression coefficient (the slope) is called *ordinary least squares,* or OLS. OLS estimates the slope by minimizing the sum of squared differences between each predicted ($a + bX$) and the actual value of Y. One reason for squaring these distances is to ensure that all distances are positive.

2. To determine the criterion validity of this measure (see Chapter 5), the analyst also compared the average employee rating per facility with that of an outside evaluator who recently evaluated the productivity of each

facility. Although measured on different scales, using the Spearman rank correlation coefficient test (Chapter 4), the analyst concludes that two rankings are similar. This is also confirmed by visual inspection of the data.

3. The standard error of Y for predictions that are not based on the mean of X is larger than the SEE, according to the following formula:

$$SEE' = SEE \sqrt{1 + \frac{1}{N} + \frac{(x_i - \bar{x})^2}{(N-1)s_x^2}},$$

where s_x^2 is the variance of x, that is, $\Sigma(x - \bar{x})^2/(N-1)$. As can be seen, $SEE' = SEE$ only when N is large and the predicted values of Y are calcu-

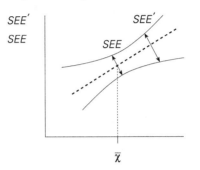

lated for the mean value of x (that is, $x_i = \bar{x}$). Graphically, the relationship between SEE' and x is as follows:

4. Nomothetic explanations are contrasted by *idiographic* explanations, which identify all factors affecting a dependent variable. Idiographic models are quite difficult in multiple regression because the number of factors that affect dependent variables often is very, very large, including unique factors that affect only a small subset of observations. Empirical data about all these factors are typically missing, hence, the use of nomothetic strategies.

5. Figure 6.3 is adapted from the actual computer-generated error term plot associated with Table 6.2. Figure 6.3 illustrates the random (or lack of) relationship that is sought. The actual error term plot for this model is shown in Box 7.1 (next chapter).

6. Although the global F-test is not particularly useful, one variation is the *partial F-test*. Here, the analyst wants to know whether adding additional independent variables adds to the explanation of the dependent variable. The initial model is called the restricted model (R), and the model with additional independent variables is called the unrestricted model (UR).

The F statistic for testing the statistical significance of the additional variables is defined as:

$$F = \frac{(R^2_{UR} - R^2_R)/m}{(1 - R^2_{UR})/(N-k)},$$

where N = number of observations, k = number of variables in the unrestricted model, and m = the number of variables in the unrestricted model minus the number of variables in the restricted model. To test this test statistic, the denominator df is defined as $(N-k)$ and the numerator df is defined as m.

7. Statistical software packages vary in their response to this problem. SPSS automatically deletes one variable that causes the perfect correlation, whereas other programs report error messages.

8. For example, if we thought that performance is also affected by region, we could specify the above model in Table 6.3 as: Productivity = f (Teamwork, Ability, Authority, Inducement, Fairness, Northeast, South, West), where f indicates that Productivity is a function of the variables that are between brackets. Note that using a dummy variable assumes that the regression models are statistically similar among all groups. If there are reasons to suspect that there may be differences, analysts may also wish to run regression models for each separate group.

CHAPTER

7

Regression II:
Testing Assumptions, Time Series

CHAPTER OBJECTIVES

After reading this chapter, you should be able to:
- Test multiple regression assumptions
- Correct violations of multiple regression assumptions
- Understand the challenges of working with time series data
- Know how to evaluate policy impacts
- Use lagged variables
- Make and validate forecasts

Multiple regression is indeed a powerful tool for examining rival hypotheses. But, as noted in the previous chapter, multiple regression always involves the testing of assumptions. A key purpose of assumption testing is to ensure that our regression results are robust and not unduly affected by a few unusual observations or other features of the data. The first part of this chapter examines the assumptions of multiple regression and discusses how to test for and correct violations that may occur. The second part focuses on time series analysis, a statistical method that allows analysts to examine and compare data that have been collected over time, such as through surveys. Time series analysis can help us to evaluate the effectiveness of public poli-

Figure 7.1 ————————〰—Impact of Outliers

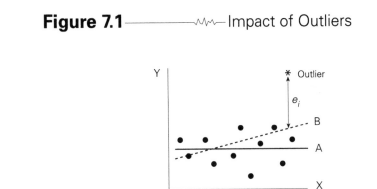

cies and it is also used to forecast the future. Analysts can use these techniques to put together strong, valid information that informs and helps shape policy.

TESTING ASSUMPTIONS

Many regression assumptions involve a test of the error term, which can help reveal problems with the model or data. As discussed in the previous chapter, ideally, the relationship between the error term and the predicted dependent variable, shown in an *error term plot,* should be random. However, several problems can occur that cause this pattern *not* to be random. The art of testing assumptions involves the analysis of these patterns.

Outliers

Outliers are observations with uncommon values, both with regard to single variables as well as combinations of variables. For example, although students with both high grade point averages (GPAs) and scholastic awards are not uncommon, any such student who commits frequent acts of school violence would likely be an outlier even among students who commit crimes. Outliers are common in multiple regression, and are of concern because they may affect the statistical significance of regression coefficients.

This problem of outliers is graphically shown in Figure 7.1. Regression line A is estimated based on the black observations only. It is calculated without the uncharacteristic outlier, shown as the single starred observation; the regression slope is not significantly different from $b = 0$. Line B is the recalculated regression line that now includes the starred observation. The additional observation alters the direction of the regression line such that $b > 0$, hence leading to the conclusion that the independent variable is significantly associated with the dependent variable. Clearly, conclusions that are so strongly affected by just a few observations are not robust. We need to identify outliers, report their impact, and consider dropping them from analysis.

Figure 7.2———————Outlier Detection

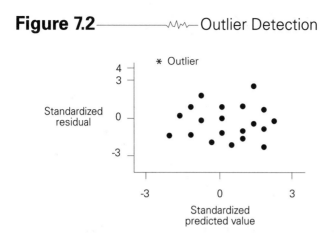

Detection. Outliers are commonly identified by the size of their residual. Note how the residual (or error, e_i, defined as $Y_i - \hat{Y}_i$) is larger for the additional starred observation than for any of the black observations in Figure 7.1. Outliers are usually first identified when the error term plot is examined (see Figure 7.2). Observations are defined as outliers when their residuals exceed three standard deviations; clearly, such observations are unusual relative to others, assuming that errors are normally distributed. Statistical software packages can flag these residuals that exceed a user-specified value (such as three standard deviations) and plot error term plots.

How to resolve. The effect of outliers on regression conclusions is examined by first removing outliers, then reestimating the model and examining conclusions for substantive robustness. Statistical software packages allow users to save residuals associated with each observation. These are then used for the purpose of removing observations that are outliers from subsequent analysis. The primary concern is with significant coefficients that become insignificant, and vice versa. Change in the direction (sign) of regression coefficients is also important. The final reported results should be robust for the presence of atypical observations; hence, they should exclude outliers that substantively affect conclusions.

Multicollinearity

The problem of ***multicollinearity*** (pronounced "multi-KOH-li-nee-air-i-tee") is that two independent variables may be correlated to such a high degree that their effects on the dependent variable are indistinguishably similar. For example, it is possible that in a study of high school violence the variables "off-campus crimes" and "off-campus misdemeanors" might be highly correlated. Then, the regression coefficients of these two independent variables may be statistically insignificant because, net of the other(s), they

Figure 7.3————〜〜〜—Multicollinearity

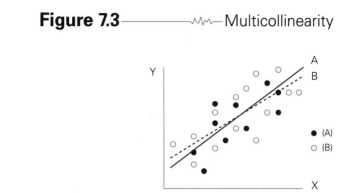

have little or no residual effect on the dependent variable, school violence. This problem is graphically shown in Figure 7.3. The black and white observations produce regression lines so similar that, given their respective standard errors, they are statistically indistinguishable.

Detection. Multicollinearity is usually first suspected when the regression coefficients of independent variables in multiple regression are statistically insignificant, which, in bivariate relationships, are known to be highly significant (for example, $r^2 > 0.60$). This is a good reason for always doing bivariate analysis before multiple regression. Multiple regression R^2 values may also be high when each of the variables is strongly associated with the dependent variable. Formally, multicollinearity is detected by calculating the *variance inflation factor* (VIF) of each independent variable. VIF is a measure of the extent to which an independent variable is predicted by all other independent variables in the model.[1] This statistic is routinely produced by statistical software packages. Values greater than 5 or 10 indicate multicollinearity; values of variables that do not exhibit multicollinearity usually are between 1.0 and 2.0.

Multicollinearity is not a common occurrence in cross-sectional data with few independent variables, but it is more likely to occur as more independent variables are entered into the model. The more independent variables entered, the more likely that some will be highly correlated with each other. For this reason, multiple regression models often limit the number of independent variables. Multicollinearity is quite common, however, in time series data because, over time, many variables tend to move in the same direction. Strategies for dealing with time series data frequently resolve this problem and are discussed later in this chapter.

How to resolve. To correct for multicollinearity, researchers need to remove the collinear variables from the model. When the variables are substantively

Figure 7.4————————Curvilinear Relationship
with Regression Line

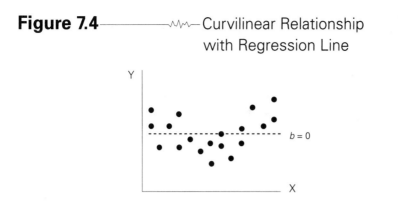

related, they might be combined to create a new index variable. For instance, in the above example concerning high school violence it may be possible to combine the variables "off-campus crimes" and "off-campus misdemeanors" into a single, new index variable. When variables are not substantively related to each other, analysts should consider substituting one of the collinear variables for a similar measurement that is less highly correlated with the other variables. When no other similar variables are available, analysts might consider dropping one of the variables from the model.

Linearity

Multiple regression estimates a *straight* regression line; it assumes that independent variables are *linearly* correlated with the dependent variable. **Curvilinear** relationships are relationships that are not linear, such as $y = \sqrt{x}$ or x^2. For example, certain forms of pollution have curvilinear relationships with population density. In those cases, a straight regression line is a poor fit, and the regression coefficients underestimate the significance of the relationship. In the worst cases, the regression coefficient will be estimated as being insignificant when it is not; this extreme problem is shown in Figure 7.4. Linear estimation is a poor fit for any curvilinear relationship, regardless of size or direction of the regression slope.

Detection. Diagnosis of curvilinear relationships centers on examining the curvilinear pattern of error terms as shown in Figure 7.5. Subsequent bivariate analysis is then used to identify *which* independent-dependent variable relationship is curvilinear. Many statistical packages also produce so-called **partial regression plots,** which show the relationship between the dependent variable and each independent variable, when controlled for the other independent variables. When examining such plots, analysts should decide whether the relationship is linear, curvilinear, or simply not present.

Figure 7.5————⌇⌇—Detecting Curvilinearity

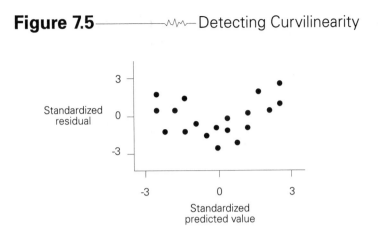

How to resolve. Curvilinearity is typically corrected by transforming the independent variable; square root, quadratic, and logarithmic transformations are used (see Chapter 5). For example, if a curvilinear relationship exists between the dependent variable and independent variable x_1, then the initial relationship might be transformed in the following manner:

$$\text{Initial relationship: } y = a + b_1 x_1 + b_2 x_2 + \ldots$$
$$\text{Transformed relationship: } y = a + b_1 \sqrt{x_1} + b_2 x_2 + \ldots$$

Of course, any other transformation of x_1 is acceptable that results in a linear relationship between y and this independent variable. In rare instances, it may be necessary to transform the dependent variable when it is curvilinearly related to all or most independent variables.[2]

Heteroscedasticity

Heteroscedasticity (pronounced "heh-troh-SKUH-das-ti-ci-tee") is the problem of unequal variances of the error term. For example, when examining expenditures by unit size, the residuals of larger units vary more than those of a smaller size because larger jurisdictions and households with larger incomes usually have more discretion in their spending patterns than those of smaller size. The extent to which heteroscedasticity occurs in public management and policy varies with the nature of one's data or problems. Unequal variances of the error term is a violation of random distribution of the error term (see Chapter 6), and it causes the statistical significance of regression coefficients to be underestimated. Heteroscedasticity usually occurs when data include heterogeneous subunits, such as households with greatly varying levels of income or jurisdictions of vastly different populations.

Figure 7.6————————Heteroscedasticity

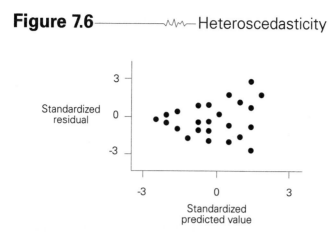

Heteroscedasticity is graphically detected by examination of the error term plot for unequal variance as shown in Figure 7.6. The figure shows a trumpet-like distribution of the error terms. Although the trumpet opening is shown in Figure 7.6, it can also occur to the left or even in the middle if that is the range in which error terms have relatively longer variances. When heteroscedasticity is suspected, the error terms (e) may also be plotted against each independent variable ($x_1, x_2, \ldots$) in order to determine *which* dependent-independent variable relationship is heteroscedastic. The above pattern is then replicated for the error term plot of the independent variable(s) causing heteroscedasticity. Some analysts believe that this graphical approach may sometimes fail to detect heteroscedasticity. They suggest analyzing the relationship between e^2 and each independent variable. This is also known as the **Park test**. Squaring of the error term causes a positive relationship to occur with the independent variable if heteroscedasticity is present (see Figure 7.7). To determine whether a relationship exists between e^2 and x, the following simple regression is used. The log transformation is used to ensure that the relationship is linear, rather than curvilinear, which may occur because of the squaring:

$$\ln e^2 = a + b_i \ln(x).$$

When the slope (b_i) is significant, a heteroscedastic relationship exists between the error term and the independent variable, as shown in Figure 7.7.

How to resolve. Heteroscedasticity is overcome by transforming one or more variables. The scale adjustment reduces the sizes of differences between variables, hence minimizing unequal variance. Often, a logarithmic transforma-

Figure 7.7 ——————⁓⁓⁓— Heteroscedasticity: Park Test

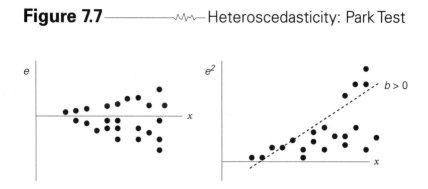

tion of *both* the dependent and the independent variables sufficiently corrects for the problem:

Initial relationship: $y = a + b_1x_1 + b_2x_2 + \ldots$
Transformed relationship: $\ln(y) = a + b_1 \ln(x_1) + b_2 \ln(x_2) + \ldots$

The log transformation is useful when large error terms are associated with large values of the (in)dependent variables because the log transformation reduces large values much more than small values. However, this approach may fail when heteroscedasticity is caused by a more complex relationship between the error term and one or more variables. *Weighted least squares* (WLS) is a procedure that mathematically calculates the requisite transformation based on the observed variance and its relationship to a specific variable. WLS is available in most statistical software packages.[3] Box 7.1 provides an example of testing for the above assumptions.

Measurement and Specification
Multiple regression further assumes (1) that the variables are accurately measured, (2) that the model does not omit important variables, and (3) that the model does not include irrelevant variables. Unlike the above assumptions, detection and resolution are largely based on theoretical rather than empirical grounds.

   Measurement error is defined as inaccurate measurement of the underlying study concept; variables that have measurement error are substantively invalid or have systematic biases. Measurement validity was discussed earlier as part of validating index variables (see Chapter 5). Accurate measurement is especially important for the *dependent* variable because inaccurate measurement may render it impossible for independent variables to achieve requisite levels of statistical significance. One instance in which inaccurate measurement of the dependent variable occurs is when there are few

In Greater Depth...

Box 7.1   Assumption Testing

in Multiple Regression

Chapter 6 discussed the example of a workplace productivity analysis, the results of which are shown in Table 6.2. In that example, perceptions of productivity is the dependent variable, and teamwork, job knowledge, authority, days sick, and fairness are independent variables. Table 6.2 shows that $\bar{R}^2 = 0.263$, and teamwork, job knowledge, and authority are significant at the 1 percent level. Fairness is significant at the 5 percent level. How do we test for assumptions?

The first step is to plot the error terms against the predicted values. The figure shows the error term plot. The error term plot does not show the presence of any outliers, which would have been indicated by values of the regression standardized residual (shown on the Y-axis) smaller than –3 or greater than +3. We do note that one observation has a value that is close to –3; it is circled in the figure. To examine its impact on regression results (as we would have done for all observations with standardized residuals smaller than –3 or greater than +3), we remove this observation from the sample and rerun the regression model to test for robustness. We then observe that removing this observation does not affect the reported levels of statistical significance which, hence, are robust for outliers.

Figure 7.1A————〰〰—Dependent Variable: Productivity

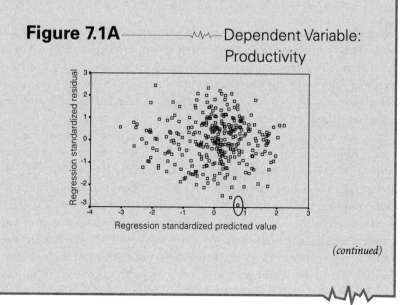

(continued)

Box 7.1 *(continued)*

We also test for multicollinearity. The reported values of the variance inflation factors (VIFs) are, respectively, for teamwork (1.025), job knowledge (1.037), authority (1.074), days sick (1.011), and fairness (1.056). These VIFs are well below the threshold of 5, and thus we conclude that multicollinearity does not affect the statistical significance of the independent variables. This result is reflected by the Pearson's correlation coefficients of the bivariate correlations among the independent variables. The largest bivariate correlation coefficient is a mere 0.202, occurring between the variables "fairness" and "authority."

Although the scatterplot shown here does not suggest heteroscedasticity (there is no obvious trumpet-shaped pattern), the Park test does find evidence of slight heteroscedasticity between the error term and the variable authority (t-test statistic 2.69, $p < .01$). Using the weighted least squares procedure, we rerun the above model with "authority" as the weight variable. $\bar{R}^2$ is now slightly lower (0.237), but the levels of statistical significance reported above remain unchanged.

Finally, we see no evidence of curvilinearity in the plot. This is further verified by examining the partial regression plots of each of the independent variables. In all, then, we conclude that the previously reported results are robust. They are unaffected by any of the potential problems noted.

categories, such as when using a dependent variable with a five-point Likert scale. This typically causes an upward or downward sloping pattern of the error terms. To improve measurement, an index variable, which increases the range of values and improves substantive relevance (by encompassing more dimensions of the concept), should be used. Researchers usually give heightened importance to measurement of the dependent variable.

As has been previously stated, full model specification allows for a family of plausible models. Random distribution of the error term does not imply that any set of independent variables is the only plausible set; relevant, independent variables may have been excluded. *Specification error* involves both omitting relevant variables and including irrelevant ones. The effect of *omitting a relevant variable* is to inflate the value of t-test statistics of independent variables that are included. Analysts should ask whether any theoretically relevant (control) variable has been excluded from their model. Indeed, adding a relevant control variable may affect the levels of statistical significance that are observed. Excluding relevant variables also biases the estimate of the intercept, which may affect prediction. To avoid these problems, analysts need to give full, theoretical consideration to the broadest possible set of relevant variables when they are model building.

The effect of *including irrelevant variables* is the opposite of that of omitting a relevant value; namely, it understates the importance of other independent variables. Analysts should ask whether all variables included in the model are theoretically sound. The problem of including irrelevant variables often arises as analysts verify how existing models hold up under the impact of a broader range of variables. Generally, irrelevant variables should not be included because they reduce the level of statistical significance of other variables, increase the possibility of multicollinearity, and work against model parsimony. Also, theoretically irrelevant variables cannot be justified, no matter how statistically significant they may be. Thus, a guarded stance is usually appropriate regarding irrelevant variables.[4]

TIME SERIES ANALYSIS

Managers and policy analysts frequently use data that have been collected over time. Examples of these data include administrative data, such as activity logs, customer complaints, budget data, and inspection reports that have been completed or gathered in different periods, as well as survey data that are completed on a regular basis, such as client, citizen, and business surveys. Time series data are used for similar purposes as cross-sectional data but have additional applications in forecasting and policy evaluation.

Detecting Autocorrelation

With time series data, the assumption of random distribution of error terms usually is violated. This is because the adjacent, time-ordered values of observations are highly correlated with each other: knowledge of today's value is a good predictor of tomorrow's. **Autocorrelation,** also called **serial correlation,** reflects correlation in the order (or series) in which observations are measured. The error term plot, when plotted against the sequence of time-ordered observations, typically exhibits a "snake-like" pattern as shown in Figure 7.8. Note that the figure examines the residuals against time (the order in which the observations are made) rather than the (standardized) predicted dependent variable $\hat{Y}$. Plotting the error term against $\hat{Y}$ will *not* show the pattern of Figure 7.8. The problem with autocorrelation is that it severely exaggerates the statistical significance of variables, hence leading to the erroneous conclusion that variables are statistically associated when they are not.

Serial correlation is usually anticipated when working with time series data. Serial correlation is detected through the graph shown as Figure 7.8 or the **Durbin-Watson test statistic.** Statistical software packages do not always

Figure 7.8————————〜〜〜—Autocorrelation

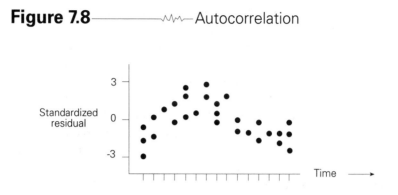

easily produce such a figure, and many analysts rely on the Durbin-Watson statistic. The Durbin-Watson test statistic ranges from 0 to 4. Values close to 2 indicate the lack of serial correlation; values closer to 0 and 4 indicate serial correlation. Values less than 2 indicate positive serial correlation, whereas values greater than 2 indicate negative serial correlation. Positive serial correlation occurs when successive error terms are positively correlated with each other, which is most common. Negative serial correlation implies the opposite.

Durbin-Watson critical values differ from other test statistics in two ways: each critical value has an upper and lower limit, and the test tests for both positive and negative serial correlation. Software packages do not always produce the level at which the test statistic is statistically significant; analysts need to refer to the table of critical values in the Appendix. Critical values are determined by the number of observations (n) and number of independent variables (k). For example, when $n = 30$ and $k = 2$, the lower critical value (d_l) is 1.28 and the upper critical value (d_u) is 1.57 ($p = .05$). Values less than d_l and greater than $4 - d_l$ indicate the presence of correlation, but values between d_l and d_u, and $4 - d_l$ and $4 - d_u$, are considered inconclusive in determining serial correlation. These are critical values at the level of 5 percent significance. Figure 7.9 shows the critical regions for this test statistic. Thus, in the above example, values less than 1.28 and greater than 2.72 indicate autocorrelation; values between 1.57 and 1.28 and between 2.43 and 2.72 are inconclusive. Values between 1.57 and 2.43 indicate the absence of autocorrelation.

Correcting Autocorrelation

Two strategies are available for correcting serial correlation: the first strategy is to add a trend variable to the model, and the second strategy is to examine the relationship in so-called first-order differences.

Figure 7.9 ——— ᴧᴧᴧ— Durbin-Watson Critical Values

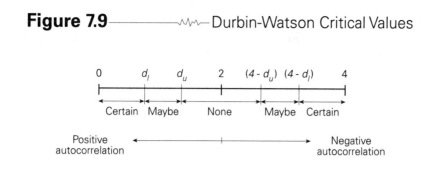

The rationale for adding a trend variable is to control for the fact that over time many variables increase; the trend variable controls for growth over time and, hence, any spurious correlation between the dependent variable and independent variables. A **trend** (or counter) **variable** is simply a variable that records the order in which observations appear (1, 2, 3, 4, 5 . . . , shown as the variable "Time" in Table 7.1). When adding a trend variable, the relationship is changed in the following manner:

Initial relationship: $y = a + b_1x_1 + b_2x_2 + \ldots$
Transformed relationship: $y = a + b_1x_1 + b_2x_2 + \ldots + b_n\text{Time}.$

A second strategy is using **first-order differences.** These are the differences between successive observations, as shown below. The rationale for first-order differences (also called first-differences) is the logical proposition that if it is true that (the levels of) two variables are correlated with each other over time, then their increases also should be correlated over time. For example, the value of ΔY for Time = 2 in Table 7.1 is the difference between the value of Vary in Time = 2 and Time = 1, or 25 − 23 = 2. The first observation is always lost because of the differencing. Statistical packages routinely calculate first-order differences. Thus, the relationship is transformed as follows:

Initial relationship: $y = a + b_1x_1 + b_2x_2 + \ldots$
Transformed relationship: $\Delta y = a + b_1\Delta x_1 + b_2\Delta x_2 + \ldots .$

Relationships in first-difference form often eliminate problems of serial correlation because differenced data exhibit far more variability than levels data. This is clearly shown in Table 7.1, in which the differenced data do not show an upward bias that the levels data do.

Comparing these two strategies, one sees the regression of first-order differences is considered a far more stringent test than adding a trend vari-

Table 7.1 ⎯⎯⎯⎯⎯⎯⎯⎯ⵊⵜⵊ⎯ Calculating First-Order Differences

TIME	VARY	VARX1	VARX2	ΔY	$\Delta X1$	$\Delta X2$
1	23	1	5	.	.	.
2	25	2	8	2	1	3
3	27	4	10	2	2	2
4	29	5	13	2	1	3
5	31	6	18	2	1	5
6	30	8	16	−1	2	−2
7	33	9	14	3	1	−2
8	34	11	14	1	2	0

able and is therefore preferred. Adding a trend variable is a prophylactic strategy that attempts to control for the problem. Regressing first-order differences is a preventive strategy that aims to avoid the problem.

Policy Evaluation

Time series data are excellent for evaluating the impact of a policy or program. Levels of performance or service utilization are tracked and compared with the moment or period in which a policy is implemented. Time series data are fundamental to the use of (quasi-) experimental designs in public management and policy, as discussed in Chapter 1.

Policy variables measure when and how policies affect the dependent variables. Policy variables indicate when the policy has caused an effect. Policy variables can be modeled in different ways, as shown in Figure 7.10. The initial zeroes indicate the pre-policy time period, the first "1" indicates the first period in which the policy or program is implemented, and so on. These variables are easily added to any data set, with values as shown in Figure 7.10. The pulse and period variables reflect a policy or program that is used for only a limited time. For example, these policy variables might be used to measure, respectively, a one-time or limited-period intervention, such as a one-night or month-long effort by roadway police to apprehend drunken drivers. The period after the policy or program is terminated is called the post-policy period. By contrast, the step and increasing impact variables signify an ongoing policy or program. (By definition, no post-policy periods are associated with these on-going programs or policies.) These variables differ only with regard to the level of impact over time. For example, some programs are plausibly hypothesized to have a near-constant effect over time, such as a permanent increase of the speed limit. However, benefit programs, such as after-school services, often have an increasing effect over time as more and more beneficiaries are affected by the policy or enrolled in the program. It is typically a matter of empirical trial-and-error as to which

Figure 7.10 —————〰〰—Policy Variables

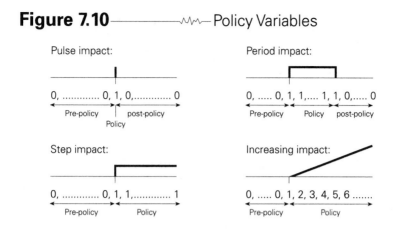

Pulse impact:

0, ... 0, 1, 0,............. 0

Pre-policy Policy post-policy

Period impact:

0, ... 0, 1, 1,.... 1, 1, 0,..... 0

Pre-policy Policy post-policy

Step impact:

0, ... 0, 1, 1,............. 1

Pre-policy Policy

Increasing impact:

0, ... 0, 1, 2, 3, 4, 5, 6 ....

Pre-policy Policy

policy form best approximates the actual impact of the policy. To examine for policy impacts, the relationship without policy impacts is modified in the following way:

Without policy impacts: $\Delta y = a + b_1 \Delta x_1 + b_2 \Delta x_2 + \ldots$
  With policy impacts: $\Delta y = a + b_1 \Delta x_1 + b_2 \Delta x_2 + \ldots + b_n P_n + b_m P_m + \ldots,$

where $b_n P_n, \ldots$ are alternative specifications of the policy impact. A significant coefficient of any policy variable signifies that the policy has had an impact on the outcome Δy. The above model can also be written in levels form with an added trend variable.

Consider the following hypothetical example. In response to a growing concern about classroom violence discussed in Chapter 1, a high school has begun an anger awareness and management program. Teachers are asked to record the number of incidents that involve physical contact. The total number of weekly incidences are tallied. There exist eight weeks of data from before the anger management program and eight weeks of data from the beginning of it. The following data (average number of classroom incidents) are available on a per classroom basis: 6.3, 6.4, 6.8, 7.0, 7.2, 7.3, 7.1, 7.5, 6.6, 6.5, 6.2, 6.0, 5.8, 5.5, 5.2, and 4.9. Is the decline sufficient to conclude that the program has a statistically significant impact? Table 7.2 shows the regression output. The data set has sixteen observations, one for each week. Values for the variable "trend" are 1, 2, 3 . . . 14, 15, 16. Values for the variable "Step impact" are 0,0,0,0,0,0,0,0,1,1,1,1,1,1,1,1, and the values for the variable "Increasing impact" are 0,0,0,0,0,0,0,0,1,2,3,4,5,6,7,8. It also shows the results for the dependent variable in levels form with a trend variable. The first order of business is to determine whether the model violates regression assumptions. The Durbin-Watson test statistic is 1.597. With three explanatory vari-

Table 7.2 〰️ Time Series Regression Output

Model Fit

R	R-square	Adjusted R-square	SEE	Durbin-Watson
0.989	0.979	0.973	0.125	1.597

Dependent variable: Violent classroom incidents (Level)

Coefficients

Model	Unstandardized coefficients		t	Sig.
	b	SE		
Constant	6.221	.097	63.916	0.000
Trend	.162	.019	8.399	0.000
Step impact	−0.570	.126	−4.511	0.001
Increasing impact	−0.408	.027	−14.979	0.000

Note: SE = Standard error, Sig. = Significance

ables and sixteen observations, $d_l = 0.86$ and $d_u = 1.73$. Hence, the Durbin-Watson statistic is in the inconclusive range, and we decide that there is insufficient evidence of serial correlation. We also examine the error term plot and determine that no outliers are present, using procedures discussed earlier in this chapter. The results in Table 7.2 show that the program, modeled as both a step and an increasing impact, is significantly associated with the reduction in classroom incidents. These results are plausible, as behavioral programs often have effects that increase over time.

The results find support in first-order difference form. Then, the Durbin-Watson statistic is 2.801, which is again in the inconclusive range. T-test test statistics are shown in parentheses:

$$\Delta \text{Incidents} = 0.171 - 0.668^{**}\text{Step} + 0.0038 \text{ Increase}$$
$$(-3.43) \qquad (1.10)$$
$$^{**}) \, p < .01; \, ^{*}) \, p < .05.$$

This result is consistent with that above because the dependent variable measures differences; the significance of the Step variable suggests that the rate of change is constant.

Lagged Variables

A *lagged variable* is one whose impact on the dependent variable is delayed. Even though a policy is implemented on a certain date, it sometimes takes some time before measurable effects on the dependent variable occur. In the above example, the impact of a juvenile curfew on juvenile crime might be delayed a little, perhaps because it requires a few time periods for police

Δx_2	.52	.48	.62	.38	.45	.58	.63	.56	.67
$\Delta x_{2, t\text{-}1}$	.	.52	.48	.62	.38	.45	.58	.63	.56
$\Delta x_{2, t\text{-}2}$	.	.	.52	.48	.62	.38	.45	.58	.63

staffing levels to take full effect, or because it takes a few weeks before juveniles become fully aware of the curfew. Thus, we wish to lag the effect of the curfew policy variable.

Statistical software packages can readily lag variables. To indicate that, for example, Δx_2 is lagged one time period, the relationship "$\Delta y = a + b_1 \Delta x_1 + b_2 \Delta x_2 + \ldots$" becomes: $\Delta y = a + b_1 \Delta x_1 + b_2 \Delta x_{2, t-1} + \ldots$. The notation "$t-1$" indicates the one-period lag. For illustration, $\Delta x_{2, t-2}$ is shown above. An empirical question concerns the length of the lag: should Δx_2 be lagged one, two, three, or even more periods? Analysts can determine this on a trial-and-error basis. When effects are lagged, regression coefficients (and t-test statistics) often show a nice bell-shaped (or inverted-V) pattern for successive lags. For example, the regression coefficients of Δx_2 when lagged three through seven periods might be −2.25, 11.50, 73.89, 35.32, −1.83, suggesting that a lag of five is most appropriate, hence, $\Delta x_{2, t-5}$.[5]

On occasion, the dependent variable might be lagged, too: $\Delta y = a + b_1 \Delta y_{t-1} + b_2 \Delta x_2 + \ldots$. This signifies that the dependent variable is affected by its own immediate past: perhaps, juvenile delinquency is seen as feeding on itself. The specification of a lagged dependent variable is called autoregression and further reduces problems of serial correlation. The Durbin-Watson statistic is not appropriate for autoregressive models. Instead, the Durbin $\hbar$ statistic is used.[6]

Regarding the above example, we find no evidence of lagged effect. For example, the t-test statistics of the Increasing Impact variable are: −14.979 (no lag), −12.869 ($t=-1$), −11.680 ($t-2$), and −5.466 ($t-3$). These results are obtained by running the above model separately for each lag. Thus, the impact of this variable is strongest when there is no lag. Similarly, the t-test statistics for the Step variable are, respectively, −4.511, −0.873, −0.055, and −1.051. This, too, does not show a lagged impact.

FORECASTING

Frequently, public managers and analysts are called upon to forecast. In this section, we provide some useful forecast methods. To avoid confusion, the term *forecast* is used to refer to predicted observations in the *future*. By contrast, the predicted values of *known* observations are called predicted values, $\hat{Y}$, not forecasts.

Multiple regression often is of limited use for forecasting because *future* values of independent variables are unknown. At best, when all of the independent variables are lagged, some near-term forecasts are possible, based on known values of independent variables. Rather, simple regression is then used to make forecasts in which Time is the (sole) independent variable. Various advanced, statistical regression techniques estimate time series that take trends and seasonal fluctuations into account. These advanced techniques are often used in financial forecasting (for example, stock markets), but they have found little application in public management and policy to date. One limitation is that they often require more observations than are available to managers; few managers have twenty or more time-based observations. By contrast, the following spreadsheet-based approaches do not require many observations, and these are discussed below. An overview of regression-based forecasting strategies is provided in the next chapter.

Validation is critical in forecasting. Generally, the first step in forecasting is ascertaining that the model accurately predicts current values. We cannot place much credence in forecasting a model that does a poor job of predicting today's known values. To this end, the models are recalculated based on a smaller sample that excludes recent observations. Recent observations are then used to compare the predicted and actual values. If the model is found to make accurate predictions of recent known values, which is usually determined by visual comparison of the actual and predicted values, then existing values are included and predictions are made of future conditions.

Forecasting with Few Observations

Managers are frequently asked to make forecasts on the basis of few previous observations. This problem sometimes is encountered when managers are asked to forecast budget expenditures on the basis of just a few years or months of prior data. The lack of an adequate number of observations makes the use of time series regression impractical. When one is working with expenditures and revenues, it is common to use constant dollars, that is, to remove inflationary growth from other sources of growth. Hence, expenditures are deflated before making forecasts. Assume that annual inflation rates are as shown in Table 7.3 (in percentages). All data are first recalculated in constant year T dollars, which are then forecasted. This is shown in the table.[7] Inflation rates affect the current year's expenditures. Hence, $57.5 in $T - 1$ is equivalent to ($57.5 * 1.033) = $59.4 in time period T. The amount $54.3 in Table 7.2 is equivalent to ($54.3 * 1.027 * 1.033) = $57.6 in time period T. Any forecasted expenditures will now be net of any inflation. The result shows that despite the overall increase in current dollars, for most of the period budget expenditures have been about level; expenditures at time T are in fact less than $T - 5$, when both are expressed in constant $t = T$ dollars.

Several approaches exist to forecasting data. Each has its own bias. A conservative approach is the use of ***prior moving averages*** (also called PMA).

Table 7.3 ⎯⎯⎯〜〜⎯ Annual Inflation Rates: Percentages

Year	T–5	T–4	T–3	T–2	T–1	T	T+1	T+2	T+3
Inflation rate (%)	2.8	3.1	4.0	2.7	3.3	.			
Budget (current $s)	52.1	50.5	52.5	54.3	57.5	60.4			
Budget (constant $s)	60.9	57.4	57.9	57.6	59.4	60.4			

In this approach, the average of the current preceding observations is used to predict the following period. The problem with this widely used approach is that it *under*estimates future values by basing forecasts on the average of the recent past. Typically, a time span of three periods is used, hence, the three most recent periods are used to predict the next period. At the end of existing observations, predicted observations become part of the series used to predict the next period, and so on. Whenever possible, actual rather than predicted values should be used. The results are shown in Table 7.4. For example, the predicted value of the budget in the $T-2$ period is the mean of $60.9, $57.4, and $57.9, which is $58.7 (see Table 7.3). Similarly, the predicted value for the $T-1$ period is the mean of $57.4, $57.9, and $57.6, which is $57.6. The forecasted value of the budget in period $T+1$ is the mean of $57.6, $59.4, and $60.4 which is $59.1. Note that the values that are used to forecast the budget in $T+1$ are the actual numbers, not the predicted numbers. The forecasted value in $T+2$ is the mean of $59.4, $60.4, and $59.1, which is $59.6. Here, the value of $T+1$ is the forecasted value because no actual value exists. Comparing predicted against actual values for purposes of validation, we see the downward tendency for T and $T-1$.

A second approach, which we call **prior moving changes,** forecasts on the basis of *changes* in preceding periods. Often, the average of the last three increases are used to predict the next period. Then, future values are defined as the immediate past level plus the average of the last three increases. The idea is that future changes in expenditures should resemble past increases. Using the average increases of three prior years, we obtain the results shown in Table 7.5. For example, the change from $T-5$ to $T-4$ is ($57.4 – $60.9) = $–3.50. The average of changes in the three periods prior to $T-1$ is the mean of $–3.5, $0.5, and $–0.3, which is $–1.1. Hence, the predicted value for $T-1$ is the actual budget of $T-2$, or $57.6 – $1.1, which is $56.5. The

Table 7.4 ⎯⎯⎯〜〜⎯ Forecasted Budget Using PMA

Year	T–5	T–4	T–3	T–2	T–1	T	T+1	T+2	T+3
Predicted budget (constant $s)	.	.	.	58.7	57.6	58.3	59.1	59.6	59.7

Table 7.5: ———— ∿∿— Forecasted Budget Using Average Changes

Year	T–5	T–4	T–3	T–2	T–1	T	T+1	T+2	T+3
Change from prior period		–3.5	0.5	–0.3	1.8	1.0	0.8	1.2	
Average change				–1.1	0.7	0.8	1.2	1.0	
Actual budget (constant $s)	60.9	57.4	57.9	57.6	59.4	60.4			
Predicted/forecasted budget (constant $s)					56.5	60.1	61.2	62.4	63.4

other values are calculated similarly. For example, the forecasted value of $T + 1$ is calculated as the value of T, $60.4, plus the average of the last three increases ($–0.3, $1.8, and $1), or $0.83, which is $61.2. This is ($61.2 – $60.4) = $0.8 higher than in time period T. (We prefer to use actual rather than predicted values wherever possible; hence, we use the actual value of $60.4 rather than the predicted value of $60.1.) This information is used for calculating the average increases for forecasts in the next time period, $T + 2$, and so on. Comparing these two approaches, we find that forecasts based on average increases are far less conservative than PMA.[8] From the perspective of validation, we find that the predicted values of $T – 1$ and T are slightly better than those using PMA.

These results can sometimes be improved, or at least validated, through a third approach, which forecasts expenditures based on known *forecast ratios*. Tests involve other variables, such as work orders, client requests, or populations. Assume, for example, that expenditures are known to be related to the population size, the source of service requests. Then these forecasts can be triangulated by forecasts of population growth, shown below for $T + 1$ and beyond. These forecasts are made as shown in Table 7.6. The average ratio is

Table 7.6 ———— ∿∿— Predicted Budget: Forecast Ratio

Year	T–5	T–4	T–3	T–2	T–1	T	T+1	T+2	T+3
Budget (constant $s)	60.9	57.4	57.9	57.6	59.4	60.4			
Population	250	253	258	260	266	273	275	280	282
Ratio	0.244	0.227	0.224	0.221	0.223	0.221			
Forecasted budget (constant $s) Mean of all ratios							62.4	63.6	64.0
Forecasted budget (constant $) Mean of last three ratios							61.1	62.2	62.6

Table 7.7 ———〜〜— Weekly and Monthly Activity: Forecasted
Values

Month	Week	Activity	Mean monthly activity	Deviation from mean	Predicted activity for week 5
1	1	10		−5.00	
1	2	14		−1.00	
1	3	15		0.00	
1	4	21	15.00	+6.00	
2	1	12		−4.75	
2	2	15		−1.75	
2	3	17		+0.25	
2	4	23	16.75	+6.25	
3	1	14		−4.00	
3	2	16		−2.00	
3	3	16		−2.00	
3	4	26	18.00	+8.00	
4	1	16		−3.25	
4	2	16		−3.25	
4	3	20		+0.75	
4	4	25	19.25	+5.75	
Forecasted:					
5	1		20.67	−4.25	16.42
5	2		20.67	−2.00	18.67
5	3		20.67	−0.25	20.42
5	4		20.67	+6.50	27.17

0.227. Hence, the predicted budget for $T + 1$ is (275 $*$ 0.227 =) $62.4. These values seem consistent with the forecasting approach based on prior moving changes. If the ratios of only the last three periods are used, whose mean is 0.222, then the forecasted values are somewhat lower. Of course, the credibility of these forecasts hinges on the constancy and theoretical justification of the ratio. If credible, the forecasted values heighten the importance of incorporating estimated demand in expenditure forecasts.

Forecasting with Periodic Effects
A rather different problem involves forecasting when data exhibit *periodicity* (or *seasonality*), that is, systematically fluctuating (or modulating) values. Some examples of these problems are daily activities that exhibit lower workloads on Mondays and weekly activities that exhibit more activity toward the end of the month. Table 7.7 lays out an example of such data. When only PMA is used, the last three values of Month 4 will greatly

Figure 7.11 ⟶ ∿∿ Workload

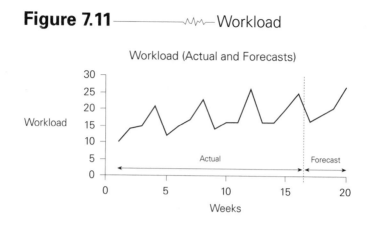

overestimate the value of Week 1 in Month 5. This is because the three prior observations (the last three weeks in Month 4) fail to take into account that, on average, Week 1 activity levels are low for all months. The strategy of forecasting Month 5, Week 1, requires that we take this information into account. The methodology is a straightforward, albeit cumbersome, three-step process. First, average workloads are calculated for each period, on the basis of which a forecast is made for the entire Month 5. Specifically, we forecast an average for Month 5 as the average of Month 4 plus the mean increase of preceding months. Second, the mean deviations are determined for each week of preceding months. Third, these deviations are used to adjust the weekly forecasts in Month 5. The calculations are done as follows:

The column mean monthly activity clearly shows an upward trend. Because these are not expenditures, we do not deflate them. The first step is to forecast all of Month 5. To this end, we calculate the *mean increase* from month to month. For example, the increase from Month 1 to Month 2 is 16.75 − 15.00 = 1.75. In this manner, the mean increase is the mean of 1.75, 1.25, and 1.25, which is 1.42. Thus, it seems reasonable to forecast the average activity in Month 5 as 19.25 (the mean of Month 4) plus 1.42, which is 20.67.

Second, we calculate the deviations for each week and average them. For example, the mean deviation across all Week 1s (for each Month) is the mean of −5.00, −4.75, −4.00, and −3.25, shown in italics, or −4.25. Similarly, mean deviations are calculated for other weeks. Third, the forecasted mean value for Month 5 is adjusted for these weekly deviations. For example, Week 1 in Month 5 is (20.67 − 4.25 =) 16.42. Values for other periods in Month 5 are similarly calculated. The results are shown in Table 7.7 and Figure 7.11.

CONCLUSION

To further strengthen their research, analysts should always test their regression models for assumption violations. Doing so is critical to establishing validity and robustness. Assumption violations—outliers, multicollinearity, curvilinearity, heteroscedasticity, misspecification, measurement errors, and autocorrelation—are relatively easy to detect and correct. Please keep in mind that multiple regression is often used in studying the effects of control variables but is seldom the first step in analysis and does not replace the study of bivariate relationships. Relationships that hold under the scrutiny of multiple regression should also be significant in bivariate form. Typically, analysis of bivariate relations remains vital to understanding the practical significance of data, and it further enhances the usefulness of any study.

Analysts should also be familiar with the correct usage of time series data. Time series data can be used for testing the impact of policy and can also incorporate the effects of time lags between policy implementation and policy effect. Time series data frequently exhibits autocorrelation, which can be corrected by including a trend variable or examining the relationship in first-difference form. Through time series data, analysts can also forecast on the basis of past results. Most accurate when involving only a few periods in the future, forecasts are validated by comparing predictions in recent periods against known values. Forecasting does not necessarily involve regression, as shown by examples in this chapter, and it provides analysts with additional opportunities for contributing to decision-making processes by giving their audience insight into things that may come.

Through careful application of these techniques and thorough testing of models, researchers can put together a strong set of results that shapes policy decision-making.

KEY TERMS

Autocorrelation (pp. 145–147)

Curvilinear (p. 139)

Durbin-Watson test statistic (p. 145)

Error term plot (p. 136)

First-order differences (p. 147)

Forecast (p. 151)

Forecast Ratios (p. 154)

Heteroscedasticity (p. 140)

Lagged variable (p. 150)

Measurement error (p. 142)

Multicollinearity (p. 137)

Outliers (p. 136)

Park test (p. 141)

Partial regression plot (p. 139)

Periodicity (p. 155)

Policy variable (p. 148)

Prior moving averages (pp. 152–153)

Prior moving changes (p. 153)

Seasonality (p. 155)

Serial correlation (p. 145)

Specification error (p. 144)

Trend variable (p. 147)

Notes

1. VIF = 1/Tolerance, where Tolerance = $1 - R^2$, and R^2 is calculated for the model in which an independent variable is predicted by all of the other independent variables.

2. A special instance occurs when the dependent variable is a fraction p, ranging from 0.0 to 1.0. Then, a so-called logit transformation, which is defined as $\ln[1/(1-p)]$, is recommended.

3. A thorough discussion of WLS is beyond this text. For a discussion and example of WLS, see SPSS, *Regression Models 10.0* (Chicago: SPSS, Inc., 1999 or latest edition), or Damodar Gujarati, *Basic Econometrics*, 3rd ed. (New York: McGraw-Hill, 1999).

4. Some analysts also consider as a criterion whether $\bar{R}^2$ increases as a result of adding a variable. Increases in $\bar{R}^2$ imply that more variance of the dependent variable is explained. However, the ultimate basis for including or excluding variables should be theoretical; it cannot be solely based on empirical considerations.

5. Statistical packages often have a cross-correlation function (CCF), which examines lags between two variables. This is used to estimate the number of lags. The CCF should only be used when variables are stationary, that is, exhibit stable mean and variances over time. This is typically accomplished by taking first-order differences. The discussion of CCF is beyond the scope of this text. See, for example, SPSS, *SPSS Trends 10.0* (Chicago: SPSS, Inc., 1999 or later editions).

6. Durbin $\hbar$ is defined as

$$(1 - 0.5DW)\sqrt{\frac{N}{1 - N[se(b_{y_{t-1}})]^2}},$$

where N = sample size, DW = Durbin-Watson statistic, and $[se(b_{y_{t-1}})]^2$ is the squared standard error of the regression coefficient of the lagged dependent variable (that is, b_1, in the model $\Delta y = a + b_1\Delta y_{t-1} + b_2\Delta x_2 + \ldots$). Durbin $\hbar$ is normally distributed; hence, values greater than $|\hbar| > 1.96$ indicate serial correlation.

7. For ease of calculation, only one decimal is retained in the following data and tables. Actual results (such as when using a spreadsheet) will vary slightly due to rounding.

8. Some analysts might prefer using the average of prior expenditures, rather than the last expenditure as the basis for future prediction. This, of course, has a downward effect on prediction. For example, the prediction for $T - 1$ is the average of T through $T - 2$, or $57.6, $59.4, and $60.4, or $59.1, plus the average increase of $T - 1$ through $T - 3$, $0.67, or $59.8. This value falls between the two approaches discussed in the text.

Advanced Statistics

CHAPTER OBJECTIVES

After reading this chapter, you should be able to understand:
- How logistic regression is used for estimating the probability of an event
- How path analysis uses multiple dependent variables
- How survival analysis deals with events that have not yet occurred
- How regression-based forecasting results in a wide range of forecasts
- Other advanced techniques that are sometimes used

This last chapter provides an overview of other advanced statistical techniques. Each of these multivariate techniques expands on previous techniques in ways that help managers to work with some rather special situations. These methods are quite popular, although less so than multiple regression. Specifically, analysts use logistic analysis when the dependent variable is dichotomous. Logistic regression is often used in political science, for example, to predict the likelihood of winning an election. When analysts are faced with variables that are interrelated in complex ways, they turn to path analysis. Survival analysis deals with the problem that records may reflect events that have not yet happened but still may occur, for exam-

Figure 8.1 ————————— Logistic Curve

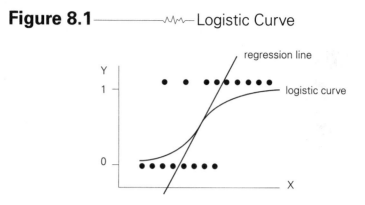

ple, the probability that clients will drop out of a welfare program. Finally, we discuss regression-based forecasting and other advanced techniques.

LOGISTIC REGRESSION

Logistic regression deals with the situation that, at times, the dependent variable is dichotomous rather than continuous. Examples of dichotomous variables include winning a political election, receiving a death penalty, and having an abortion. In these instances, the dependent variable is dichotomous by nature since it is impossible to win half an election or to be somewhat put to death.

A dichotomous dependent variable violates the regression assumption that it should be continuous. The specific statistical problem is that linear regression poorly predicts the dichotomous variable, a situation that is shown graphically in Figure 8.1. When using the straight regression line, it is seen that predicted values of the dependent variable can be less than zero and greater than one. This is problematic if we interpret the predicted values as the probability that the dependent variable event occurs. Obviously, the chance of winning an election can neither be negative nor be greater than one. To resolve this problem, an S-shaped curve (also called a "logistic" curve) is fitted to the observations. The values of this curve always lie between zero and one.

The mathematics of logistic curves are more complicated than those of linear regression. The probability of an event occurring is expressed as:

$$\text{Probability (event occurs)} = 1/1 + e^{-(a + b_1x_1 + b_2x_2 + \ldots)}$$

This formula is used to calculate event probabilities (the likelihood of the event's occurring). Assume, hypothetically, that data exist about teenagers who have been involved in incidents of classroom violence. We do not know

Table 8.1 ————⋀⋀⋀— Logistic Regression Output

Model Fit

Model	-2 log likelihood (-2LL) Sig. (base model)	Cox and Snell R²	Nagelkerke R²	Hosmer and Lemeshow test Chi-square	Sig.
66.001	0.000	0.392	0.535	8.397	.396

Dependent variable: Student classroom incident

Coefficients

Model	Unstandardized coefficients b	SE	Wald chi-square	Sig.
Constant	-7.405	5.202	2.027	0.155
Gender	-4.464	1.319	11.450	0.001
Education	1.558	0.544	8.212	0.004
GPA	-2.716	0.722	14.140	0.000

Classification Table

Observed Variable	Group	Predicted Violence 0	1	Percent correct
Violence	0	44	6	88.0
	1	11	19	63.3
Overall percentage				78.8

Note: Sig. = significance; GPA = grade point average; SE = standard error.

how many incidents they have been involved in, only that they have been involved. Hence, the dependent variable is dichotomous. Assume further that we want to know whether grade level, educational attainment (grade point average, or GPA), and gender are predictors of classroom violence. Data are available for thirty students who have been involved in such incidents, as well as for an additional random sample of fifty students who have not been involved. The population is drawn only from high school students. The results shown in Table 8.1 are obtained. This output yields many new statistics because the estimation methodology is different from multiple regression.[1] The first statistic is a measure of the overall fit, analogous to the global F-test. The absolute value (66.001) has no interpretation; the statistic shows that the model with the three variables is significantly better than the base (or null) model that lacks these variables. This is hardly a surprise, given that all three independent variables are statistically significant.

Table 8.2 ——————～∿∿— Calculating Event Probability

Gender	Education	GPA	$a + bx + \ldots$	$e^{-(a + bx + \ldots)}$	$1/(1 + e^{-(a + bx + \ldots)})$
0	10	3.0	0.027	0.973	0.507
1	10	3.0	−4.437	84.521	0.012
0	10	2.0	2.743	0.064	0.939
0	10	4.0	−2.689	14.717	0.064
1	12	3.0	−1.321	3.747	0.211

The two leftmost header group is labeled **Variables** and the rightmost is **Probability**.

Note: GPA = grade point averages; 0 = male; 1 = female.

Cox and Snell R^2 is analogous to R^2 in multiple regression but has the limitation that it cannot reach 1.0. The *Nagelkerke R^2* is a modification that overcomes this problem. The interpretation of the results shows that 53.5 percent of the variance in students involved in classroom incidents is explained by the model—a modest amount. The classification table shown in Table 8.1 confirms this finding and shows the percentage of corrected predicted observations. The minimum is 50 percent, indicating the lack of useful prediction. Typically, standards of 80–85 percent indicate "good" model prediction. Our model falls somewhat short (78.8 percent correct); we acknowledge the desirability of a better model. (The analysis also suggested two observations that might be classified as outliers; however, removing them did not substantively affect these results.) The *Hosmer and Lemeshow test* is a measure of overall model fit, comparing the observed and predicted values. A good model fit has close correspondence between observed and predicted values and, hence, an insignificant chi-square value for this test.

The results show that all three variables are statistically significant: gender, grade level, and scholastic performance are all predictors of a student's becoming involved in a violent classroom incident. Using the above formula, we can now calculate the probability of a student's becoming involved for different levels of the independent variables. Many combinations are possible, allowing for interesting what-if analyses. These calculations are readily performed on a spreadsheet (Table 8.2). The results for tenth-grade students show that classroom violence is primarily associated with being male; for students with a GPA of 3.0, the odds of being involved in a violent classroom incident are much lower. The odds for the two groups are, respectively, 50.7 percent for males and 1.2 percent for females. Among tenth-grade males, the probability of being involved in a violent incident is greatly affected by school performance: for male students with a GPA of 2.0 the chance is 93.9 percent, but for those with a 4.0 GPA the chance is only 6.4 percent. Further analysis shows that the chance of violence increases with

Figure 8.2———————〜〜〜—Path Analysis

Relationship between Job Training, Job Interviews, and Employment

grade level. It is highest in the twelfth grade; females with a 3.0 GPA have a probability of 21.1 percent of being involved in violence. It bears repeating that these are hypothetical data.

PATH ANALYSIS

Path analysis is a technique for estimating models with complex interrelationships among variables. Regression analysis does a poor job of modeling complex reality. Linear regression assesses the impacts of all variables on one dependent variable; what if reality allows for indirect effects? Consider the following hypothetical scenario from a welfare employment agency. Unemployed persons are provided the opportunity to participate in job training, which includes training in job interview techniques as well as some remedial education. The question is whether or not job training is successful. Managers suspect job training affects employment (that is, whether a job seeker secures employment within a certain time) in the manner shown in Figure 8.2. Job training is hypothesized to increase the employment of job seekers, but it also causes them to participate in more job interviews because part of the job training includes interviewing skills. This, in turn, also increases employment. Thus, the hypothesized effect of job training is both direct and indirect. Figure 8.2 can be further elaborated by including the effects of having dependents and substance abuse problems (see Figure 8.3).

Path analysis is a causal modeling technique for estimating such complex models. However, an important limitation of path analysis is that it may not be used when feedback loops are present. Feedback loops are relationships in which two or more variables are directly or indirectly caused by each other; no such relationships are present in Figure 8.3. (Feedback loops would have existed *if* additional paths had been added that go from "job interviews" to "job training," or from "job interviews" to "having dependents." Of course, these additional paths make little theoretical sense in our model.)[2] Models without feedback loops are called *recursive models.* When no feedback loops

Figure 8.3 ——————⋎⋏⋎⋏— Path Analysis

Relationship between Job Training, Job Interviews, and Employment
with Effects of Dependents and Substance Abuse

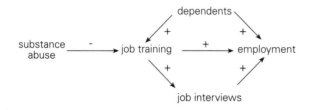

are present, each path can be estimated with OLS regression.[3] Specifically, in
the above case, the following regression models are estimated:

Employment $= a_1 + b_1$ Job interviews $+ b_2$ Job training $+ b_3$ Dependents $+ e_1$.
Job interviews $= a_2 + b_4$ Job training $+ e_2$.
Job training $= a_3 + b_5$ Dependents $+ b_6$ Substance abuse $+ e_3$.

Note that in causal models, the terminology of independent and dependent
variables often is inconclusive: the variable Job interviews is both an independent variable (causing Employment) and a dependent variable (caused
by Job training, Having dependents, and Substance abuse). Then, causal
modeling distinguishes between *exogenous variables,* which are variables
that are unaffected by other variables in the model (such as Substance
abuse), and *endogenous variables,* which are affected by other variables
(such as Employment and Job interviews).

For each model, the impact of each variable is stated by the beta coefficient. Assume that the results in Figure 8.4 are available. The numbers along
the arrows are the beta coefficients. The error terms that are shown are
sometimes calculated as $\sqrt{1-R^2}$.[4] Then, direct and indirect effects of the variables are calculated in Table 8.3. *Direct effects* are simply the beta coefficients
of the variables that immediately affect another variable. *Indirect effects* are
calculated as the product of beta coefficients of each pathway. Note that both
Dependents and Substance abuse have two indirect pathways to Employment
(Table 8.3). The results shown in the table are interesting because they show
that, although interviewing has a greater direct effect on employment than
training, the indirect effects of training are substantial. The total effect of job
training exceeds that of interviewing. If only multiple regression had been
used (with Employment as a dependent variable), this indirect effect would
have gone undetected. The results also show that substance abuse and having
dependents have less impact on employment than the other two variables.

Figure 8.4 ───────〜〜〜─ Path Analysis Results

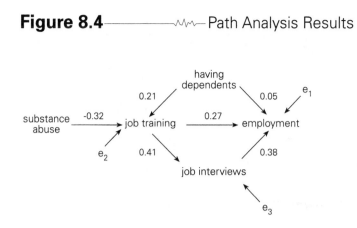

Path analysis is a relatively simple extension of multiple regression. The standards for its proper use are the following:

- The model must be theory-based. Although many different models can be constructed from even a modest number of variables, the relationships that they depict must "make sense" (have face validity). Typically, analysts specify a family of plausible models and even though only one model might be reported, all models should have similar substantive conclusions.
- There are no feedback loops and all models satisfy standard regression assumptions. Thus, problems of outliers, heteroscedasticity, linearity, autocorrelation, and multicollinearity should be identified and addressed.
- All error terms should be uncorrelated with all exogenous variables. The correlation of an error term with an exogenous variable suggests that that variable has an effect on the endogenous variable associated with the error term. In such a case, another path should be drawn that reflects the impact of the exogenous variable with the endogenous variable. The absence of such correlation does not prove that the model is correctly specified, only that it is not incorrectly specified.

Table 8.3 ───────〜〜〜─ Calculating Direct and Indirect Effects on Employment

Variable	Effects		
	Indirect	Direct	Total
Job training	0.41*0.38 = 0.16	0.27	0.43
Job interviews	—	0.38	0.38
Dependents	0.21*0.27 + 0.21*0.41*0.38 = 0.09	0.05	0.14
Substance abuse	−.32*.27 + −0.32*0.41*0.38 = −0.14	—	−0.14

Table 8.4 ⎯⎯⎯⎯⎯⎯⎯ Censored Observations

Obs	Week	Emp	Obs	Week	Emp	Obs	Week	Emp
1	0	0	6	2	0	11	4	1
2	0	0	7	2	0	12	4	0
3	1	1	8	3	1	13	5	1
4	1	0	9	3	0	14	5	1
5	1	0	10	4	1	15	5	0

Note: Obs = observations (clients); Emp = employment; 0 = has not yet found employment; 1 = has found employment.

SURVIVAL ANALYSIS

Another limitation of regression is that it assumes that complete information is available about all observations. *Survival analysis* deals with techniques that analyze information about events that is not yet available. Assume that a welfare manager in the above example (see path analysis) takes a snapshot of the status of the welfare clients. Some clients may have obtained employment and others not yet. Clients will also vary as to the amount of time that they have been receiving welfare. Examine the following data in Table 8.4. It shows that neither of the two clients, who have yet to complete their first week on welfare, has found employment; one of the three clients who have completed one week of welfare has found employment. *Censored observations* are observations for which the specified outcome has yet to occur. It is assumed that all clients who have not yet found employment are still waiting for this event to occur. Thus, the sample should not include clients who are not seeking employment. It is also important to note that a censored observation is very different from one that has missing data, which might occur because the manager does not know whether the client has found employment. As with regression, records with missing data are excluded from analysis. A censored observation is simply an observation for which a specified outcome has not yet occurred.

Assume that data exist from a random sample of 100 clients who are seeking, or have found, employment. *Survival analysis* is the statistical procedure for analyzing these data. The name of this procedure stems from its use in medical research. In clinical trials, researchers want to know the survival (or disease) rate of patients as a function of the duration of their treatment. For patients in the middle of their trial, the specified outcome may not yet have occurred. We obtain the following results (also called a *life table*) from analyzing hypothetical data from welfare records (Table 8.5). The terminology *terminal* signifies that the event has occurred. In this instance, the client has found employment. At start time zero, 100 cases enter the interval.

Table 8.5 ———⌁⌁— Life Table Results

Start time	# Entering interval	# Terminal events	Cum. prop. surviving until end of interval	Probability density
0.0	100.0	0.0	1.0000	0.0000
1.0	91.0	2.0	0.9762	0.0238
2.0	75.0	5.0	0.9055	0.0707
3.0	58.0	6.0	0.7979	0.1076
4.0	37.0	9.0	0.5867	0.2112
5.0	22.0	14.0	0.1304	0.4563

Note: The median survival time is 5.19.

During the first period, there are no "terminal cases" and nine censored cases. Thus, ninety-one cases enter the next period. In this second period, two clients find employment and fourteen do not, resulting in seventy-five cases that enter the following period. The column "Cumulative proportion surviving until end of interval" is an estimate of probability of surviving (not finding employment) until the end of the stated interval.[5] The column Probability density is an estimate of the probability of the terminal event occurring (that is, finding employment) during the time interval. The results also report that the "median survival time" is 5.19. That is, half of the clients find employment in 5.19 weeks.

Survival analysis can also examine survival rates for different "treatments" or conditions. Assume that data are available about the number of dependents that each client has. Table 8.5 is readily produced for each subset of this condition. For example, by comparing the survival rates of those with and those without dependents, the ***probability density*** figure, which shows the likelihood of an event's occurring, can be obtained (Figure 8.5). This figure suggests that having dependents is associated with clients' finding employment somewhat faster.

REGRESSION-BASED FORECASTING

In the previous chapter, we used spreadsheet-based techniques to make forecasts that can also be performed by hand. This is intentional, because many of the ***regression-based forecasting*** techniques are quite sophisticated and often require more data than are available to managers. There are four types of regression-based forecasting techniques: forecasting with leading indicators, curve estimation, exponential smoothing, and ARIMA (Auto Regressive Integrated Moving Averages). A brief overview of each is provided. *Note:* as

Figure 8.5————————ᴧᴧ—Probability Density

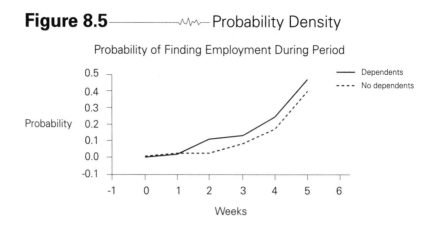

Probability of Finding Employment During Period

before, to avoid linguistic confusion, the term *forecast* is used to refer to predicted future observations. The predicted values of known observations are called predicted values, $\hat{Y}$, not forecasts.

Forecasting with Leading Indicators

Forecasting with leading indicators involves regression with independent variables that are all lagged (leading indicators). When independent variables are lagged, it is possible to forecast near-term observations by using the known, present values of the lagged independent variables to predict future values of the dependent variable. If the current predicted and observed values are close, then the forecasted values should be reasonably accurate. The problem is, of course, that most time series models include a mix of lagged and not-lagged independent variables. Hence, the usefulness of this approach may be quite limited and, in any event, limited to forecasts that are no longer than the shortest of the lagged periods.

Curve Estimation

Curve estimation estimates the shape of a trend variable and makes forecasts based on it. Curve estimation is available on many statistical software packages. Typically, various linear, quadratic, and logarithmic models are estimated (fitted), where Time is the sole independent variable. Thus, for example, a quadratic function is estimated as $y(t) = a + b_1 t + b_2 t^2$, and a logarithmic function is estimated as $y(t) = a + b_1 \log(t)$. Although R-square values are reported for each model, models should be selected that best seem to fit the observed curve. In regard to Chapter 7 (forecasting), we note that these models provide for level and trend but not for seasonality. If the analyst believes that a model accurately fits, model parameters can be used as a basis for making forecasts. An example is shown in Figure 8.6. The

Figure 8.6 ——————⋀⋀⋀—Curve Estimation I

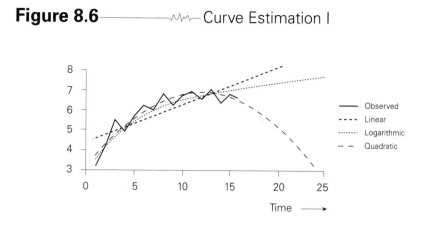

figure shows linear, logarithmic, and quadratic model results in vastly different forecasts. This is quite common with such estimations. Although the R^2 values of these models are quite respectable (respectively, 0.455, 0.747, and 0.895), both the linear and quadratic models seem way off the mark for even near-term predictions.

Curve estimation procedures can also be used to calculate confidence intervals. Confidence intervals are somewhat smaller for known values and become larger for forecasts that lie further into the future. For the curves in Figure 8.6, the 95 percent level confidence intervals are considerable, varying from ± 0.87 to ± 2.31 for each of the estimated curves. Figure 8.7 shows the 95 percent confidence interval for the logarithmic curve.

Exponential Smoothing

Exponential smoothing is a technique that estimates the dependent variables based on their level, trend, and seasonality: $y(t) = f$ (level, trend,

Figure 8.7 ——————⋀⋀⋀—Curve Estimation II

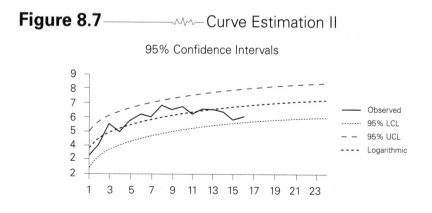

Figure 8.8 ———————— Exponential Smoothing

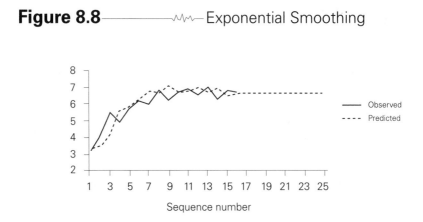

seasonality). The estimation methodology involves an iterative testing of alternative parameters that define level, trend, and seasonality components. There are four parameters: alpha (specifying the relative weight given to recent observations in calculating the current level), gamma (specifying the relative weight given to recent observations in determining the trend), and delta (specifying the relative weight given to recent observations in determining seasonality). In addition, some models also have a parameter phi, which specifies the extent to which the trend is dampened (that is, dies out) over time.

The computer conducts a so-called grid search, which is iterative testing of combinations of parameters to minimize the *sum of squared errors* (SSE, not to be confused with SEE; see Chapter 6), defined as the squared differences between actual and predicted values. The model with the lowest SSE best fits the observations. Predictions with exponential smoothing often rely heavily on recent observations. Then, forecasted values closely resemble most recent observations, modified according to any trend that is present in the most immediate observations, and any seasonality that is present. This is shown in Figure 8.8. The forecasted values closely match the last observation. Note how the most recent observations are also devoid of any trend. Figure 8.8 does not include a seasonality component. If seasonality had been specified and present, the forecast would have been modulated to reflect the estimated seasonality. The model can also be made to give more weight to past observations. Then the forecasted values will show an upward trend. However, based on the criterion of choosing a model with the lowest SSEs, the above model is preferred. We also note that in this instance the predicted observations do not always closely match the actual observations; the predicted values seem to follow actual observations by about one period. In fact, manually lagging the predicted values further reduces the SSE.[6]

Figure 8.9 ————————〜〜—ARIMA

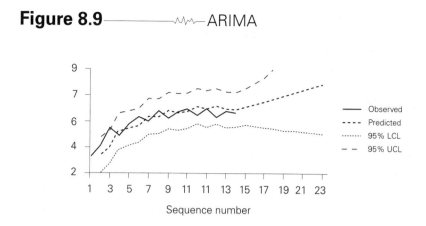

Sequence number

ARIMA

Autoregressive Integrated Moving Average (ARIMA) is a highly advanced technique that is often used for financial forecasting (for example, stock markets) but has found little application in public management and policy to date. ARIMA models require users to specify the nature of moving averages, autoregression, and seasonality. When the purpose is only prediction (not forecasting), independent variables can be used, too. The first step in ARIMA modeling is to make the data stationary, that is, to ensure that the variable has the same mean and variance across the entire range. This typically is achieved by taking first-order differences. The second step is determining the nature of parameters through myriad diagnostics that are part of ARIMA procedures. The third step is estimation and evaluation of the model by comparing actual and predicted values. Following these procedures, we obtain the predicted values and forecasts shown in Figure 8.9. We use first-order differences and no seasonality.

In comparison, ARIMA gives more weight to past observations than Figure 8.8, hence resulting in an upward trend. ARIMA also produces confidence intervals. Forecasts that are further into the future are more uncertain and thus have larger confidence intervals (CIs). The forecast methods of Chapter 7 also give more weight to recent observations and increases; the smoothing of recent fluctuations quickly results in a constant forecast of about 6.7—the last observation, similar to the exponential smoothing forecast shown in Figure 8.8.

PRECIS OF OTHER TECHNIQUES

The field of regression-based statistics is very broad and increasingly more common as advances in computing and user-friendly software make these techniques more accessible. This final section details some other advanced strategies. A brief discussion emphasizes the rationale and application for each approach, so that analysts can have a quick, easy reference to when and how to use these techniques.

Beyond Logistic Regression

Logistic regression extends multiple regression by allowing for a dichotomous dependent variable. But what if the dependent variable has more than two categories, yet it is not continuous? *Discriminant analysis* and *multinomial logistic regression* are two techniques for predicting group membership when the dependent variable is nominal. For example, we might want to predict parents' choice of school voucher program out of three or more types, or the characteristics or learning styles of students that might result in being more often involved in different types of classroom incidents. In both instances, the dependent variable is *nominal:* there is no ordering among type of voucher program or student characteristic. The differences between discriminant analysis and multinomial logistic regression are computational; either can be used for this purpose. Discriminant analysis is used to calculate regression lines that distinguish among nominal groups (the categories of the dependent variable) and others that predict group membership. Multinomial logistic regression is used to calculate regression lines that predict group membership on the basis of which probabilities of group membership are calculated (in a manner similar to logistic regression).

When the dependent variable is ordinal, *ordinal regression* can be used. Like multinomial logistic regression, ordinal regression often is used to predict group membership. *Probit* and *logit* regression is similar to logistic regression but has additional features that make it effective for medical applications in which treatments such as drug doses may interact with each other, and in which tests for dealing with equivalency of different treatment groups arise.

Exploratory Analysis

Factor analysis is a technique that aids in creating index variables. Chapter 5 discusses the use of Cronbach alpha to empirically justify the selection of variables that make up an index, but analysts must justify the selection of variables that are considered for the index. By contrast, factor analysis analyzes a large number of variables (often twenty to thirty) and classifies them into groups based on empirical similarities and dissimilarities. This empirical assessment can aid analysts' judgment regarding variables that might be grouped together. *Multidimensional scaling* and *cluster analysis* aim to identify key dimensions along which observations (rather than variables) differ. These techniques differ from factor analysis in that they allow for a hierarchy of classification dimensions. Some also use graphics to aid in visualizing the extent of differences and help in identifying the similarity or dissimilarity of observations. These techniques are called exploratory because they help analysts better understand their data and variables. These techniques usually precede regression and other analyses and are used whenever analysts have a large number of variables or observations on a related subject matter.

Beyond Life Tables

Life tables require that the interval (time) variable be measured on a discrete scale. When the time variable is continuous, *Kaplan-Meier survival analysis* is used. This procedure is quite analogous to life tables analysis. *Cox regression* is similar to Kaplan-Meier but allows for considering a larger number of independent variables (called covariates). In all instances, the purpose is to examine the effect of treatment on the survival of observations, that is, the occurrence of a dichotomous event.

Beyond One-Way ANOVA

Chapter 5 discussed the use of ANOVA in examining the impact of one discrete (noncontinuous) variable on a continuous variable. This is also called one-way ANOVA. This scenario is easily generalized to accommodate more than one independent variable. These independent variables are either discrete (called factors) or continuous (called covariates). This is called n-way ANOVA. This scenario is even further generalized to allow for testing on two or more *dependent* variables. This is called *MANOVA*, or multiple analysis of variance. MANOVA, like ANOVA, has its own vocabulary of tests that is quite different from regression. Historically, it has often been used in medical research. Both ANOVA and MANOVA allow for users to specify "contrasts" (that is, differences among treatments) in which they are especially interested. Although many analysts feel that ANOVA and regression are largely equivalent, the advantage of MANOVA is that it deals with multiple variables. Both n-way ANOVA and MANOVA are quite sensitive to departures of test assumptions. We can graphically depict MANOVA in the following way:

Figure 8.10 ⎯⎯⎯⎯⎯⎯⎯〰〰⎯ MANOVA

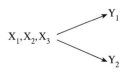

Beyond Path Analysis

Path analysis is limited to models that have no feedback loops. When feedback loops are present, error term assumptions are violated. Causal models with feedback loops are called *nonrecursive* models. *Two-stage least squares* (known as 2SLS) is an econometric technique (that is, a statistical method used in economic research) for estimating two regression models that have feedback loops such as:

(1) $$X_{10} \leftarrow X_{11}, X_{12}$$
(2) $$X_{11} \leftarrow X_{13}, X_{14}, X_{10}$$

In model 1, X_{11} is endogenous and X_{12} is exogenous. The basic strategy of 2SLS is to use a modified version of X_{11} in model 1 that does not violate error term assumptions. The name "two stage" indicates a two-step process for estimating such systems of models. The purpose of the first step is to estimate the modified variable, here, X_{11}. Typically, X_{11} is predicted by other variables that are, hence, called instrumental variables. The predicted variable X_{11} is denoted $\hat{X}_{11}$. In the second stage, $\hat{X}_{11}$, is used to predict the dependent variable X_{10}, hence, $X_{10} = f(\hat{X}_{11}, X_{12})$.

In recent years, advances in software interfaces have increased the popularity of *structural equation models* (SEM). These are models that simultaneously estimate (1) the relationship between observed variables and their factor constructs and (2) relationships among variables and constructs that involve feedback loops. Estimation requires specific software such as LISREL or AMOS. Figure 8.11 shows an example of a SEM model. In the model, classroom violence is composed of measures of physical contact, weapons, and verbal assaults. GPA is measured through math and verbal scores. The impact on classroom violence is predicted through the same variables as in the logistic regression example earlier in this chapter, namely, gender, grade level, and GPA. However, this model also, and simultaneously, examines the impact of classroom violence on GPA. The estimation methodology is quite complex, and analysts test for the robustness and validity in ways that are dissimilar from multiple regression.

CONCLUSION

A vast array of statistical methods exists. In this concluding chapter we examined how logistic analysis can be applied in situations with dichotomous dependent variables, how path analysis handles multiple dependent variables (but without feedback loops), and how survival analysis tackles censored data. The overview of other regression-based forecasting tech-

Figure 8.11 ——————— SEM Model

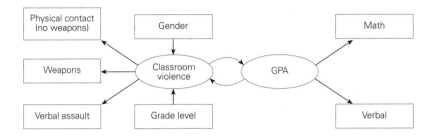

niques gives analysts even more tools to work with when faced with problematic situations.

It is still true that in many instances managers will need only simple approaches to calculate the means of their variables, produce a few good graphs that tell the story, make simple forecasts, and test for significant differences among a few groups. Why, then, bother with these more advanced techniques? Because they are part of the analytical world in which managers operate. Through research and consulting, managers cannot help but come in contact with them. It is hoped that these last chapters whet the appetite and provide a useful reference for managers and students alike.

KEY TERMS

ARIMA (p. 171)
Curve estimation (p. 168)
Direct effect (p. 164)
Endogenous variable (p. 164)
Exogenous variable (p. 164)
Exponential smoothing (p. 169)
Forecasting with leading indicators
    (p. 168)

Indirect effect (p. 164)
Logistic regression (p. 160)
Path analysis (p. 163)
Probability density (p. 167)
Recursive models (p. 163)
Regression-based forecasting
    (p. 167)
Survival analysis (p. 166)

Notes

1. Specifically, multiple regression uses ordinary least squares (OLS), whereas logistic regression uses maximum likelihood (ML). In OLS, the regression line minimizes the sum of error terms; ML chooses the regression coefficients such that wrong predictions of group membership (of the dependent variable) are minimized. ML is an iterative process.

2. Two types of feedback loops are:

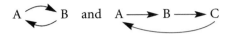

3. When feedback loops are present, error terms of the different models will be correlated with exogenous variables, violating an error term assumption for such models. Then, alternative estimation methodologies are necessary, such as two-stage least squares and others discussed later in this chapter.

4. Some models may show double-headed arrows among error terms. These show the correlation between error terms, which is of no importance in estimating the beta coefficients.

5. The functions used to estimate probabilities are rather complex. They are so-called Weibull distributions, which are defined as $h(t) = \alpha\lambda(\lambda t)^{\alpha-1}$, where α and λ are chosen to best fit the data.

6. In this regard, exponential smoothing with seasonal trend nearly identically matches the predicted observations shown in Figure 7.11. The mean discrepancy between these forecasts is 2.4 percent. Without seasonality, the fitted model merely shows the general trend.

APPENDIX

Appendix A
Normal Distribution

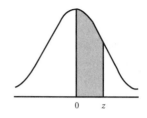

z	.00	.01	.02	.03	.04	.05	.06	.07	.08	.09
0.0	.0000	.0040	.0080	.0120	.0160	.0199	.0239	.0279	.0319	.0359
0.1	.0398	.0438	.0478	.0517	.0557	.0596	.0636	.0675	.0714	.0753
0.2	.0793	.0832	.0871	.0910	.0948	.0987	.1026	.1064	.1103	.1141
0.3	.1179	.1217	.1255	.1293	.1331	.1368	.1406	.1443	.1480	.1517
0.4	.1554	.1591	.1628	.1664	.1700	.1736	.1772	.1808	.1844	.1879
0.5	.1915	.1950	.1985	.2019	.2054	.2088	.2123	.2157	.2190	.2224
0.6	.2257	.2291	.2324	.2357	.2389	.2422	.2454	.2486	.2517	.2549
0.7	.2580	.2611	.2642	.2673	.2704	.2734	.2764	.2794	.2823	.2852
0.8	.2881	.2910	.2939	.2967	.2995	.3023	.3051	.3078	.3106	.3133
0.9	.3159	.3186	.3212	.3238	.3264	.3289	.3315	.3340	.3365	.3389
1.0	.3413	.3438	.3461	.3485	.3508	.3531	.3554	.3577	.3599	.3621
1.1	.3643	.3665	.3686	.3708	.3729	.3749	.3770	.3790	.3810	.3830
1.2	.3849	.3869	.3888	.3907	.3925	.3944	.3962	.3980	.3997	.4015
1.3	.4032	.4049	.4066	.4082	.4099	.4115	.4131	.4147	.4162	.4177
1.4	.4192	.4207	.4222	.4236	.4251	.4265	.4279	.4292	.4306	.4319
1.5	.4332	.4345	.4357	.4370	.4382	.4394	.4406	.4418	.4429	.4441
1.6	.4452	.4463	.4474	.4484	.4495	.4505	.4515	.4525	.4535	.4545
1.7	.4554	.4564	.4573	.4582	.4591	.4599	.4608	.4616	.4625	.4633
1.8	.4641	.4649	.4656	.4664	.4671	.4678	.4686	.4693	.4699	.4706
1.9	.4713	.4719	.4726	.4732	.4738	.4744	.4750	.4756	.4761	.4767
2.0	.4772	.4778	.4783	.4788	.4793	.4798	.4803	.4808	.4812	.4817
2.1	.4821	.4826	.4830	.4834	.4838	.4842	.4846	.4850	.4854	.4857
2.2	.4861	.4864	.4868	.4871	.4875	.4878	.4881	.4884	.4887	.4890
2.3	.4893	.4896	.4898	.4901	.4904	.4906	.4909	.4911	.4913	.4916
2.4	.4918	.4920	.4922	.4925	.4927	.4929	.4931	.4932	.4934	.4936
2.5	.4938	.4940	.4941	.4943	.4945	.4946	.4948	.4949	.4951	.4952
2.6	.4953	.4955	.4956	.4957	.4959	.4960	.4961	.4962	.4963	.4964
2.7	.4965	.4966	.4967	.4968	.4969	.4970	.4971	.4972	.4973	.4974
2.8	.4974	.4975	.4976	.4977	.4977	.4978	.4979	.4979	.4980	.4981
2.9	.4981	.4982	.4982	.4983	.4984	.4984	.4985	.4985	.4986	.4986
3.0	.4987	.4987	.4987	.4988	.4988	.4989	.4989	.4989	.4990	.4990

Source: Adapted from Table II of R. A. Fisher and F. Yates, *Statistical Tables for Biological, Agricultural, and Medical Research,* 6th edition, Longman Group, Ltd., London, 1974. (Previously published by Oliver & Boyle, Ltd., Edinburgh). Used with permission of the authors and publishers.

Appendix B
Chi-square (χ^2) Distribution

Degree of Freedom (df)	0.10	0.05	0.01	.001
1	2.706	3.841	6.635	10.827
2	4.605	5.991	9.210	13.815
3	6.251	7.815	11.341	16.266
4	7.779	9.488	13.277	18.467
5	9.236	11.070	15.086	20.515
6	10.645	12.592	16.812	22.457
7	12.017	14.067	18.475	24.322
8	13.362	15.507	20.090	26.125
9	14.684	16.919	21.666	27.877
10	15.987	18.307	23.209	29.588
11	17.275	19.675	24.725	31.264
12	18.549	21.026	26.217	32.909
13	19.812	22.362	27.688	34.528
14	21.064	23.685	29.141	36.123
15	22.307	24.996	30.578	37.697
16	23.542	26.296	32.000	39.252
17	24.769	27.587	33.409	40.790
18	25.989	28.869	34.805	42.312
19	27.204	30.144	36.191	43.820
20	28.412	31.410	37.566	45.315
21	29.615	32.671	38.932	46.797
22	30.813	33.924	40.289	48.268
23	32.007	35.172	41.638	49.728
24	33.196	36.415	42.980	51.179
25	34.382	37.652	44.314	52.620
26	35.563	38.885	45.642	54.052
27	36.741	40.113	46.963	55.476
28	37.916	41.337	48.278	56.893
29	39.087	42.557	49.588	58.302
30	40.256	43.773	50.892	59.703

Source: Adapted from Table IV of R. A. Fisher and F. Yates, *Statistical Tables for Biological, Agricultural, and Medical Research,* 6th edition, Longman Group, Ltd., London, 1974. (Previously published by Oliver & Boyd, Ltd., Edinburgh). Used with permission of the authors and publishers.

Appendix C
T-test Distribution

	Alpha Level for One-Tailed Test					
	.10	.05	.025	.01	.005	.0025
Degree of Freedom (df)	Alpha Level for Two-Tailed Test					
	.20	.10	.05	.02	.01	.005
1	3.078	6.314	12.706	31.821	63.657	127.32
2	1.886	2.920	4.303	6.965	9.925	14.089
3	1.638	2.353	3.182	4.541	5.841	7.453
4	1.533	2.132	2.776	3.747	4.604	5.598
5	1.476	2.015	2.571	3.365	4.032	4.773
6	1.440	1.943	2.447	3.143	3.707	4.317
7	1.415	1.895	2.365	2.998	3.499	4.029
8	1.397	1.869	2.306	2.896	3.355	3.833
9	1.383	1.833	2.262	2.821	3.250	3.690
10	1.372	1.812	2.228	2.764	3.169	3.581
11	1.363	1.796	2.201	2.718	3.106	3.497
12	1.356	1.782	2.179	2.681	3.055	3.428
13	1.350	1.771	2.160	2.650	3.012	3.372
14	1.345	1.761	2.145	2.624	2.977	3.326
15	1.341	1.753	2.131	2.602	2.947	3.286
16	1.337	1.746	2.120	2.583	2.921	3.252
17	1.333	1.740	2.110	2.567	2.898	3.222
18	1.330	1.734	2.101	2.552	2.878	3.197
19	1.328	1.729	2.093	2.539	2.861	3.174
20	1.325	1.725	2.086	2.528	2.845	3.153
21	1.323	1.721	2.080	2.518	2.831	3.135
22	1.321	1.717	2.074	2.508	2.819	3.119
23	1.319	1.714	2.069	2.500	2.807	3.104
24	1.318	1.711	2.064	2.492	2.797	3.091
25	1.316	1.708	2.060	2.485	2.787	3.078
26	1.315	1.706	2.056	2.479	2.779	3.067
27	1.314	1.703	2.052	2.473	2.771	3.057
28	1.313	1.701	2.048	2.467	2.763	3.047
29	1.311	1.699	2.045	2.462	2.756	3.038
30	1.310	1.697	2.042	2.457	2.750	3.030
40	1.303	1.684	2.021	2.423	2.704	2.971
60	1.296	1.671	2.000	2.390	2.660	2.915
120	1.289	1.658	1.980	2.358	2.617	2.860
∞	1.282	1.645	1.960	2.326	2.576	2.807

Source: Adapted from Table III of R. A. Fisher and F. Yates, *Statistical Tables for Biological, Agricultural, and Medical Research,* 6th edition, Longman Group, Ltd., London, 1974. (Previously published by Oliver & Boyd, Ltd., Edinburgh). Used with permission of the authors and publishers.

Appendix D
F-test Distribution $\alpha = .05$

Degree of freedom (df) within groups [denominator]

	Degree of freedom (df) between groups [numerator]																		
nominator]	1	2	3	4	5	6	7	8	9	10	12	15	20	24	30	40	60	120	∞
1	161.4	199.5	215.7	224.6	230.2	234.0	236.8	238.9	240.5	241.9	243.9	245.9	248.0	249.1	250.1	251.1	252.2	253.3	254.3
2	18.51	19.00	19.16	19.25	19.30	19.33	19.35	19.37	19.38	19.40	19.41	19.43	19.45	19.45	19.48	19.47	19.48	19.49	19.50
3	10.13	9.55	9.28	9.12	9.01	8.94	8.89	8.85	8.81	8.79	8.74	8.70	8.66	8.64	8.62	8.59	8.57	8.55	8.53
4	7.71	6.94	6.59	6.39	6.26	6.16	6.09	6.04	6.00	5.96	5.91	5.86	5.80	5.77	5.75	5.72	5.69	5.66	5.63
5	6.61	5.79	5.41	5.19	5.05	4.95	4.88	4.82	4.77	4.74	4.68	4.62	4.56	4.53	4.50	4.46	4.43	4.40	4.36
6	5.99	5.14	4.76	4.53	4.39	4.28	4.21	4.15	4.10	4.06	4.00	3.94	3.87	3.84	3.81	3.77	3.74	3.70	3.67
7	5.59	4.74	4.35	4.12	3.97	3.87	3.79	3.73	3.68	3.64	3.57	3.51	3.44	3.41	3.38	3.34	3.30	3.27	3.23
8	5.32	4.46	4.07	3.84	3.69	3.58	3.50	3.44	3.39	3.35	3.28	3.22	3.15	3.12	3.08	3.04	3.01	2.97	2.93
9	5.12	4.26	3.86	3.63	3.48	3.37	3.29	3.23	3.18	3.14	3.07	3.01	2.94	2.90	2.86	2.83	2.79	2.75	2.71
10	4.96	4.10	3.71	3.48	3.33	3.22	3.14	3.07	3.02	2.98	2.91	2.85	2.77	2.74	2.70	2.66	2.62	2.58	2.54
11	4.84	3.98	3.59	3.36	3.20	3.09	3.01	2.95	2.90	2.85	2.79	2.72	2.65	2.61	2.57	2.53	2.49	2.45	2.40
12	4.75	3.89	3.49	3.26	3.11	3.00	2.91	2.85	2.80	2.75	2.69	2.62	2.54	2.51	2.47	2.43	2.38	2.34	2.30
13	4.67	3.81	3.41	3.18	3.03	2.92	2.83	2.77	2.71	2.67	2.60	2.53	2.46	2.42	2.38	2.34	2.30	2.25	2.21
14	4.60	3.74	3.34	3.11	2.96	2.85	2.76	2.70	2.65	2.60	2.53	2.46	2.39	2.35	2.31	2.27	2.22	2.18	2.13
15	4.54	3.68	3.29	3.06	2.90	2.79	2.71	2.64	2.59	2.54	2.48	2.40	2.33	2.29	2.25	2.20	2.16	2.11	2.07
16	4.49	3.63	3.24	3.01	2.85	2.74	2.66	2.59	2.54	2.49	2.42	2.35	2.28	2.24	2.19	2.15	2.11	2.06	2.01
17	4.45	3.59	3.20	2.96	2.81	2.70	2.61	2.55	2.49	2.45	2.38	2.31	2.23	2.19	2.15	2.10	2.06	2.01	1.96

(continued)

Appendix D Continued
F-test Distribution $\propto = .05$

Degree of freedom (df) within groups [denominator] \ Degree of freedom (df) between groups [numerator]

[denominator]	1	2	3	4	5	6	7	8	9	10	12	15	20	24	30	40	60	120	∞
18	4.41	3.55	3.16	2.93	2.77	2.66	2.58	2.51	2.46	2.41	2.34	2.27	2.19	2.15	2.11	2.06	2.02	1.97	1.92
19	4.38	3.52	3.13	2.90	2.74	2.63	2.54	2.48	2.42	2.38	2.31	2.23	2.16	2.11	2.07	2.03	1.98	1.93	1.88
20	4.35	3.49	3.10	2.87	2.71	2.60	2.51	2.45	2.39	2.35	2.28	2.20	2.12	2.08	2.04	1.99	1.95	1.90	1.84
21	4.32	3.47	3.07	2.84	2.68	2.57	2.49	2.42	2.37	2.32	2.25	2.18	2.10	2.05	2.01	1.96	1.92	1.87	1.81
22	4.30	3.44	3.05	2.82	2.66	2.55	2.46	2.40	2.34	2.30	2.23	2.15	2.07	2.03	1.98	1.94	1.89	1.84	1.78
23	4.28	3.42	3.03	2.80	2.64	2.53	2.44	2.37	2.32	2.27	2.20	2.13	2.05	2.01	1.96	1.91	1.86	1.81	1.76
24	4.26	3.40	3.01	2.78	2.62	2.51	2.42	2.36	2.30	2.25	2.18	2.11	2.03	1.98	1.94	1.89	1.84	1.79	1.73
25	4.24	3.39	2.99	2.76	2.60	2.49	2.40	2.34	2.28	2.24	2.16	2.09	2.01	1.96	1.92	1.87	1.82	1.77	1.71
26	4.23	3.37	2.98	2.74	2.59	2.47	2.39	2.32	2.27	2.22	2.15	2.07	1.99	1.95	1.90	1.85	1.80	1.75	1.69
27	4.21	3.35	2.96	2.73	2.57	2.46	2.37	2.31	2.25	2.20	2.13	2.06	1.97	1.93	1.88	1.84	1.79	1.73	1.67
28	4.20	3.34	2.95	2.71	2.56	2.45	2.36	2.29	2.24	2.19	2.12	2.04	1.96	1.91	1.87	1.82	1.77	1.71	1.65
29	4.18	3.33	2.93	2.70	2.55	2.43	2.35	2.28	2.22	2.18	2.10	2.03	1.94	1.90	1.85	1.81	1.75	1.70	1.64
30	4.17	3.32	2.92	2.69	2.53	2.42	2.33	2.27	2.21	2.16	2.09	2.01	1.93	1.89	1.84	1.79	1.74	1.68	1.62
40	4.08	3.23	2.84	2.61	2.45	2.34	2.25	2.18	2.12	2.08	2.00	1.92	1.84	1.79	1.74	1.69	1.64	1.58	1.51
60	4.00	3.15	2.76	2.53	2.37	2.25	2.17	2.10	2.04	1.99	1.92	1.84	1.75	1.70	1.65	1.59	1.53	1.47	1.39
120	3.92	3.07	2.68	2.45	2.29	2.17	2.09	2.02	1.96	1.91	1.83	1.75	1.66	1.61	1.55	1.50	1.43	1.35	1.25
∞	3.84	3.00	2.60	2.37	2.21	2.10	2.01	1.94	1.88	1.83	1.75	1.67	1.57	1.52	1.46	1.39	1.32	1.22	1.00

(continued)

Appendix D Continued
F-test Distribution ∝ = .01

Degree of freedom (df) between groups [numerator]

Degree of freedom (df) within groups [denominator]	1	2	3	4	5	6	7	8	9	10	12	15	20	24	30	40	60	120	∞
1	4052	4999.5	5403	5625	5764	5859	5928	5981	6022	6056	6106	6157	6209	6235	6261	6287	6313	6339	6366
2	98.58	99.00	99.17	99.25	99.30	99.33	99.36	99.37	99.39	99.40	99.42	99.43	99.45	99.46	99.47	99.47	99.48	99.49	99.50
3	34.12	30.82	29.46	28.71	28.24	27.91	27.67	27.49	27.35	27.23	27.05	26.87	26.69	26.60	26.50	26.41	26.32	26.22	26.13
4	21.20	18.00	16.69	15.98	15.52	15.21	14.98	14.80	14.66	14.55	14.37	14.20	14.02	13.93	13.64	13.75	13.65	13.56	13.46
5	16.26	13.27	12.06	11.39	10.97	10.67	10.46	10.29	10.16	10.05	9.89	9.72	9.55	9.47	9.38	9.29	9.20	9.11	9.02
6	13.75	10.92	9.78	9.15	8.75	8.47	8.26	8.10	7.98	7.87	7.72	7.56	7.40	7.31	7.23	7.14	7.06	6.97	6.88
7	12.25	9.55	8.45	7.85	7.46	7.19	6.99	6.84	6.72	6.62	6.47	6.31	6.16	6.07	5.99	5.91	5.82	5.74	5.65
8	11.26	8.65	7.59	7.01	6.63	6.37	6.18	6.03	5.91	5.81	5.67	5.52	5.36	5.28	5.20	5.12	5.03	4.95	4.86
9	10.56	8.02	6.99	6.42	6.06	5.80	5.61	5.47	5.35	5.26	5.11	4.96	4.81	4.73	4.65	4.57	4.48	4.40	4.31
10	10.04	7.56	6.55	5.99	5.64	5.39	5.20	5.06	4.94	4.85	4.71	4.56	4.41	4.33	4.25	4.17	4.08	4.00	3.91
11	9.65	7.21	6.22	5.67	5.32	5.07	4.89	4.74	4.63	4.54	4.40	4.25	4.10	4.02	3.94	3.86	3.78	3.69	3.60
12	9.33	6.93	5.95	5.41	5.06	4.82	4.64	4.50	4.39	4.30	4.16	4.01	3.86	3.78	3.70	3.62	3.54	3.45	3.36
13	9.07	6.70	5.74	5.21	4.86	4.62	4.44	4.30	4.19	4.10	3.96	3.82	3.66	3.59	3.51	3.43	3.34	3.25	3.17
14	8.86	6.51	5.56	5.04	4.69	4.46	4.28	4.14	4.03	3.94	3.80	3.66	3.51	3.43	3.35	3.27	3.18	3.09	3.00
15	8.68	6.36	5.42	4.89	4.56	4.32	4.14	4.00	3.89	3.80	3.67	3.52	3.37	3.29	3.21	3.13	3.05	2.96	2.87
16	8.53	6.23	5.29	4.77	4.44	4.20	4.03	3.89	3.78	3.69	3.55	3.41	3.26	3.18	3.10	3.02	2.93	2.84	2.75
17	8.40	6.11	5.18	4.67	4.34	4.10	3.93	3.79	3.68	3.59	3.46	3.31	3.16	3.08	3.00	2.92	2.83	2.75	2.65
18	8.29	6.01	5.09	4.58	4.25	4.01	3.84	3.71	3.60	3.51	3.37	3.23	3.08	3.00	2.92	2.84	2.75	2.66	2.57
19	8.18	5.93	5.01	4.50	4.17	3.94	3.77	3.63	3.52	3.43	3.30	3.15	3.00	2.92	2.84	2.76	2.67	2.58	2.49

(continued)

Appendix D   Continued
F-test Distribution ∝ = .01

Degree of freedom (df) within groups [denominator]	\multicolumn{19}{c|}{Degree of freedom (df) between groups [numerator]}

nominator]	1	2	3	4	5	6	7	8	9	10	12	15	20	24	30	40	60	120	∞
20	8.10	5.85	4.94	4.43	4.10	3.87	3.70	3.56	3.46	3.37	3.23	3.09	2.94	2.86	2.78	2.69	2.61	2.52	2.42
21	8.02	5.78	4.87	4.37	4.04	3.81	3.64	3.51	3.40	3.31	3.17	3.03	2.88	2.80	2.72	2.64	2.55	2.46	2.36
22	7.95	5.72	4.82	4.31	3.99	3.76	3.59	3.45	3.35	3.26	3.12	2.98	2.83	2.75	2.67	2.58	2.50	2.40	2.31
23	7.88	5.66	4.76	4.26	3.94	3.71	3.54	3.41	3.30	3.21	3.07	2.93	2.78	2.70	2.62	2.54	2.45	2.35	2.26
24	7.82	5.61	4.72	4.22	3.90	3.67	3.50	3.36	3.26	3.17	3.03	2.89	2.74	2.66	2.58	2.49	2.40	2.31	2.21
25	7.77	5.57	4.68	4.18	3.85	3.63	3.46	3.32	3.22	3.13	2.99	2.85	2.70	2.62	2.54	2.45	2.36	2.27	2.17
26	7.72	5.53	4.64	4.14	3.82	3.59	3.42	3.29	3.18	3.09	2.96	2.81	2.66	2.58	2.50	2.42	2.33	2.23	2.13
27	7.68	5.49	4.60	4.11	3.78	3.56	3.39	3.26	3.15	3.06	2.93	2.78	2.63	2.55	2.47	2.38	2.29	2.20	2.10
28	7.64	5.45	4.57	4.07	3.75	3.53	3.36	3.23	3.12	3.03	2.90	2.75	2.60	2.52	2.44	2.35	2.26	2.17	2.06
29	7.60	5.42	4.54	4.04	3.73	3.50	3.33	3.20	3.09	3.00	2.87	2.73	2.57	2.49	2.41	2.33	2.23	2.14	2.03
30	7.56	5.39	4.51	4.02	3.70	3.47	3.30	3.17	3.07	2.98	2.84	2.70	2.55	2.47	2.39	2.30	2.21	2.11	2.01
40	7.31	5.18	4.31	3.83	3.51	3.29	3.12	2.99	2.89	2.80	2.66	2.52	2.37	2.29	2.20	2.11	2.02	1.92	1.80
60	7.08	4.98	4.13	3.65	3.34	3.12	2.95	2.82	2.72	2.63	2.50	2.35	2.20	2.12	2.03	1.94	1.84	1.73	1.60
120	6.85	4.79	3.95	3.48	3.17	2.96	2.79	2.66	2.56	2.47	2.34	2.19	2.03	1.95	1.86	1.76	1.66	1.53	1.38
∞	6.63	4.61	3.78	3.32	3.02	2.80	2.64	2.51	2.11	2.32	2.18	2.04	1.88	1.79	1.70	1.59	1.47	1.32	1.00

Source: Adapted from Table II of R. A. Fisher and F. Yates, *Statistical Tables for Biological, Agricultural, and Medical Research*, 6th edition, Longman Group, Ltd., London, 1974. (Previously published by Oliver & Boyd, Ltd., Edinburgh). Used with permission of the authors and publishers.

Appendix E
Durbin-Watson Distribution
Five percent significance points of d_l and d_u for Durbin-Watson test[†]

N	$k = 1$		$k = 2$		$k = 3$		$k = 4$		$k = 5$	
	d_l	d_u	d_l	d_u	d_l	d_u	d_l	d_u	d_l	d_u
15	1.08	1.36	0.95	1.54	0.82	1.75	0.69	1.97	0.56	2.21
16	1.10	1.37	0.98	1.54	0.86	1.73	0.74	1.93	0.62	2.15
17	1.13	1.38	1.02	1.54	0.90	1.71	0.78	1.90	0.67	2.10
18	1.16	1.39	1.05	1.53	0.93	1.69	0.82	1.87	0.71	2.06
19	1.18	1.40	1.08	1.53	0.97	1.68	0.86	1.85	0.75	2.02
20	1.20	1.41	1.10	1.54	1.00	1.68	0.90	1.83	0.79	1.99
21	1.22	1.42	1.13	1.54	1.03	1.67	0.93	1.81	0.83	1.96
22	1.24	1.43	1.15	1.54	1.05	1.66	0.96	1.80	0.86	1.94
23	1.26	1.44	1.17	1.54	1.08	1.66	0.99	1.79	0.90	1.92
24	1.27	1.45	1.19	1.55	1.10	1.66	1.01	1.78	0.93	1.90
25	1.29	1.45	1.21	1.55	1.12	1.66	1.04	1.77	0.95	1.89
26	1.30	1.46	1.22	1.55	1.14	1.65	1.06	1.76	0.98	1.88
27	1.32	1.47	1.24	1.56	1.16	1.65	1.08	1.76	1.01	1.86
28	1.33	1.48	1.26	1.56	1.18	1.65	1.10	1.75	1.03	1.85
29	1.34	1.48	1.27	1.56	1.20	1.65	1.12	1.74	1.05	1.84
30	1.35	1.49	1.28	1.57	1.21	1.65	1.14	1.74	1.07	1.83
31	1.36	1.50	1.30	1.57	1.23	1.65	1.16	1.74	1.09	1.83
32	1.37	1.50	1.31	1.57	1.24	1.65	1.18	1.73	1.11	1.82
33	1.38	1.51	1.32	1.58	1.26	1.65	1.19	1.73	1.13	1.81
34	1.39	1.51	1.33	1.58	1.27	1.65	1.21	1.73	1.15	1.81
35	1.40	1.52	1.34	1.53	1.28	1.65	1.22	1.73	1.16	1.80
36	1.41	1.52	1.35	1.59	1.29	1.65	1.24	1.73	1.18	1.80
37	1.42	1.53	1.36	1.59	1.31	1.66	1.25	1.72	1.19	1.80
38	1.43	1.54	1.37	1.59	1.32	1.66	1.26	1.72	1.21	1.79
39	1.43	1.54	1.38	1.60	1.33	1.66	1.27	1.72	1.22	1.79
40	1.44	1.54	1.39	1.60	1.34	1.66	1.29	1.72	1.23	1.79
45	1.48	1.57	1.43	1.62	1.38	1.67	1.34	1.72	1.29	1.78
50	1.50	1.59	1.46	1.63	1.42	1.67	1.38	1.72	1.34	1.77
55	1.53	1.60	1.49	1.64	1.45	1.68	1.41	1.72	1.38	1.77
60	1.55	1.62	1.51	1.65	1.48	1.69	1.44	1.73	1.41	1.77
65	1.57	1.63	1.54	1.66	1.50	1.70	1.47	1.73	1.44	1.77
70	1.58	1.64	1.55	1.67	1.52	1.70	1.49	1.74	1.46	1.77
75	1.60	1.65	1.57	1.68	1.54	1.71	1.51	1.74	1.49	1.77
80	1.61	1.66	1.59	1.69	1.56	1.72	1.53	1.74	1.51	1.77
85	1.62	1.67	1.60	1.70	1.57	1.72	1.55	1.75	1.52	1.17
90	1.63	1.68	1.61	1.70	1.59	1.73	1.57	1.75	1.54	1.78
95	1.64	1.69	1.62	1.71	1.60	1.73	1.58	1.75	1.56	1.78
100	1.65	1.69	1.63	1.72	1.61	1.74	1.59	1.76	1.57	1.78

[†]N = number of observations; k = number of explanatory variables (excluding the constant term).

Source: Reprinted with permission from J. Durbin and G. S. Watson, "Testing for Serial Correlation in Least Squares Regression," *Biometrika*, vol. 38, 1951, pp. 159–177.

INDEX